Philippians

BHGNT
Baylor Handbook on the Greek New Testament
Lidija Novakovic
General Editor

OTHER BOOKS IN THIS SERIES

Matthew 1–14	Wesley G. Olmstead
Matthew 15–28	Wesley G. Olmstead
Mark 1–8	Rodney J. Decker
Mark 9–16	Rodney J. Decker
Luke	Martin M. Culy, Mikeal C. Parsons, and Joshua J. Stigall
John 1–10	Lidija Novakovic
John 11–21	Lidija Novakovic
Acts	Martin M. Culy and Mikeal C. Parsons
1 Corinthians 1–9	Timothy A. Brookins and Bruce W. Longenecker
1 Corinthians 10–16	Timothy A. Brookins and Bruce W. Longenecker
2 Corinthians	Fredrick J. Long
Galatians	David A. deSilva
Ephesians	William J. Larkin
Colossians and Philemon	Constantine R. Campbell
The Pastoral Letters	Larry J. Perkins
James	A. K. M. Adam
1 Peter	Mark Dubis
2 Peter and Jude	Peter H. Davids
1, 2, 3 John	Martin M. Culy
Revelation	David L. Mathewson

Philippians

A Handbook on the Greek Text

Lidija Novakovic

BAYLOR UNIVERSITY PRESS

© 2020 by Baylor University Press
Waco, Texas 76798

All Rights Reserved. No part of this publication may be reproduced, stored in a retrieval system, or transmitted, in any form or by any means, electronic, mechanical, photocopying, recording, or otherwise, without the prior permission in writing of Baylor University Press.

Typesetting by Scribe Inc.
Series cover design by Pamela Poll

Paperback ISBN: 978-1-4813-0771-0
Library of Congress Control Number: 2020936999

CONTENTS

Series Introduction	vii
Preface	xiii
Abbreviations	xv
Introduction	xix
Philippians 1:1-2	1
Philippians 1:3-11	4
Philippians 1:12-18a	16
Philippians 1:18b-26	25
Philippians 1:27-30	35
Philippians 2:1-4	41
Philippians 2:5-11	47
Philippians 2:12-18	56
Philippians 2:19-24	63
Philippians 2:25-30	68
Philippians 3:1-11	74
Philippians 3:12-16	90
Philippians 3:17-21	97
Philippians 4:1-3	103
Philippians 4:4-7	106

Philippians 4:8-9	111
Philippians 4:10-20	114
Philippians 4:21-23	127
Glossary	131
Works Cited	139
Author Index	145
Grammar Index	147

SERIES INTRODUCTION

The Baylor Handbook on the Greek New Testament (BHGNT) is designed to guide new readers and seasoned scholars alike through the intricacies of the Greek text. Each handbook provides a verse-by-verse treatment of the biblical text. Unlike traditional commentaries, however, the BHGNT makes no attempt to expound on the theological meaning or significance of the document under consideration. Instead, the handbooks serve as supplements to commentary proper. Readers of traditional commentaries are sometimes dismayed by the fact that even those that are labeled "exegetical" or "critical" frequently have little to say about the mechanics of the Greek text and all too often completely ignore the more perplexing grammatical issues. In contrast, the BHGNT offers an accessible and comprehensive, though not exhaustive, treatment of the Greek New Testament, with particular attention given to the grammar of the text. In order to make the handbooks more user friendly, authors have only selectively interacted with secondary literature. Where there is significant debate on an issue, the handbooks provide a representative sample of scholars espousing each position; when authors adopt a less known stance on the text, they generally list any other scholars who have embraced that position.

The BHGNT, however, is more than a reliable guide to the Greek text of the New Testament. Each author brings unique strengths to the task of preparing the handbook, such as textual criticism, lexical semantics, discourse analysis, or other areas. As a result, students and scholars alike will at times be introduced to ways of looking at the Greek language that they have not encountered before. This feature makes the handbooks valuable not only for intermediate and advanced Greek courses, but also for students and scholars who no longer have the luxury of increasing their Greek proficiency within a classroom context. While handbook authors do not consider modern linguistic theory to be a panacea for all questions exegetical, the BHGNT does aim both to help move linguistic insights into the mainstream of New Testament reference works and, at the same time, to help weed out some of the myths about the Greek language that continue to appear in both scholarly and popular treatments of the New Testament.

Using the Baylor Handbook on the Greek New Testament

Each handbook consists of the following features. The introduction draws readers' attention to some of the distinctive characteristics of the New Testament document under consideration and treats some of the broader issues relating to the text as a whole in a more thorough fashion. In the handbook proper, the biblical text is divided into sections, each of which is introduced with a translation that illustrates how the insights gleaned from the analysis that follows may be expressed in modern English. Following the translation is the heart of the handbook, an extensive analysis of the Greek text. Here, the Greek text of each verse is followed by comments on grammatical, lexical, and text-critical issues. Every verb is parsed for the sake of pedagogical expediency, while nouns are parsed only when the form is unusual or requires additional explanation. Handbook authors may also make use of other features, such as passage overviews between the translation and notes.

Each page of the handbook includes a header to help readers quickly locate comments on a particular passage. Terminology used in the comments that is potentially unfamiliar is included in a glossary in the back of the handbook and/or cross-referenced with the first occurrence of the expression, where an explanation may be found. This is followed by a bibliography of works cited, providing helpful guidance in identifying resources for further research on the Greek text. Each volume concludes with a grammar index and an author index. The list of grammatical phenomena occurring in the biblical text provides a valuable resource for students of Greek wanting to study a particular construction more carefully or Greek instructors needing to develop illustrations, exercises, or exams.

The handbooks assume that users will possess a minimal level of competence with Greek morphology and syntax. Series authors generally utilize traditional labels such as those found in Daniel Wallace's *Greek Grammar beyond the Basics*. Labels that are drawn from the broader field of modern linguistics are explained at their first occurrence and included in the glossary. Common labels that users may be unfamiliar with are also included in the glossary.

The primary exception to the broad adoption of traditional syntactic labels relates to verb tenses. Most New Testament Greek grammars describe the tense system as being formally fairly simple (only six tenses) but functionally complex. The aorist tense, it is frequently said, can function in a wide variety of ways that are associated with labels such as "ingressive," "gnomic," "constative," "epistolary," "proleptic," and so forth. Similar functional complexity is posited for the other tenses. Positing such functions, however, typically stems not from a careful analysis of Greek syntax but rather from grappling with the challenges of translating Greek verbs into English. When we carefully examine the Greek verb tenses, we find that the tense forms do not themselves denote semantic features such as ingressive, iterative, or conative; at best they may allow for ingressive, iterative, or conative translations. In addition, the tense labels have frequently led to exegetical claims that go beyond the syntax. For this reason, handbook authors do not generally utilize these labels but seek to express nuances typically associated with them in the translation.

Avoidance of traditional tense labels is based on the insights gained from the discussions about verbal aspect theory over the past three decades, which distinguish *Aktionsart* (kind of action) from aspect (subjective portrayal of an action). Many contributors to the BHGNT series agree with the basic premise of verbal aspect theory that tense forms do not grammaticalize time and adopt a three-aspect paradigm that differentiates between perfective aspect, imperfective aspect, and stative aspect. Some authors also concur with Stanley Porter's (1989; 1994) claim about different levels of semantic density or markedness, i.e., the concept of the perfective aspect as the least marked (background), the imperfective aspect as more marked (foreground), and the stative aspect as the most marked aspect (frontground). There is, however, still significant scholarly disagreement concerning the nature of verbal aspects and their semantic functions. Constantine Campbell (2008), for example, identifies the Greek perfect not with stative aspect, like Porter and others, but with imperfective aspect with heightened remoteness, which he describes as a dynamic action in progress. Steven Runge (2014), conversely, challenges the foundational idea of Porter's verbal aspect theory that Greek tense forms do not have temporal references and argues for a mixed time-aspect system. Handbook authors are encouraged to interact with these and other discussions about verbal aspect and incorporate their insights in the analysis of the Greek text.

Deponency

Although series authors will vary in the theoretical approaches they bring to the text, the BHGNT has adopted the same general approach on one important issue: deponency. Traditionally, the label "deponent" has been applied to verbs with middle, passive, or middle/passive morphology that are thought to be "active" in meaning. Introductory grammars tend to put a significant number of middle verbs in the New Testament in this category, despite the fact that some of the standard reference grammars have questioned the validity of the label. Archibald Robertson (332), for example, argues that the label "should not be used at all."

In recent years, a number of scholars have taken up Robertson's quiet call to abandon this label. Carl Conrad's posts on the B-Greek Internet discussion list (beginning in 1997) and his subsequent formalization of those concerns in unpublished papers available on his website have helped flesh out the concerns raised by earlier scholars. In his essay, "New Observations on Voice in the Ancient Greek Verb," Conrad argues that the Greek voice system is not built upon trichotomy (active, middle, and passive) but upon a bipolar basis (active and middle/passive). He further claims that the verbs that have been traditionally termed "deponent" are by their nature subject focused, like the forms that are regarded as genuine middle, and suggests that "both term and concept of 'Deponency' should be eliminated forever from formal categories and thinking about ancient Greek voice" (11). Similar conclusions are reached by Jonathan Pennington (60–64), who helpfully summarizes the rationale for dispensing with the label, maintaining that widespread use of the term "deponent" stems from two key factors: (1) the tendency to analyze Greek syntax through reference to English translation—if a workable translation of a middle form appears "active" in English, we conclude that the verb must be active in meaning even though it is middle in form; and (2) the imposition of Latin categories on Greek grammar. Pennington concludes, "[M]ost if not all verbs that are considered 'deponent' are in fact truly middle in meaning" (61).

The questions that have been raised regarding deponency as a syntactic category, then, are not simply issues that interest a few Greek scholars and linguists without much bearing on how one understands the text. Rather, the notion of deponency has, at least in some cases, effectively obscured the semantic significance of the middle voice, leading to imprecise readings of the text (see also Bakker; Taylor). It is not only middle-voice verbs, however, that are the focus of attention in this debate. Conrad, Pennington, and others also maintain that deponency is an invalid category for passive verbs that have traditionally been placed in this category. To account for putative passive deponent verbs, these scholars have turned to the evolution of voice morphology in the Greek language. They draw attention to the fact that middle morphology was being replaced by passive morphology (the θη morpheme) during the Koine period (see esp. Conrad, 3, 5–6; cf. Pennington, 68; Taylor, 175; Caragounis, 153). Consequently, in the Common Era we find "an increasing number of passive forms without a distinctive passive idea . . . replacing older middle forms" (Pennington, 68). This diachronic argument leads Conrad (5) to conclude that the θη morpheme should be treated as a middle/passive rather than a passive morpheme. Such arguments have a sound linguistic foundation and raise serious questions about the legitimacy of the notion "passive deponent."

Should, then, the label "deponent" be abandoned altogether? While more research needs to be done to account for middle/passive morphology in Koine Greek fully, the arguments are both compelling and exegetically significant. Consequently, users of the BHGNT will discover that verbs that are typically labeled "deponent," including some with θη morphology, tend to be listed as "middle" or "middle/passive."

In recognizing that so-called deponent verbs should be viewed as true middles, users of the BHGNT should not fall into the trap of concluding that the middle form emphasizes the subject's involvement in the action of the verb. At times, the middle voice appears simply to be a morphological flag indicating that the verb is intransitive. More frequently, the middle morphology tends to be driven by the "middle" semantics of the verb itself. In other words, the middle voice is sometimes used with the verb not in order to place a focus on the subject's involvement in the action, but precisely because the sense of the lexical form itself involves subject focus.

It is the hope of Baylor University Press, the series editors, and each of the authors that these handbooks will help advance our understanding of the Greek New Testament, be used to equip further pastors and other church leaders for the work of ministry, and fan into flame a love for the Greek New Testament among a new generation of students and scholars.

Martin M. Culy
Founding Series Editor

Lidija Novakovic
Series Editor

PREFACE

I wish to express my gratitude to John Genter, who checked the accuracy of my grammatical analysis and all bibliographical references, and to Taylor Brown, who proofread the final draft of the manuscript and prepared the glossary. I dedicate this handbook to my husband, Ivo, in memory of our encounter at the camp Činta on the Adriatic island Ugljan back in the summer of 1977 and the beginning of our courtship, which started with our lively conversation about the meaning of Paul's declaration in Phil 3:8-9: "I continue to consider all things to be loss because of the surpassing greatness of the knowledge of Christ Jesus my Lord, for the sake of whom I have suffered the loss of all things and continue to consider [them] garbage, in order that I may gain Christ and may be found in him, not having a righteousness of my own that [is] from the law but [one] that [is] through faith in Christ—the righteousness from God based on faith."

ABBREVIATIONS

1st	first person
2nd	second person
2 Pet	2 Peter
3rd	third person
acc	accusative
act	active
a.k.a.	also known as
aor	aorist
ASV	American Standard Version
BBE	Bible in Basic English
BCE	Before the Common Era
BDAG	Danker, *A Greek-English Lexicon of the New Testament*, 2000
BDF	Blass, Debrunner, Funk, *A Greek Grammar of the New Testament*
CEB	Common English Bible
ch.	chapter
cf.	compare (*confer*)
dat	dative
DBY	The Darby Bible
e.g.	for example (*exempli gratia*)
ESV	English Standard Version
et al.	and others (*et alii*)

fem	feminine
fut	future
gen	genitive
GNT	Good News Translation
GW	God's Word
HCSB	Holman Christian Standard Bible
i.e.	that is (*id est*)
impf	imperfect
impv	imperative
ind	indicative
inf	infinitive
KJV	King James Version
LEB	The Lexham English Bible
lit.	literally
LN	Louw and Nida, *Greek-English Lexicon*
LSJ	Liddell, Scott, Jones, *A Greek-English Lexicon*
LXX	Septuagint
masc	masculine
MHT	Moulton, Howard, Turner, *A Grammar of New Testament Greek*, 4 vols.
mid	middle
MSG	The Message
MSS/mss	manuscripts
n.	note
NA28	Nestle-Aland, *Novum Testamentum Graece*, 28th ed.
NAB	New American Bible
NASB	New American Standard Bible
NCV	New Century Version
NEB	New English Bible
NET	New English Translation
neut	neuter
NIV	New International Version

NJB	New Jerusalem Bible
NKJV	New King James Version
NLT	New Living Translation
nom	nominative
NRSV	New Revised Standard Version
NT	New Testament
opt	optative
OT	Old Testament
pace	with deference to
pass	passive
pl	plural
plprf	pluperfect
PP	prepositional phrase
pres	present
prf	perfect
ptc	participle
REB	Revised English Bible
RHE	Douay-Rheims Catholic Bible (English translation of the Vulgate)
RSV	Revised Standard Version
SBLGNT	The SBL Greek New Testament
sg	singular
subj	subjunctive
TDNT	Kittel, *Theological Dictionary of the New Testament*, 10 vols.
TSKS	article-substantive-καί-substantive (relating to Granville Sharp's rule)
TYN	Tyndale Bible
UBS5	The United Bible Societies' Greek New Testament, 5th ed.
v./vv.	verse/verses
voc	vocative
WBT	Webster Bible
WEB	World English Bible
WH	Westcott-Hort

INTRODUCTION

The Letter to the Philippians, which is usually classified as a "letter of friendship" or a "letter of consolation," is replete with expressions of joy and appeals to the Christian community in the Roman colony of Philippi to rejoice in the Lord. One of its most famous features is the "Christ hymn" (2:6-11), an early Christian composition that describes Christ's transition from being "in the form of God" to becoming a human being. Another distinctive characteristic of the letter is the complete absence of explicit quotations of Israel's Scripture. The only exception may be Phil 1:19, which contains a verbatim parallel to LXX Job 13:16a, but since it is not introduced by an explicit citation formula, it is better to regard it as an intertextual scriptural echo (Hays, 21–24).

The Pauline authorship of the letter is universally assumed. There is less agreement, however, regarding the letter's provenance. Paul indicates that he writes from prison (1:7, 17), but he provides no specific information about the location of his incarceration. Three major candidates are Rome (Fee, 34–37; Silva, 5–8; Bockmuehl, 25–32), Ephesus (Duncan; Ferguson, 85–87), and Caesarea (Hawthorne, xli–xliv; Soards, 33–34, 113–14). The references to "the whole praetorian guard" (ἐν ὅλῳ τῷ πραιτωρίῳ) in Phil 1:13 and to "the emperor's household" (οἱ ἐκ τῆς Καίσαρος οἰκίας) in Phil 4:22 favor the Roman setting, although a non-Roman imprisonment, especially in an imperial province such as Judea, is also conceivable. The usual objection to Rome as well as to Caesarea is the significant geographical distance between these localities and Philippi, which requires more travel time than the letter seems to presuppose. The proximity of Ephesus to Philippi, conversely, offers a better explanation of frequent contacts between Paul and the Philippians than a Roman or Caesarean imprisonment, but the references to the praetorian guard and the emperor's household appear anomalous in a senatorial province such as Asia. These and other arguments for or against a particular locale indicate that none of the reconstructions of the letter's provenance could be conclusive.

Literary Unity

The hypothesis that Philippians is a composite work rather than a single letter, which emerged in the 1960s and quickly gained scholarly support (Koester; Collange, 5–15; Sellew; Patte; Beare, 2–5, 24–25; Reumann, 8–13), is based on several observations: (1) the clause Τὸ λοιπόν, ἀδελφοί μου, χαίρετε ἐν κυρίῳ in Phil 3:1a may function as a farewell formula (cf. NRSV: "Finally, my brothers and sisters, rejoice in the Lord"), signaling the conclusion of a letter; (2) Phil 3:2 ("Beware of the dogs, beware of the evil workers, beware of the mutilation") marks the beginning of a new section extending through Phil 4:3, which is characterized by a sharply polemical tone that stands in contrast to the rest of the letter; (3) Phil 4:4 ("Rejoice in the Lord always! Again I will say, rejoice!") seems to be a continuation of Phil 3:1a (". . . rejoice in the Lord"); and (4) the thank-you note in Phil 4:10-20 appears out of place because such an expression of gratitude would normally be expected much earlier in the letter. The fragmentation hypothesis is supported by Polycarp's statement that Paul, when he was absent, wrote letters to the Philippians (Pol. *Phil.* 3.2). The proponents of this view typically regard the canonical Philippians as a compilation of three letter fragments: Letter A (4:10-20), Letter B (1:1-3:1 and possibly 4:4-9, 21-23), and Letter C (3:2-4:3).

The traditional view, which understands Philippians as a unified text, was revived in 1985 with the publication of Garland's article, in which he calls attention to several literary factors that support the idea of the unity of the letter. He rightly points out that the appeal to Τὸ λοιπόν in Phil 3:1a is inconclusive because this adverbial phrase could function not only as a closing formula but also as a transitional particle (149–50; cf. O'Brien, 348; Alexander, 96–97). More important for the integrity of Philippians, however, is the occurrence of parallel ideas and vocabulary in chs. 1–2 and 3–4, respectively, giving a thematic and linguistic coherence to the letter as a whole (Garland, 157–62; cf. Dalton, 100).

humility and self-abasement	2:2, 7	3:3, 8, 12-15
acceptance of suffering	1:29; 2:17	3:10
progress in the Christian life	2:12-14	3:12-16
partnership and sharing	1:5, 7; 2:1, 2, 17, 18	3:10, 17, 21; 4:14, 15

standing firm in one spirit / in the Lord	1:27	4:1
verbs χαίρω and συγχαίρω	1:18; 2:17, 18, 28	3:1; 4:4, 10
verb ὑπάρχω	2:6	3:20
verb φρονέω	1:7; 2:2, 5	3:15, 19; 4:2, 10
verb ἡγέομαι	2:3, 6, 25	3:7, 8
verb συναθλέω	1:27	4:3
noun θάνατος	2:8	3:10
μορφ-cognates	2:6, 7	3:10, 21
σχημ-cognates	2:7	3:21
ταπεινο-cognates	2:8	3:21
πολιτευ-cognates	1:27	3:20

This handbook follows the growing trend in Pauline studies that presumes the literary integrity of the letter (Watson 1988, 57–88; Guthrie; Levinsohn 1995; O'Brien, 10–18; Silva, 12–14; Reed 1996, 63–90). As is customary in the BHGNT series, however, even when I express preferences for certain readings, my comments regularly include references to alternative explanations of the meaning and function of individual words and phrases in the Greek text of Philippians.

Language

Philippians is a relatively short text, consisting of 1,633 words, 36 of which are NT *hapax legomena* (not counting the proper names). The language of the letter is characterized by the use of terms and formulations that convey affection, longing, reciprocity, and participation. For example, Paul calls the Philippians his "beloved and longed-for brothers [and sisters]" (ἀδελφοί μου ἀγαπητοὶ καὶ ἐπιπόθητοι [4:1; cf. 2:12]), talks about their "taking part in [his] trouble" (συγκοινωνήσαντές μου τῇ θλίψει [4:14]) and sharing with him "in the matter of giving and receiving" (εἰς λόγον δόσεως καὶ λήμψεως [4:15]), and frequently mentions his own (τὰ κατ' ἐμὲ) and their (τὰ περὶ ὑμῶν) circumstances (1:12, 27; 2:19, 20, 23). The most frequent lexemes are those conveying joy: χαρά (1:4, 25; 2:2, 29), χαίρω (1:18; 2:17, 18, 28; 3:1; 4:4, 10), and συγχαίρω (2:17, 18).

Paul's infrequent use of the explanatory conjunction γάρ (1:8, 18a, 19, 21, 23; 2:13, 20, 21; 3:3, 18, 20; 4:11) and the inferential conjunction οὖν (2:1, 23, 28, 29; 3:8, 15) indicate that his style in this letter is rarely argumentative. When we add to this the observation that Paul's usual theological vocabulary is either absent (ἐλπίζω, σῴζω) or rare (σωτηρία [1:28; 2:12]; ἐλπίς [1:20]; πιστεύω [2:29]; πίστις [2:17; 3:9]; χάρις [1:2, 7; 4:23]), we could probably conclude with Fee (20) that "[i]f this were the only Pauline letter to have survived, it would be well-nigh impossible to reconstruct his theology adequately; nor would we have any sense at all that Paul's apostleship counted for something!"

Verbal Aspect

The basic assumption of verbal aspect theory is that a speaker or writer grammaticalizes a view of a particular situation by selecting a particular verb form in the verbal system: the aorist tense if the situation is viewed as a complete event without regard for its progress (perfective aspect), the present or imperfect tense if the situation is viewed as in progress without regard for its beginning and end (imperfective aspect), and the perfect or pluperfect tense if a writer depicts a state of affairs that exists with no reference to any progress (stative aspect).

To help readers apply these insights to the biblical text, I have regularly commented on aspectual characteristics of various verb forms in Philippians. For example, in Phil 1:21 I note Paul's choice of the present infinitive ζῆν to describe the process of living and of the aorist infinitive ἀποθανεῖν to describe the transition from life to death, which is obscured in the English translations that use the gerunds "living" and "dying." I have also called attention to the aspectual difference between the perfect-tense ἥγημαι in Phil 3:7, which describes Paul's current view of his past privileges (stative aspect), and the present-tense ἡγοῦμαι in Phil 3:8, which expresses his ongoing view of all things (imperfective aspect). By using four aorist verbs (ἐμάθετε, παρελάβετε, ἠκούσατε, and εἴδετε) in Phil 4:9, Paul portrays each activity of the Philippians as a complete event, in contrast to the present imperative πράσσετε, which draws attention to the ongoing character of their implementation of the things that they have learned, accepted, heard, and seen in Paul. I have paid particular attention to Paul's use of the perfect tense and its prominence in the text (e.g., πεπληρωμένοι in 1:11; διεστραμμένης in 2:15; πεπλήρωμαι in 4:18), as well as to contextual clues that could indicate a prior occurrence of an event that produced a certain result (e.g., πεπληρωμένοι in 1:11; ἐλήλυθεν in 1:12). I therefore do not share Silva's view that "the significance of [aspectual] distinctions for biblical interpretation has been greatly overestimated.... Aspectual choices are usually restricted by factors of a grammatical or contextual nature, and so only seldom do they reflect a conscious semantic motivation" (11). While it is certainly true that Paul's use of some verb forms, such as οἶδα, is grammatically constrained, his choice of the verb forms is mostly purposeful and rhetorically effective.

Regarding the contentious question of whether Greek tenses carry any temporal references, I side with scholars who think that in the indicative mood Greek verbs do encode time. I am not persuaded by Porter's (1989, 75–83) test of contrastive substitution, i.e., the reasoning that if different tense forms could be used in the same context or, conversely, if the identical tense form could be used in different temporal contexts, we must conclude that Greek verbs do not grammaticalize time (Porter 1993, 32; for a critique of Porter's argument, see Runge 2014, 154–73). To expect that a verb tense must always have the same temporal reference is to create an absolute category into which no language could fit. The existence of two tense forms (the present and the imperfect) that convey imperfective aspect and two tense forms (the perfect and the pluperfect) that convey stative aspect also supports the idea that in the indicative mood Greek verbs encode time.

Most aorist indicative verbs in Philippians are past-referring. For example, ἐταπείνωσεν in Phil 2:8 describes Christ's self-imposed humiliation as an event that occurred in the past. Likewise, the verbs ὑπερύψωσεν and ἐχαρίσατο in the next verse depict God's vindication of Jesus in response to his death on the cross. The present-tense verbs are typically used to describe the current experiences of Paul or the Philippians. Since this is not a narrative, it is not surprising that no historical present can be found.

Word Order

I have regularly noted word order that differs from the default order of a Greek clause in which the finite verb is placed in the initial position (Levinsohn 2000, 38). When other elements of a clause are placed before the verb, i.e., when they are "fronted," they receive more prominence, but the actual reason for such fronting does not need to be emphasis. According to Runge, "Placing nonfocal information in [the] clause-initial position has the effect of establishing an explicit frame of reference for the clause that follows. It does not result in emphasis. By definition, emphasis refers to taking what was already most important in a clause and placing it ... at the beginning of the clause" (2010, 224). I have applied Runge's principle to the text of Philippians, using the *Lexham Discourse Greek New Testament* as an aid, and distinguished among three types of fronting: "fronted for emphasis," "fronted as a topical frame," and "fronted as a temporal frame." I have also called attention to the word order in which the verb is placed in final position, becoming the focal point of a clause.

Following Runge's suggestion, I have interpreted various cleft constructions linguistically as either left-dislocations, "where the new entity is dislocated to the beginning of the clause and then resumed in the main clause through the use of a pronominal trace" (2010, 289), or right-dislocations, which entail "referring to a participant in the midst of a clause using a pronoun or generic phrase and then adding more information about the same participant at the end of the clause" (317). I have identified nine relative clauses in Philippians that stand in left-dislocations: one in 3:7 (ἅτινα ἦν μοι κέρδη), one in 3:16 (εἰς ὃ ἐφθάσαμεν), six in 4:8 (ὅσα ἐστὶν ἀληθῆ, ὅσα σεμνά, ὅσα δίκαια, ὅσα ἁγνά, ὅσα προσφιλῆ, ὅσα εὔφημα), and one in 4:9 (ἃ καὶ ἐμάθετε καὶ παρελάβετε καὶ ἠκούσατε καὶ εἴδετε ἐν ἐμοί). Right-dislocations are more diverse and include adverbs (1:17), attributive modifiers (3:9), and appositions (3:9, 20; 4:18). In my English translations, which seek to approximate the word order and syntax of the Greek text for pedagogical purposes, I have used em dashes (—) to indicate the end of left-dislocations and the beginning of the main clauses. Right-dislocations are marked off either by commas or em dashes, depending on the function they have in the sentences in which they occur.

A HANDBOOK ON THE GREEK TEXT OF PHILIPPIANS

Philippians 1:1-2

¹Paul and Timothy, slaves of Christ Jesus, to all the saints in Christ Jesus who are in Philippi, together with the overseers and assistants: ²Grace to you and peace from God our Father and [from] the Lord Jesus Christ.

These two verses follow the conventional format for a salutation in an ancient Greek letter: a sender (in the nominative), a recipient (in the dative), and a greeting.

1:1 Παῦλος καὶ Τιμόθεος δοῦλοι Χριστοῦ Ἰησοῦ πᾶσιν τοῖς ἁγίοις ἐν Χριστῷ Ἰησοῦ τοῖς οὖσιν ἐν Φιλίπποις σὺν ἐπισκόποις καὶ διακόνοις,

Παῦλος . . . Τιμόθεος. Nominative absolutes. Paul's Greek name, Παῦλος, is the first word in all letters attributed to him (Rom 1:1; 1 Cor 1:1; 2 Cor 1:1; Gal 1:1; Eph 1:1; Phil 1:1; Col 1:1; 1 Thess 1:1; 2 Thess 1:1; 1 Tim 1:1; 2 Tim 1:1; Titus 1:1; Phlm 1). Τιμόθεος is mentioned, in addition to this letter, in the salutation of 2 Corinthians, Colossians, 1 Thessalonians, 2 Thessalonians, and Philemon.

καὶ. Coordinating conjunction, linking two nominative absolutes.
δοῦλοι. Nominative in apposition to Παῦλος καὶ Τιμόθεος.
Χριστοῦ Ἰησοῦ. Possessive genitive ("slaves belonging to Jesus Christ"; cf. Porter 1994, 93) or objective genitive qualifying δοῦλοι ("slaves serving Jesus Christ"). The term Χριστός is a Greek translation of the Hebrew term מָשִׁיחַ ("Anointed One"). Its earliest occurrence as a *terminus technicus* for the future deliverer of Israel ("the Messiah")

is in Pss. Sol. 17:32; 18:5, 7. Although it is generally assumed that in this construction Χριστός functions not as a messianic title but as a proper name ascribed to Jesus (Hengel; BDAG, 1091.2; TDNT 9:540), some scholars contend that in Paul's letters the term Χριστός retains its titular force (Dahl, 15–25; Wright 2009, 42; 2013, 817–25). An alternate view is offered by Novenson, who argues that Χριστός functions neither as a title nor as a name but as an "honorific, comparable in form to Epiphanes, Augustus, or Bar Kokhba" (174).

πᾶσιν τοῖς ἁγίοις. Dative of recipient. As Wallace explains, this type of dative "would ordinarily be an indirect object, except that it appears in *verbless constructions* (such as in titles and salutations)" (1996, 148). The article indicates that the adjective ἁγίοις ("dedicated or consecrated to the service of God" [BDAG, 10.1]) functions as a substantive ("the saints"; cf. BDAG, 11.2.d.β). The pronominal adjective πᾶσιν has attributive function ("all the saints") although it stands in the first predicate position (adjective-article-noun) (Wallace 1996, 307–8).

ἐν Χριστῷ Ἰησοῦ. According to BDAG (327.4.c), Paul uses the PP with ἐν "to designate a close personal relation in which the referent of the ἐν-term is viewed as the controlling influence." In his comprehensive analysis of this expression in the Pauline corpus, Campbell argues that the PP ἐν Χριστῷ and other related expressions (ἐν κυρίῳ, ἐν αὐτῷ, and ἐν ᾧ) "can express instrumentality, close association, agency, recognition, cause, kind and manner, locality, specification or substance, circumstance or condition, the object of faith, incorporation, union, reference or respect, and participation" (2012, 199; see also Wedderburn, 83–87; Reumann, 59–61). Since in the current context, ἐν Χριστῷ Ἰησοῦ qualifies the previous expression πᾶσιν τοῖς ἁγίοις (it is attributive in effect although it is not preceded by the article τοῖς; cf. Reumann, 58), its sense is either (1) instrumental/causal, explaining "how those in Philippi came to be 'saints'"; (2) locative, conveying that the saints in Philippi exist "in the sphere of [Christ's] power, spatially" (Reumann, 84; cf. Hansen, 40); or (3) relational, describing the recipients' union / close association with Christ (O'Brien, 46; Hansen, 40) and identifying them as Christians (Campbell 2012, 124). While the reverse word order, Ἰησοῦς Χριστός, frequently occurs in Paul's letters (e.g., Rom 1:4, 6, 7, 8; 3:22; 1 Cor 1:2, 3, 7, 9, 10; 6:11; Gal 1:1, 3, 12; 2:16; 3:1, 22; Phil 1:2, 11, 19; 2:11, 21; 4:23), in the prepositional phrases with ἐν he always uses the order Χριστός Ἰησοῦς (e.g., Rom 3:24; 6:11; 8:1; 1 Cor 1:2, 4, 30; Gal 2:4; 3:14, 26, 28; Phil 1:1, 26; 2:5; 3:3, 14; 4:7, 19, 21; 1 Thess 2:14; 5:18; Phlm 23), as here.

τοῖς οὖσιν. Pres act ptc masc dat pl εἰμί (attributive). The participle modifies τοῖς ἁγίοις, standing in the second attributive position (article-noun-article-attributive participle) (Wallace 1996, 306–7, 618).

ἐν Φιλίπποις. Locative.
σὺν ἐπισκόποις καὶ διακόνοις. Accompaniment. Two groups of church officials are included among the recipients (τοῖς ἁγίοις ἐν Χριστῷ Ἰησοῦ τοῖς οὖσιν ἐν Φιλίπποις). Although καί could mark a hendiadys—a "co-ordination of two ideas, one of which is dependent on the other" (BDF §442.16)—ἐπισκόποις and διακόνοις probably refer to two distinct groups. ἐπίσκοπος denotes "one who has a definite function or fixed office of guardianship and related activity within a group" (BDAG, 379.2). The variant συνεπισκόποις (B² D² K P^vid 075 33 1241 1739 1881 et al.) is a later scribal modification, which "arose no doubt from dogmatic or ecclesiastical interests" (Metzger, 544). Although some English translations use the term "bishop" as a rendering of ἐπίσκοπος (ASV; NRSV; REB; KJV), this "ecclesiastical loanword . . . is too technical and loaded with late historical baggage for precise signification of usage of ἐπίσκοπος and cognates in our lit[erature], esp. the NT" (BDAG, 379.2). It is therefore better to use more neutral terms, such as "overseer" or "supervisor." In this context, διάκονος denotes "one identified for special ministerial service in a Christian community" (BDAG, 231.2). Since the English derivatives "deacon" and "deaconess" are technical terms that have been variously used in church history, they are "inadequate for rendering NT usage of δ[ιάκονος]" (BDAG, 230–31.2). I have therefore opted for the term "assistant" as a less loaded translation, which adequately conveys the sense of the Greek term.

1:2 χάρις ὑμῖν καὶ εἰρήνη ἀπὸ θεοῦ πατρὸς ἡμῶν καὶ κυρίου Ἰησοῦ Χριστοῦ.

χάρις ὑμῖν καὶ εἰρήνη ἀπὸ θεοῦ πατρὸς ἡμῶν καὶ κυρίου Ἰησοῦ Χριστοῦ. Paul's customary greeting found in Rom 1:7; 1 Cor 1:3; 2 Cor 1:2; Gal 1:3; Eph 1:2; Phil 1:2; 2 Thess 1:2; Phlm 3.
χάρις . . . καὶ εἰρήνη. Nominative subjects of a verbless clause. The omission of the verb is "normal in formulaic wishes like εἰρήνη ὑμῖν etc." (BDF §128.5). Paul replaces the standard form of Hellenistic epistolary greeting χαίρειν with χάρις and adds the traditional Jewish greeting εἰρήνη corresponding to the Hebrew שָׁלוֹם ("peace") (BDAG, 287–88.2.a; cf. LXX Judg 6:23; 19:20; 2 Kgs 5:22).
ὑμῖν. Dative of advantage.
ἀπὸ θεοῦ . . . καὶ . . . κυρίου. Source. BDF (§254.1) explains that "θεός and κύριος (= יהוה but also Christ) designate beings of which there is only one of a kind, and these words (especially κύριος) frequently come very close to being proper names; the article appears when the specific Jewish or Christian God or Lord is meant (not 'a being of divine nature'

or 'a Lord'), but it is sometimes missing, especially after prepositions," as here. Turner notes that "in rather formal wording, as in the opening of an epistle, κύριος or θεός will occur without art[icle], followed by an anarthrous appositional phrase" (MHT 3:206).

πατρός. Genitive in apposition to θεοῦ. On the absence of the article before πατρός, see ἀπὸ θεοῦ ... καὶ ... κυρίου above.

ἡμῶν. Genitive of relationship modifying πατρός.

Ἰησοῦ Χριστοῦ. Genitive in apposition to κυρίου.

Philippians 1:3-11

³I thank my God at [my] every remembrance of you, ⁴always in my every prayer for all of you, making the prayer with joy, ⁵because of your participation in [the furtherance of] the gospel from the first day until now, ⁶since I am confident of this very thing, that the one who began a good work among you will complete [it] until the day of Christ Jesus. ⁷So it is right for me to think this about all of you because I hold you in my heart—all of you who are partakers with me of grace, both in my imprisonment and in the defense and confirmation of the gospel. ⁸For God [is] my witness how I long for all of you with the affection of Christ Jesus. ⁹And this I pray, that your love may abound still more and more in knowledge and every discernment, ¹⁰so that you may approve the things that really matter, in order that you may be sincere and blameless in the day of Christ, ¹¹having been filled with the fruit of righteousness that comes through Jesus Christ, for the glory and praise of God.

1:3 Εὐχαριστῶ τῷ θεῷ μου ἐπὶ πάσῃ τῇ μνείᾳ ὑμῶν

Εὐχαριστῶ. Pres act ind 1st sg εὐχαριστέω. Εὐχαριστῶ ("to express appreciation for benefits or blessings" [BDAG, 415.2]) functions as the governing verb of the long sentence that begins in v. 3 and ends in v. 6.

τῷ θεῷ. Dative complement of Εὐχαριστῶ.

μου. Genitive of subordination modifying θεῷ. Paul regularly uses the expression "my God" after εὐχαριστέω when the verb is in the singular (Rom 1:8; 1 Cor 1:4; Phlm 4; and here; see also the expression ὁ θεός μου in Phil 4:19 and 2 Cor 12:21). When εὐχαριστέω is in the plural, the personal pronoun is missing (1 Thess 1:2; 2:13; Col 1:3).

ἐπὶ πάσῃ τῇ μνείᾳ. Temporal (BDF §235.5; Fee, 78–80; Reed 1997, 201) or causal (O'Brien, 58–61). The noun μνεία means either "remembrance, memory" (BDAG, 654.1; LN 29.7) or "mention (in prayer)" (BDAG, 654.2). While the expression πάσῃ τῇ μνείᾳ technically denotes "the whole of my remembrance" (BDF §275.3; MHT 3:200), it probably means "every remembrance" because, as Fee notes, "in reality the remembrance of them happened from time to time, especially in prayer" (79 n. 38). This conclusion is consistent with Turner's observation that "the distinction of an anarthrous and articular noun with πᾶς is not very clear in NT, even to the extent that πᾶς with an articular noun can approach the meaning of *any*" (MHT 3:200). Temporal interpretation of ἐπὶ πάσῃ τῇ μνείᾳ requires understanding ὑμῶν as the objective genitive: "every time I remember you" (NRSV) or "whenever I remember you" (WEB). Causal interpretation of the PP can be combined with both possible functions of ὑμῶν. If ὑμῶν is taken as the objective genitive, the meaning is "for every remembrance of you" (HCSB) or "for all the memories I have of you" (GW). If ὑμῶν is taken as the subjective genitive, the meaning is "because of your every remembrance of me" (Hellerman 2015, 19; O'Brien, 58–61). Because temporal rendering of the expression ἐπὶ πάσῃ τῇ μνείᾳ makes more sense in its current context (see ὑμῶν below), I have adopted it in my translation above.

ὑμῶν. Objective genitive ("remembering you" or "mentioning you"; cf. ASV; ESV; LEB; NIV; NRSV; REB) or subjective genitive modifying μνείᾳ ("your remembrance [of me]"; cf. O'Brien, 58–61; Reumann, 149). While interpreting ὑμῶν subjectively makes good sense in the larger context of the letter because it calls attention to the Philippians' generosity and contribution to Paul's needs (4:10-20), the objective meaning is supported by the next verse, in which Paul speaks about his prayer for the readers (ὑπὲρ πάντων ὑμῶν). Besides, in other occurrences of μνεία + genitive in the LXX (Job 14:13; Ps 110:4; Wis 5:14; Zech 13:2; Isa 23:16; Jer 38:20) and the NT (Rom 1:9; 3:6; Phlm 4), the genitive is regularly the object of the remembering. To this we should add Fee's astute remark that interpreting ὑμῶν as a subjective genitive "creates a most unusual Pauline thanksgiving, namely that '*always*, in *my every prayer for you all*' what I thank God is your gift to me!" (79 n. 37). Considering these observations, taking ὑμῶν as the objective genitive makes the best sense of Paul's syntax in this verse.

1:4 πάντοτε ἐν πάσῃ δεήσει μου ὑπὲρ πάντων ὑμῶν, μετὰ χαρᾶς τὴν δέησιν ποιούμενος,

πάντοτε ἐν πάσῃ δεήσει μου ὑπὲρ πάντων ὑμῶν. Although this temporal clarification could go with the participial clause that follows (μετὰ χαρᾶς τὴν δέησιν ποιούμενος), it is better to take it with the previous clause in v. 3 (Εὐχαριστῶ τῷ θεῷ μου ἐπὶ πάσῃ τῇ μνείᾳ ὑμῶν). The alliteration created by the repetition of the πά-initial sound (πάσῃ . . .

πάντοτε . . . πάσῃ . . . πάντων) also shows that vv. 3-4a should be kept together.

πάντοτε. Temporal adverb.

ἐν πάσῃ δεήσει. Temporal. πάσῃ modifies δεήσει ("urgent request to meet a need, exclusively addressed to God" [BDAG, 213]), standing in the first (anarthrous) attributive position (adjective-noun) (Wallace 1996, 309–10).

μου. Subjective genitive qualifying δεήσει.

ὑπὲρ πάντων ὑμῶν. Reference/respect or advantage. This use of ὑπέρ is close to the sense of περί (Robertson, 632; Harris, 210–11). Wallace (1996, 85 n. 41) rightly points out that ὑμῶν is not a partitive genitive. His own suggestion that ὑμῶν should be regarded as an apposition to πάντων presumes that πάντων functions as a substantive. A better explanation, in my view, is to understand πάντων as an adjective modifying the personal pronoun ὑμῶν (cf. BDAG, 783.1.c.α; see also πάντας ὑμᾶς in 1:7, 8).

μετὰ χαρᾶς. Manner. Fronted for emphasis.

τὴν δέησιν. Accusative direct object of ποιούμενος.

ποιούμενος. Pres mid ptc masc nom sg ποιέω (manner [Reumann, 104] or temporal [Wallace 1996, 627]). Runge argues that adverbial participles that follow the main verb, as here, "have a somewhat different effect from those that precede it, in that they elaborate the action of the main verb, often providing more specific explanation of what is meant by the main action. . . . Rather than offering a distinct action in its own right, the participle relegates its action to supporting the main action" (2010, 262–63). Although the post-main-verb participles are typically more important than the pre-main-verb participles in relation to the main verb, they do not provide the foreground information because, as Buth points out, "they are ranked with lower prominence than the main head verbs because they are participles" (282 n. 9).

1:5 ἐπὶ τῇ κοινωνίᾳ ὑμῶν εἰς τὸ εὐαγγέλιον ἀπὸ τῆς πρώτης ἡμέρας ἄχρι τοῦ νῦν,

ἐπὶ τῇ κοινωνίᾳ. Causal (Zerwick §126; Reumann, 106). If ἐπὶ πάσῃ τῇ μνείᾳ in v. 3 is understood temporally, as I suggest, ἐπὶ τῇ κοινωνίᾳ in this verse is the only prepositional phrase in vv. 3-6 that expresses the ground for Paul's thanksgiving (Εὐχαριστῶ, v. 3). Given its proximity to the preceding participial clause (μετὰ χαρᾶς τὴν δέησιν ποιούμενος, v. 4), this PP could also be seen as providing the reason for Paul's joyful prayer (Fee, 81). In this context, the term κοινωνία denotes "close association involving mutual interests and sharing" (BDAG, 552.1) that could be translated "fellowship" (ASV; KJV), "partnership" (HCSB; ESV; NIV; RSV), "sharing" (NRSV), or "participation" (LEB; NASB). Paul's use of cognate verbs κοινωνέω and συγκοινωνέω in 4:14-15 may indicate that the noun κοινωνία here refers primarily, though not exclusively, to the Philippians' financial participation in the spread of the gospel (O'Brien, 61; Fee, 84; see also Paul's use κοινωνία + εἰς in Rom 15:26 and 2 Cor 9:13 in reference to the collection for the poor in Jerusalem).

ὑμῶν. Subjective genitive qualifying κοινωνίᾳ.

εἰς τὸ εὐαγγέλιον. Reference/respect or advantage (BDAG, 291.5; Harris, 85). In this PP, εἰς does not stand for ἐν, as the Vulgate's rendering, *in evangelio*, assumes, because Paul typically preserves the distinction between these two prepositions (MHT 3:256). Zerwick (§107) suggests that the PP εἰς τὸ εὐαγγέλιον "is to be understood as cooperation in the spread of the gospel," i.e., as the Philippians' participation in a process (furthering the gospel) rather than in a state (demonstrating the possession of the gospel in their lives). The term εὐαγγέλιον, as elsewhere in the NT, is used "only in the sense of good news relating to God's action in Jesus Christ" (BDAG, 402).

ἀπὸ τῆς πρώτης ἡμέρας. Temporal. The ordinal adjective πρώτης stands in the first attributive position (article-adjective-noun) (Wallace 1996, 306). The juxtaposition of two prepositional phrases (ἀπὸ ... ἄχρι) suggests a time interval between τῆς πρώτης ἡμέρας and τοῦ νῦν.

ἄχρι τοῦ νῦν. Temporal. ἄχρι ("until") is a temporal conjunction, which here serves as an improper preposition. The main distinction between improper and proper prepositions is that the former cannot be prefixed to verb forms. When they are used in prepositional phrases, as here, improper prepositions function in the same way as proper prepositions (Porter 1994, 140; Harris, 243). The article τοῦ functions as a nominalizer, changing the adverb νῦν into the object of the preposition ἄχρι. The PP ἄχρι τοῦ νῦν conveys duration of time, whose end point is the present moment ("now").

1:6 πεποιθὼς αὐτὸ τοῦτο, ὅτι ὁ ἐναρξάμενος ἐν ὑμῖν ἔργον ἀγαθὸν ἐπιτελέσει ἄχρι ἡμέρας Χριστοῦ Ἰησοῦ·

πεποιθὼς. Prf act ptc masc nom sg πείθω (causal). The perfect tense of πείθω ("to come to believe the certainty of something on the basis of being convinced" [LN 31.46]) has the sense of the present: "I have been persuaded and therefore am convinced" (Reumann, 111; cf. BDF §341; Zerwick and Grosvenor, 592). The participle modifies Εὐχαριστῶ in v. 3, providing another reason (see ἐπὶ τῇ κοινωνίᾳ in v. 5) for Paul's thanksgiving.

αὐτὸ τοῦτο. Accusative of respect/accusative of general reference (BDF §154). This phrase, which combines the identical adjective αὐτὸ and the demonstrative pronoun τοῦτο ("this same thing" or "this very thing"), is quite common in the Pauline corpus (Rom 9:17; 13:6; 2 Cor 5:5; 7:11; Gal 2:10; Eph 6:22; Col 4:8). While τοῦτο could be anaphoric, referring back "to the constancy emphasized in v. 5" (BDF 290.4), it is probably cataphoric, referring to the ὅτι clause that follows (O'Brien, 63; Fee, 85 n. 62; Reumann, 111).

ὅτι. Introduces a nominal clause that stands in apposition to τοῦτο (Wallace 1996, 459, 665).

ὁ ἐναρξάμενος ἐν ὑμῖν ἔργον ἀγαθὸν. Fronted as a topical frame. This type of fronting is governed by the following functional principle: "To provide a new point of departure for what follows, place the element which expresses that point of departure at the beginning of the clause or sentence concerned" (Levinsohn 1995, 61).

ὁ ἐναρξάμενος. Aor mid ptc masc nom sg ἐνάρχομαι (substantival). Nominative subject of ἐπιτελέσει. The substantival participle is used here not just to describe but also to identify God as the one who started an ἔργον ἀγαθὸν among the Philippians.

ἐν ὑμῖν. Locative. The sense of the PP is collective ("among you") rather than individual ("in you").

ἔργον ἀγαθὸν. Accusative direct object of ἐναρξάμενος. The adjective ἀγαθὸν stands in the fourth attributive position (noun-adjective) (Wallace 1996, 310–11).

ἐπιτελέσει. Fut act ind 3rd sg ἐπιτελέω. The verb ἐπιτελέω means "to bring an activity to a successful finish—'to complete, to finish, to end, to accomplish'" (LN 68.22). The portrayal of God as the one who started a good work among the recipients, on the one hand, and the temporal reference ἄχρι ἡμέρας Χριστοῦ Ἰησοῦ, on the other hand, suggest that here "the work of salvation and its completion are . . . depicted as two overlapping events—once the good work has begun it is being completed, so that the Future refers to past, present, and future events, but even more than that, to Paul's expectation of them" (Porter 1989, 426). Wallace calls this specific use of the present tense "predictive future" and thinks that in this context ἐπιτελέσει "seems to suggest a progressive idea" (1996, 568). The understood direct object of ἐπιτελέσει is αὐτό because "[i]n keeping with its economic nature, Greek regularly implies an object that was already mentioned in the preceding context, rather than restating it" (409 n. 5; cf. MHT 3:39).

ἄχρι ἡμέρας. Temporal. The article is omitted because ἡμέρα Χριστοῦ Ἰησοῦ is a set phrase referring to the parousia (Zerwick and Grosvenor,

592; Zerwick §183). Because the expression ἡμέρα Χριστοῦ Ἰησοῦ ("the day of Christ Jesus") has future implicature, the PP with the improper preposition ἄχρι (see 1:5 on ἄχρι τοῦ νῦν) describes the interval until the end point in the future is reached.

Χριστοῦ Ἰησοῦ. Aporetic genitive (cf. Wallace 1996, 79) modifying ἡμέρας ("the day of Christ Jesus" = "the day when Christ Jesus comes"). Paul uses a similar expression in 1:10 and 2:16 ("the day of Christ"). Elsewhere in his letters, he talks about "the day of our Lord Jesus" (1 Cor 1:8), "the day of the Lord" (1 Thess 5:2), or simply "that day" (1 Thess 5:4).

1:7 Καθώς ἐστιν δίκαιον ἐμοὶ τοῦτο φρονεῖν ὑπὲρ πάντων ὑμῶν διὰ τὸ ἔχειν με ἐν τῇ καρδίᾳ ὑμᾶς, ἔν τε τοῖς δεσμοῖς μου καὶ ἐν τῇ ἀπολογίᾳ καὶ βεβαιώσει τοῦ εὐαγγελίου συγκοινωνούς μου τῆς χάριτος πάντας ὑμᾶς ὄντας.

Καθώς. Introduces a causal clause. When the adverb καθώς ("just as") is used to introduce a sentence, as here, it means "since, insofar as" (BDF §453.2; BDAG, 494.3; Robertson, 968).

ἐστιν. Pres act ind 3rd sg εἰμί.

δίκαιον. Predicate adjective.

ἐμοὶ. Dative of advantage.

τοῦτο. Accusative direct object of φρονεῖν. The demonstrative pronoun is anaphoric, referring back to vv. 3-6.

φρονεῖν. Pres act inf φρονέω. The infinitival phrase, τοῦτο φρονεῖν ὑπὲρ πάντων ὑμῶν, functions as the subject of ἐστιν. The sense of φρονέω in this context is "to have an opinion with regard to someth[ing]," or more specifically, to "think or feel in a certain way about someone" (BDAG, 1065.1).

ὑπὲρ πάντων ὑμῶν. Reference/respect. This use of ὑπέρ is close to the sense of περί (Robertson, 632; Harris, 210–11); see also 1:4 on ὑπὲρ πάντων ὑμῶν.

ἔχειν. Pres act inf ἔχω. Used with διὰ τὸ to indicate cause (BDF §402.1; Wallace 1996, 597). This is the only occurrence of διὰ τὸ + infinitive in the letters of Paul.

με. Accusative subject of the infinitive ἔχειν. Since ἔχειν is followed by two accusatives, με and ὑμᾶς, either could be regarded as the subject of the infinitive. Although the NRSV ("because you hold me in your heart") and some commentaries (Hawthorne and Martin, 26; Witherington, 55; Reumann, 117, 153) take ὑμᾶς as the subject of ἔχειν, most English translations presume that με is the subject of the infinitive ("because I hold you in my heart"). This reading is supported by two considerations. The first is the word order ("in infinitive constructions in the NT where two items are found in the accusative, in the overwhelming majority of instances the subject precedes the object" [Porter 1994, 203]; cf. Reed 1991, 1–27; for Wallace [1996, 193, 196], the word order is not the primary consideration but "the factor that tips the scales"). The second is the context (cf. the explanatory clause in v. 8: "for God is my witness how I long for all of you . . .").

ἐν τῇ καρδίᾳ. Locative. τῇ καρδίᾳ is a distributive singular. Since human anatomy is involved, the article functions like a possessive pronoun (Wallace 1996, 196, 215–16).

ὑμᾶς. Accusative direct object of the infinitive ἔχειν (see με above).

ἔν . . . τοῖς δεσμοῖς. State or condition. Although τοῖς δεσμοῖς ("bonds, fetters, chains") could be understood literally (cf. Fee, 92), the plural form is probably used here as metonymy for imprisonment ("the state of being in prison" [LN 37.115]; see Phil 1:13; 2 Tim 2:9; Phlm 10, 13). The PP ἔν . . . τοῖς δεσμοῖς modifies the participial clause that follows (συγκοινωνούς μου τῆς χάριτος πάντας ὑμᾶς ὄντας).

μου. Possessive genitive modifying δεσμοῖς ("my chains").

τε . . . καί. A combination of the enclitic particle and a coordinating conjunction that is used to connect "concepts, usu[ally] of the same kind or corresponding as opposites" (BDAG, 993.2.c.α). This construction connects two prepositional phrases with ἔν (ἔν . . . τοῖς δεσμοῖς and ἐν τῇ ἀπολογίᾳ καὶ βεβαιώσει) and can be translated "both . . . and" or "not only . . . but also."

ἐν τῇ ἀπολογίᾳ καὶ βεβαιώσει. State or condition. Like the previous PP (ἔν . . . τοῖς δεσμοῖς), ἐν τῇ ἀπολογίᾳ καὶ βεβαιώσει modifies the participial clause that follows (συγκοινωνούς μου τῆς χάριτος πάντας ὑμᾶς ὄντας). While two nouns connected by καί and governed by a single article could be understood as hendiadys—"the co-ordination of two ideas, one of which is dependent on the other" (BDF §442.16; cf. Reumann, 118; Silva, 48)—it is better to regard them as an example of the TSKS (the article-substantive-καί-substantive) construction. In such formulations, according to the Granville Sharp rule, the single article indicates that both substantives have the same referent, but only if neither is impersonal, neither is plural, and neither is a proper name (Wallace 1996, 270–72). Since ἀπολογία ("the act of making a defense" [BDAG, 117.2]; cf. Acts 25:16; 2 Tim 4:16; 1 Pet 3:15) and βεβαίωσις (the "process of establishing or confirming something" [BDAG, 173]; cf. Heb 6:16) are impersonal nouns, they do not fulfill the conditions for the application of the Granville Sharp rule. Even so, impersonal TSKS constructions can indicate five semantic possibilities: (1) distinct entities, though united; (2) overlapping entities; (3) first entity subset of second; (4) second entity subset of first; and (5) identical entities (Wallace 1996, 286–90). Wallace suggests that the expression τῇ ἀπολογίᾳ καὶ βεβαιώσει represents the third option, i.e., that ἀπολογία is a subset of βεβαίωσις.

τοῦ εὐαγγελίου. Objective genitive modifying both verbal nouns in the TSKS construction, ἀπολογίᾳ and βεβαιώσει.

συγκοινωνούς. Predicate accusative. Fronted for emphasis. The noun συγκοινωνούς ("participants, partners"; cf. BDAG, 952) stands in predicate relationship to πάντας ὑμᾶς, with which it is joined by the participle ὄντας.

μου. Genitive of association modifying συγκοινωνούς ("participants with me"). μου does not modify the following noun, τῆς χάριτος, as some English translations presume (e.g., KJV: "my grace"; cf. Reumann, 120). Rather, the genitive case "indicates the one with whom the noun to which it stands related is associated. . . . The head noun to which this kind of genitival use is connected is normally prefixed with συν-" (Wallace 1996, 128), as here.

τῆς χάριτος. Genitive complement of συγκοινωνούς. BDAG (952) calls it the "gen[itive] of the thing in which one shares."

πάντας ὑμᾶς. Accusative in apposition to ὑμᾶς in v. 7a. Since this is a repetition of the previous pronoun (Robertson, 491), πάντας ὑμᾶς is pleonastic (Reumann, 119); see also 1:4 on ὑπὲρ πάντων ὑμῶν.

ὄντας. Pres act ptc masc acc pl εἰμί (attributive). The participle does not stand in apposition to πάντας ὑμᾶς (*pace* Hellerman 2015, 29) but modifies this accusative adjectivally (lit. "all of you who are partakers . . ."). Semantically, however, the participle indicates cause, providing the reasons for Paul's feeling about the Philippians (Hellerman 2015, 29). Distinguishing between the syntactical (adjectival modifier of πάντας ὑμᾶς) and semantic (causal) function of ὄντας offers a better explanation of the syntax of this long sentence than taking ὄντας as a causal participle (Hawthorne and Martin, 27; Haubeck and von Siebenthal, 1069). While many grammarians presume that oblique participles could function adverbially, Culy (2003) has demonstrated that adverbial participles are always in the nominative, agreeing with the subject of the verb, except when they modify a genitive subject (genitive absolute) or an infinitive whose semantic subject is in the accusative. Since ὄντας modifies πάντας ὑμᾶς, which stands in apposition to an earlier ὑμᾶς functioning as the accusative direct object of the infinitive ἔχειν, it does not fulfill the conditions for an adverbial participle. To emulate the syntax of the Greek sentence, I have placed the em dash (—) before "all of you" to indicate that it functions appositionally to the previous "you" in the sentence, and I have used the relative clause "who are partakers . . ."

to indicate that the participle ὄντας functions as an attributive modifier of "all of you."

1:8 μάρτυς γάρ μου ὁ θεὸς ὡς ἐπιποθῶ πάντας ὑμᾶς ἐν σπλάγχνοις Χριστοῦ Ἰησοῦ.

μάρτυς. Predicate nominative. The absence of the article shows that μάρτυς ("one who affirms or attests" [BDAG, 619.2]) functions as the predicate nominative (cf. McGaughy, 36–54; Wallace 1996, 243). Because in this clause the copula is lacking, μάρτυς cannot properly be called a preverbal predicate nominative. Its placement before the subject, however, indicates that it is fronted for emphasis.

γάρ. Postpositive conjunction introducing a clause that reinforces Paul's claim in v. 7 that he holds the Philippians in his heart. Based on insights from modern linguistic treatments of γάρ, Runge concludes that "the information introduced does not advance the discourse but adds background information that strengthens or supports what precedes" (2010, 52; cf. Levinsohn 2000, 91).

μου. Possessive genitive qualifying μάρτυς ("my witness"). The variant μοι (ℵ[3vid] D F G Ψ 0278 104 326 365 1175 1241) is a scribal correction. The omission of μου in 𝔓[46] is most likely accidental.

ὁ θεὸς. Nominative subject of an implied ἐστιν. Many scribes added ἐστιν before ὁ θεὸς (ℵ[2] A D K L P 075 0278 81 104 365 630 1175 1241 1505 1881 2464 𝔐 lat sy[h]), but the verbless clause is preferable because of its strong external support (𝔓[46] ℵ* B F G Ψ 6 33 1739 d) and its ability to explain the origin of the longer reading. In clauses in which two nouns are linked with an equative verb, either expressed or implied, if one substantive is articular and another anarthrous, as here, the noun that has the article is the subject (cf. McGaughy, 36–54; Wallace 1996, 243). Paul makes the same declaration, invoking God as a witness, in Rom 1:9 (μάρτυς γάρ μού ἐστιν ὁ θεός).

ὡς. ὡς functions here as a "marker of discourse content" (BDAG, 1105.5; LN 90.21) that introduces a declarative clause. Its use is similar to ὅτι, but it places more focus on manner (Culy and Parsons, 212).

ἐπιποθῶ. Pres act ind 1st sg ἐπιποθέω. The verb means "to have a strong desire for someth[ing], with implication of need" (BDAG, 377). In the NT, ἐπιποθέω is used almost exclusively in the Pauline corpus (nine out of eleven occurrences).

πάντας ὑμᾶς. Accusative direct object of ἐπιποθῶ (see also 1:4 on ὑπὲρ πάντων ὑμῶν).

ἐν σπλάγχνοις. Means/manner or causal. The literal meaning of the plural σπλάγχνα is "inward parts of a body, including esp. the viscera," "inward parts, entrails" (BDAG, 938.1). Used metaphorically, as here, the noun denotes "great affection and compassion for someone" (LN 25.49). The metaphorical meaning is derived from the idea that entrails are the seat and source of deep emotions, such as love and compassion. If the function of the PP is means/manner, ἐν σπλάγχνοις Χριστοῦ Ἰησοῦ characterizes "the kind of love which Paul has for the believers, for example, 'how I long for all of you, even with the kind of love Christ Jesus himself has for you'" (LN 25.49). If the function of the PP is causal, ἐν σπλάγχνοις Χριστοῦ Ἰησοῦ "may mean 'because of the compassion which Christ Jesus himself has for you' or '. . . for me'" (LN 25.49). My translation reflects the first option.

Χριστοῦ Ἰησοῦ. Subjective genitive ("the affection Christ Jesus has for you") or genitive of source qualifying σπλάγχνοις ("the affection derived from Jesus Christ").

1:9 Καὶ τοῦτο προσεύχομαι, ἵνα ἡ ἀγάπη ὑμῶν ἔτι μᾶλλον καὶ μᾶλλον περισσεύῃ ἐν ἐπιγνώσει καὶ πάσῃ αἰσθήσει

Καὶ. Coordinating conjunction linking Paul's prayer in vv. 9-11 to his expression of longing and affection in v. 8.

τοῦτο. Accusative direct object of προσεύχομαι. The near-demonstrative pronoun τοῦτο functions as a forward-pointing reference to the ἵνα clause that follows, attracting extra attention to the content of Paul's prayer. Runge explains that "it is not the part of speech used that achieves added prominence, but rather the non-default use of the expression to point forward" (2010, 68). Had Paul simply said, "And I pray that your love may abound," he would not have achieved the same rhetorical effect as when he said, "And *this* I pray, that your love may abound."

προσεύχομαι. Pres mid ind 1st sg προσεύχομαι. This is the main verb of the sentence that starts in this verse and ends in v. 11.

ἵνα. Introduces an epexegetical clause that explains τοῦτο (Haubeck and von Siebenthal, 1069; Zerwick §410; BDF §394; Moule, 145–46) or, alternatively, a substantival clause that is appositional to τοῦτο (cf. Wallace 1996, 475–76).

ἡ ἀγάπη. Nominative subject of περισσεύῃ. Fronted as a topical frame.

ὑμῶν. Subjective genitive qualifying ἡ ἀγάπη. The object of the Philippians' love is not expressed.

ἔτι. Adverb pertaining to number, denoting "that which is added to what is already at hand" (BDAG, 400.2.b).

μᾶλλον καὶ μᾶλλον. Comparative of the adverb μάλα ("more, rather"), which is doubled for emphasis (Robertson, 663–64). This expression "serves to emphasize the degree expressed in περισσεύῃ" (LN 78.31).

περισσεύῃ. Pres act subj 3rd sg περισσεύω. Subjunctive with ἵνα. Porter (1989, 331) emphasizes that the present subjunctive "grammaticaliz[es] the author's view of the action as in progress," which is further corroborated by the use of the modifiers ἔτι μᾶλλον καὶ μᾶλλον.

ἐν ἐπιγνώσει καὶ πάσῃ αἰσθήσει. Locative, indicating the sphere within which love operates (REB: "in knowledge and insight of every kind"; cf. O'Brien, 75), or means/manner through which love operates (ESV: "with knowledge and all discernment"). ἐπίγνωσις means "knowledge, recognition," which is in the LXX and the NT "limited to transcendent and moral matters" (BDAG, 369). αἴσθησις is a NT *hapax legomenon* that denotes "capacity to perceive clearly and hence to understand the real nature of something" (LN 32.28). Although the sense of the adjective πάσῃ, which modifies αἰσθήσει, could be elative (NRSV: "full insight"), it is probably distributive ("insight for all kinds of situations as they arise" [O'Brien, 77]; REB: "insight of every kind").

1:10 εἰς τὸ δοκιμάζειν ὑμᾶς τὰ διαφέροντα, ἵνα ἦτε εἰλικρινεῖς καὶ ἀπρόσκοποι εἰς ἡμέραν Χριστοῦ,

δοκιμάζειν. Pres act inf δοκιμάζω. Used with εἰς τὸ to indicate purpose (Robertson, 990–91; MHT 3:143; O'Brien, 77; Haubeck and von Siebenthal, 1070) or, less likely, result (Reumann, 126) of Paul's prayer for increased love (v. 9). Although δοκιμάζω can mean "to make a critical examination of someth[ing] to determine genuineness" (BDAG, 255.1), in the current context this verb means "to draw a conclusion about worth on the basis of testing" (BDAG, 255.2), or more specifically, "accept as proved, approve" (BDAG, 255.2.b).

ὑμᾶς. Accusative subject of the infinitive δοκιμάζειν.

τὰ διαφέροντα. Pres act ptc neut acc pl διαφέρω (substantival). Direct object of the infinitive δοκιμάζειν. διαφέρω here means to "differ to one's advantage fr[om] someone or someth[ing]," "be worth more than, be superior to" (BDAG, 239.4). In my translation, I have adopted BDAG's rendering of τὰ διαφέροντα as "the things that really matter."

ἵνα. Introduces a clause that either (1) gives the purpose of Paul's overall prayer, modifying the main verb προσεύχομαι in v. 9, (2) offers another purpose (see δοκιμάζειν above) of Paul's prayer for increased love described in the previous ἵνα clause (v. 9), or (3) provides the purpose of the preceding infinitival phrase (εἰς τὸ δοκιμάζειν ὑμᾶς τὰ διαφέροντα).

ἦτε. Pres act subj 2nd pl εἰμί. Subjunctive with ἵνα.

εἰλικρινεῖς. Predicate adjective. εἰλικρινεῖς (nom pl from εἰλικρινής) pertains "to being sincere, without hidden motives or pretense" (BDAG, 282).

καὶ. Coordinating conjunction, linking two predicate adjectives.

ἀπρόσκοποι. Predicate adjective. ἀπρόσκοπος pertains "to being without fault because of not giving offense" (BDAG, 125.1).

εἰς ἡμέραν. Temporal ("until the day of Christ" or "in the day of Christ") or purpose ("for the day of Christ").

Χριστοῦ. Aporetic genitive (cf. Wallace 1996, 79) modifying ἡμέραν ("the day of Christ" = "the day when Christ comes"); see 1:6 on Χριστοῦ Ἰησοῦ.

1:11 πεπληρωμένοι καρπὸν δικαιοσύνης τὸν διὰ Ἰησοῦ Χριστοῦ εἰς δόξαν καὶ ἔπαινον θεοῦ.

πεπληρωμένοι. Prf pass ptc masc nom pl πληρόω (causal or manner). The participle modifies ἦτε in v. 10. On adverbial participles that follow the main verb, see 1:4 on ποιούμενος. The context indicates that the implied subject of this passive participle is God (traditionally called "divine passive"; cf. Bockmuehl, 69). The state of being filled, which is frontgrounded by the stative aspect of the perfect passive participle, is here viewed from the perspective of the day of Christ. Consequently, the past action that caused the state of being filled is portrayed as concurrent with the present experience of the audience (Fee, 103 n. 30).

καρπὸν. Accusative of retained object. This accusative is the accusative direct object (thing) of a transitive verb in a double accusative person-thing construction, which is retained when the active verb is put in the passive (Wallace 1996, 197, 438–39; Porter 1994, 66; Robertson, 485; Zerwick §73; BDF §159.1). A reconstructed active clause underlining the passive construction would be ὁ θεὸς πεπλήρωκεν ὑμᾶς καρπόν ("God has filled you with fruit"). In a corresponding passive clause, the accusative of person from the active clause becomes the nominative subject, while the accusative of thing is retained: ὑμεῖς ἐστε πεπληρωμένοι καρπόν ("you have been filled with fruit").

δικαιοσύνης. Epexegetical genitive explaining καρπὸν ("fruit, which is uprightness," if δικαιοσύνη is understood ethically [BDAG, 248.3] or "fruit, which is righteousness," if δικαιοσύνη is understood forensically [BDAG, 247.2]) or genitive of origin modifying καρπὸν ("fruit that comes from righteousness"), in which case δικαιοσύνη is understood forensically. The attributive modifier τὸν διὰ Ἰησοῦ Χριστοῦ supports the second option.

τὸν διὰ Ἰησοῦ Χριστοῦ. The article functions as an adjectivizer, changing the PP διὰ Ἰησοῦ Χριστοῦ into the attributive modifier of καρπὸν (not of δικαιοσύνης, which is in the genitive).

διὰ Ἰησοῦ Χριστοῦ. Secondary (intermediate) agency (Wallace 1996, 433–34).

εἰς δόξαν καὶ ἔπαινον. Purpose. δόξα ("honor as enhancement or recognition of status or performance" [BDAG, 257.3]) and ἔπαινος ("the act of expressing admiration or approval" [BDAG, 357.1]) "functioned semantically in the context of Rome's honor culture, where public recognition and acclamation served as preeminent social commodities" (Hellerman 2015, 35).

θεοῦ. Objective genitive modifying both δόξαν and ἔπαινον ("glory and praise for God") or subjective genitive also modifying both δόξαν and ἔπαινον ("God's glory and praise"). The external evidence for three variants, (1) εἰς δόξαν καὶ ἔπαινον Χριστοῦ (D*), (2) εἰς δόξαν καὶ ἔπαινον μοι (F G Ambst), and (3) εἰς δόξαν θεοῦ καὶ ἔπαινον ἐμοὶ ($\mathfrak{P}^{46}$), is sparse and clearly inferior to a much better attested reading, εἰς δόξαν καὶ ἔπαινον θεοῦ (ℵ A B D² I K L P Ψ 075 0278 33 81 104 365 630 1175 1241 1505 1739 1881 2464 𝔐 lat sy co). Although the second variant could be described as "very remarkable," and the third as "still more astonishing" (Metzger, 544), both readings give evidence that some scribes understood θεοῦ as a subjective genitive, i.e., as a praise coming from God to human beings (Reumann, 137).

Philippians 1:12-18a

[12]Now, I want you to know, brothers [and sisters], that the things that happened to me actually resulted in the advancement of the gospel, [13]so that my imprisonment has become known [as being] in the cause of Christ throughout the whole praetorian guard and to all the rest, [14]and most of the brothers [and sisters], since they have become confident in the Lord because of my imprisonment, dare even more to speak the word fearlessly. [15]Some proclaim Christ even on account of envy and strife, but some also on account of good will. [16]The latter [do so] out of love because they know that I am placed [here] for the defense of the gospel. [17]The former proclaim Christ out of selfish ambition, not sincerely, because they intend to cause trouble concerning my imprisonment. [18a]What does it matter? Only that in every way, whether in pretense or in truth, Christ is being proclaimed, and over this I rejoice.

The order of verses 16 and 17 is reversed in D¹ K Ψ 104 630 1505 𝔐 sy[h], which is reflected in some English translations (KJV; NKJV; TYN; WBT; WEB). This order of verses (see below) is a scribal modification of Paul's chiastic order for the sake of clarity:

Philippians 1:11-12

Verse 15   Some proclaim Christ even on account of envy and strife, but some also on account of good will.

Verse 17   The former proclaim Christ out of selfish ambition, not sincerely, because they intend to cause trouble concerning my imprisonment.

Verse 16   The latter [do so] out of love because they know that I am placed [here] for the defense of the gospel.

1:12 Γινώσκειν δὲ ὑμᾶς βούλομαι, ἀδελφοί, ὅτι τὰ κατ' ἐμὲ μᾶλλον εἰς προκοπὴν τοῦ εὐαγγελίου ἐλήλυθεν,

Γινώσκειν δὲ ὑμᾶς βούλομαι. This introductory clause functions as a metacomment, an abstracted statement that interrupts the discourse to prepare the audience for something that the speaker considers of great importance (Runge 2010, 101, 106–7). In this case, the metacomment "now, I want you to know" prepares the audience for Paul's "surprising claim that these seemingly negative things actually had a positive impact regarding the advancement of the gospel" (121).

Γινώσκειν. Pres act inf γινώσκω (complementary to βούλομαι). Fronted for emphasis.

δὲ. Marker of development that here signals the shift to a new topic.

ὑμᾶς. Accusative subject of the infinitive Γινώσκειν.

βούλομαι. Pres mid ind 1st sg βούλομαι. In the current context, βούλομαι means "to desire to have or experience something, with the implication of some reasoned planning or will to accomplish the goal" (LN 25.3). Porter (1989, 489) notes that βούλομαι "most often grammaticalizes imperfective aspect," as here.

ἀδελφοί. Vocative of direct address. ἀδελφοί is used here and elsewhere in the letter (3:1, 13, 14, 17; 4:1, 8, 21) as a generic term for the fellow members of the Christian community (BDAG, 18.2.a). Although masculine in form, the sense of this plural noun is inclusive. Since this generic vocative is not required to identify the addressees, Runge (2010, 117–121) calls it a "redundant form of address," which here serves to separate the metacomment from the propositional content that it introduces.

ὅτι. Introduces the clausal complement (indirect discourse) of Γινώσκειν.

τὰ κατ' ἐμὲ. The article functions as a nominalizer, changing the PP κατ' ἐμὲ (lit. "the things concerning me" = "the things that happened to me" or "my circumstances") into the subject of ἐλήλυθεν. Paul's reference to τοὺς δεσμούς μου in the next verse (see also vv. 14 and 17) indicates that the PP τὰ κατ' ἐμὲ refers to Paul's imprisonment. Fronted as a topical frame.

κατ' ἐμὲ. Reference.

μᾶλλον. Comparative of the adverb μάλα. In this context, μᾶλλον does not mean "to a greater or higher degree," "more" (BDAG, 613.1) but *rather in the sense instead*" (BDAG, 614.3), "pointing to an unanticipated result" (Hellerman 2015, 42; cf. NEB: "helped on, rather than hindered"). The adverb + the PP it modifies (μᾶλλον εἰς προκοπὴν τοῦ εὐαγγελίου) is fronted for emphasis.

εἰς προκοπὴν. Result. The noun προκοπή denotes "a movement forward to an improved state" and can be translated as "progress, advancement, furtherance" (BDAG, 871).

τοῦ εὐαγγελίου. Objective genitive modifying προκοπὴν.

ἐλήλυθεν. Prf act ind 3rd sg ἔρχομαι. The stative aspect of the perfect tense puts emphasis on the resulting state existing in the time of Paul's writing (advancement of the gospel), but his reference to the things that happened to him (τὰ κατ' ἐμὲ) points to the previous events that produced this result.

1:13 ὥστε τοὺς δεσμούς μου φανεροὺς ἐν Χριστῷ γενέσθαι ἐν ὅλῳ τῷ πραιτωρίῳ καὶ τοῖς λοιποῖς πᾶσιν,

ὥστε. Introduces a result clause.

τοὺς δεσμούς. Accusative subject of the infinitive γενέσθαι. Fronted as a topical frame. On the plural form of δεσμός ("bond, fetter, chain") as metonymy for imprisonment, see 1:7 on ἔν . . . τοῖς δεσμοῖς.

μου. Possessive genitive modifying δεσμούς ("my chains").

φανεροὺς. Predicate accusative. Fronted for emphasis. The adjective φανεροὺς ("visible, clear, plainly to be seen, open, plain, evident, known" [BDAG, 1047.1]) stands in predicate relationship with δεσμούς, with which it is joined by the infinitive of γενέσθαι (Wallace 1996, 190–92).

ἐν Χριστῷ. The word order indicates that ἐν Χριστῷ modifies the infinitival phrase φανεροὺς . . . γενέσθαι that brackets it. It is therefore accurate to render the Greek text, as O'Brien suggests, as "my bonds have become manifest-in-Christ" (92). However, this does not mean that Christ has revealed Paul's bonds because, as Campbell notes, "Paul's chains are not secret, nor are they spiritually discerned" (2012, 125). Rather, Paul's "chains have become manifest [as being] in Christ" (Fee, 112 n. 29). What has been revealed, then, is that Paul's chains are "in Christ." Regarding the specific function of the PP ἐν Χριστῷ, two major options are participation and cause. If ἐν Χριστῷ conveys participation,

Paul's bonds have revealed his solidarity with Christ through sharing in Christ's suffering (Silva, 62). If ἐν Χριστῷ conveys cause, the PP expresses the reason for Paul's imprisonment: "Paul's chains are revealed to be *for* Christ, or *because* of him" (Campbell 2012, 125).

γενέσθαι. Aor mid inf γίνομαι. Used with ὥστε to indicate result.

ἐν ὅλῳ τῷ πραιτωρίῳ. Locative. πραιτώριον is a Latin loanword (*praetorium*), which originally denoted "the praetor's tent in camp, w[ith] its surroundings. In the course of its history . . . the word also came to designate the governor's official residence" (BDAG, 859). For example, in Matt 27:27, Mark 15:16, and John 18:28, the term πραιτώριον refers to the governor's official residence in Jerusalem. According to Acts 23:35, Herod's palace in Caesarea served as the πραιτώριον. In addition to denoting a place, πραιτώριον could also refer to a group of soldiers—"the Praetorian Guard, the emperor's own elite troops, stationed in Rome" (Fee, 113). Since the previous clause describes the public knowledge of the reason for Paul's imprisonment, the PP clearly refers to people, but which group is in view depends on one's understanding of the location from which Paul wrote this letter. "If the letter was written fr[om] Rome, the words ἐν ὅλῳ τῷ πραιτωρίῳ are best taken to mean *in the whole praetorian* (or *imperial*) *guard*. If it belongs to a non-Roman imprisonment, τὸ πραιτώριον beside οἱ λοιποί includes those who live in the governor's palace" (BDAG, 859). My translation reflects the first option.

καί. Coordinating conjunction.

τοῖς λοιποῖς πᾶσιν. Dative complement to φανερούς. The adjective φανερός frequently occurs with dative of person (BDAG, 1047.1). In this construction, πᾶσιν modifies the substantival adjective τοῖς λοιποῖς ("all the rest"). Alternatively, the dative τοῖς λοιποῖς πᾶσιν could be viewed as the second element of the prepositional phrase governed by ἐν (ἐν ὅλῳ τῷ πραιτωρίῳ καὶ τοῖς λοιποῖς πᾶσιν). My translation presumes that τοῖς λοιποῖς πᾶσιν does not belong to the PP but functions as a complement to φανερούς.

1:14 καὶ τοὺς πλείονας τῶν ἀδελφῶν ἐν κυρίῳ πεποιθότας τοῖς δεσμοῖς μου περισσοτέρως τολμᾶν ἀφόβως τὸν λόγον λαλεῖν.

καί. Coordinating conjunction, linking two infinitive clauses governed by ὥστε.

τοὺς πλείονας. Accusative subject of the infinitive τολμᾶν. πλείονας is a comparative of the adjective πολύς, which is here used as a substantive, "leaving the comparison implicit" (Wallace 1996, 299; "the majority, most" [BDAG, 848.1.b.β.ℵ]). Fronted as a topical frame.

τῶν ἀδελφῶν. Partitive genitive modifying πλείονας. This is a nice illustration of Wallace's observation that "not every instance of a comparative adjective ... followed by a genitive will necessarily involve a comparative genitive" (1996, 110–11).

ἐν κυρίῳ. This PP does not modify τῶν ἀδελφῶν as some translations (KJV: "the brethren in the Lord"; HCSB: "brothers in the Lord") and interpreters (e.g., Moule, 108; Campbell 2012, 174) assume because (1) ἐν κυρίῳ is not preceded by the article τῶν, which is needed to mark the PP as attributive in function; and (2) ἐν κυρίῳ would function as an identity marker ("those who are in the Lord" = "Christians"), which would be superfluous because τῶν ἀδελφῶν already identifies the audience as Christian. Rather, the PP ἐν κυρίῳ modifies the participle πεποιθότας ("being confident in the Lord"), expressing the ground of the Philippians' confidence (Fee, 116; Bockmuehl, 76; O'Brien, 95; for other examples of the perfect tense of πείθω + ἐν κυρίῳ, see Phil 2:24; Rom 14:14; Gal 5:10). Fronted for emphasis.

πεποιθότας. Prf act ptc masc acc pl πείθω (causal). This adverbial participle is in the accusative because it modifies the infinitive τολμᾶν, matching the case of the subject of the infinitive (τοὺς πλείονας; cf. Culy 2003, 446 n. 34). The perfect tense of πείθω ("to come to believe the certainty of something on the basis of being convinced" [LN 31.46]) has the sense of a present: "I have been persuaded and therefore am convinced" (Reumann, 111; cf. BDF §341; Zerwick and Grosvenor, 592).

τοῖς δεσμοῖς. Dative of cause (LEB: "because of my imprisonment"; cf. Wallace 1996, 168; BDF §196) or dative of means/instrument (NRSV: "by my imprisonment"; cf. Fee, 116; O'Brien, 95). On the plural form of δεσμός ("bond, fetter, chain") as metonymy for imprisonment, see 1:7 on ἔν ... τοῖς δεσμοῖς.

μου. Possessive genitive modifying δεσμοῖς ("my chains").

περισσοτέρως. Comparative of the adverb περισσῶς ("exceedingly, beyond measure, very" [BDAG, 806]), modifying the infinitive τολμᾶν ("to dare even more"). Fronted for emphasis.

τολμᾶν. Pres act inf τολμάω. Used with ὥστε in v. 13 (which governs both γενέσθαι [v. 13] and τολμᾶν) to indicate the second result of Paul's imprisonment.

ἀφόβως. Adverb ("fearlessly"), modifying the infinitive λαλεῖν. Fronted for emphasis.

τὸν λόγον. Accusative direct object of λαλεῖν. ὁ λόγος is here used as a technical term for the Christian message of salvation through Jesus Christ (BDAG, 600.1.a.β). In a number of manuscripts, this accusative is followed by τοῦ θεοῦ (א A B [D*] P Ψ 048[vid] 075 0278 33 81 104 326

365 629 1175 1241 2464 lat sy^(p.h**)co) or, less frequently, κυρίου (F G). The external attestation for τοῦ θεοῦ is strong (this reading was accepted by WH, the earlier Nestle-Aland editions, and some English versions [RSV; ASV; NASB; NLT]), but the text without a genitive modifier (attested by 𝔓⁴⁶ D² K 630 1505 1739 1881 𝔐 r vg^(ms) Mcion^T) is preferable because it better explains the origin of the other two readings (Metzger, 545).

λαλεῖν. Pres act inf λαλέω (complementary). The imperfective aspect of the present infinitive portrays speaking the word as an action in progress.

1:15 τινὲς μὲν καὶ διὰ φθόνον καὶ ἔριν, τινὲς δὲ καὶ δι' εὐδοκίαν τὸν Χριστὸν κηρύσσουσιν·

τινὲς. The first nominative subject of κηρύσσουσιν. Fronted as a topical frame. Although the indefinite pronoun τινὲς is an enclitic, it is accented because it stands at the head of its clause (BDF §301; Moule, 125; Carson, 49).

μὲν . . . δὲ. A point/counterpoint set of particles, which are here used to distinguish two groups, both of which proclaim Christ but do so with different motives. Levinsohn claims that "[t]he presence of μέν not only anticipates a corresponding sentence containing δέ but frequently, in narrative, it also downgrades the importance of the sentence containing μέν" (2000, 170). Runge contends that "[t]he downgrading effect that Levinsohn asserts is better explained by the nature of the offline information that it often introduces than by the particle itself" (2010, 76 n. 7). Since, however, the chiastic structure of vv. 15-17 puts more emphasis on the preachers who proclaim Christ from impure motives (Fee, 119; Silva, 64), the μέν clause in this verse seems to have more importance than the δέ clause.

καὶ . . . καὶ. Two parallel conjunctions precede the διά phrases in their respective clauses (καὶ διὰ φθόνον καὶ ἔριν . . . καὶ δι' εὐδοκίαν). They are not used as connectives (i.e., "both . . . and") but as adverbs, the first with ascensive force ("even") and the second with adjunctive force ("also"), although the latter could also be regarded as pleonastic and therefore omitted in translation (BDAG, 496.2.c).

διὰ φθόνον καὶ ἔριν. Causal. The conjunction καὶ links two nouns (φθόνον and ἔριν) governed by the same preposition (διὰ). Both terms are negative, φθόνος denoting "envy, jealousy" (BDAG, 1054), and ἔρις denoting "strife, discord, contention" (BDAG, 392). Both nouns appear on the list of vices in Rom 1:29 and Gal 5:20-21. This and the following PP are fronted for emphasis.

τινὲς. The second nominative subject of κηρύσσουσιν (see τινὲς above). Fronted as a topical frame.

δι' εὐδοκίαν. Causal (BDAG, 225.B.2.a). εὐδοκία denotes "state or condition of being kindly disposed," "good will" (BDAG, 404.1). The term could refer to God's good pleasure (in parallel with 2:13) or to the kind disposition of those who proclaim Christ (cf. Rom 10:1). O'Brien, for example, argues that εὐδοκία denotes God's approval of Paul's ministry, which was recognized by this group of preachers, who, "[i]mpelled by love for the apostle (v. 16), and appreciative of that divine approval which rested on his ministry, prisoner though he was, . . . took up the task of proclaiming Christ" (100; cf. Bockmuehl, 79). Most commentators, however, regard εὐδοκία as the preacher's goodwill because the contrast between two types of motivation, διὰ φθόνον καὶ ἔριν vs. δι' εὐδοκίαν, indicates that Paul talks about human emotions directed toward him, as vv. 16-17 further demonstrate.

τὸν Χριστὸν. Accusative direct object of κηρύσσουσιν. This is the first occurrence of Χριστός with the article in Philippians (see also 1:17, 27; 3:7, 17). On the question whether in Paul's letters the term Χριστός retains its titular force, see 1:1 on Χριστοῦ Ἰησοῦ.

κηρύσσουσιν. Pres act ind 3rd pl κηρύσσω. This is the only occurrence of κηρύσσω ("to proclaim" [BDAG, 543.2.b.β]) in Philippians. The imperfective aspect of the present tense portrays proclaiming Christ as an action in progress.

1:16 οἱ μὲν ἐξ ἀγάπης, εἰδότες ὅτι εἰς ἀπολογίαν τοῦ εὐαγγελίου κεῖμαι,

οἱ μὲν. Nominative subject of the implied καταγγέλλουσιν (see v. 17). The article functions as a demonstrative pronoun (BDAG, 686.1.b), referring back to the second group described in v. 15. The particle μὲν has identifying and contrastive function, distinguishing this group of preachers from those described in the next verse (see 1:15 on μὲν . . . δὲ).

ἐξ ἀγάπης. Source (BDAG, 296.3). The PP qualifies καταγγέλλουσιν in v. 17, explaining that these preachers proclaim Christ out of love. The noun ἀγάπη ("love, affection") is not followed by an objective genitive, but the context suggests that this is a reference to love for Paul (Fee, 120).

εἰδότες. Prf act ptc masc nom pl οἶδα (causal). This adverbial participle provides the reason for the preaching of those who proclaim Christ out of love. Wallace notes that perfect participles almost always indicate the cause or ground of the action of the main verb, even when they "are used as presents, such as οἶδα" (1996, 631 n. 47).

ὅτι. Introduces the clausal complement (indirect discourse) of εἰδότες.

εἰς ἀπολογίαν. Purpose. Fronted for emphasis. The noun ἀπολογία denotes "the act of making a defense" (BDAG, 117.2.b).

τοῦ εὐαγγελίου. Objective genitive qualifying ἀπολογίαν ("defending the gospel").

κεῖμαι. Pres pass ind 1st sg κεῖμαι. κεῖμαι serves as a perfect passive of τίθημι. BDAG (537.3.a) suggests that κεῖμαι ("lie, recline") is here used in a transferred sense ("be appointed, set, destined"), but a translation that is closer to the literal meaning of the verb is, in my view, more appropriate to the context (cf. NRSV: "I have been put here"; REB: "I am where I am"; NET: "I am placed here").

1:17 οἱ δὲ ἐξ ἐριθείας τὸν Χριστὸν καταγγέλλουσιν, οὐχ ἁγνῶς, οἰόμενοι θλῖψιν ἐγείρειν τοῖς δεσμοῖς μου.

οἱ δὲ. Nominative subject of καταγγέλλουσιν. The article functions as a demonstrative pronoun (BDAG, 686.1.b), referring back to the first group described in v. 15. The particle δὲ has identifying and contrastive function, distinguishing this group of preachers from those described in the previous verse (see 1:15 on μὲν . . . δὲ).

ἐξ ἐριθείας. Source. Fronted for emphasis. The precise meaning of the term ἐριθεία in the NT is uncertain. The meaning "strife, contentiousness," although possible, is disputed because it presumes that ἐριθεία is derived from ἔρις, which is doubtful given the fact that both ἔρις (sg.) and ἐριθεία (pl.) appear in the lists of vices in 2 Cor 12:20 and Gal 5:20. Many scholars prefer the meaning "selfishness, selfish ambition," which is based on the use of ἐριθεία in Aristotle, *Pol.* 5.2.1302b.4; 5.2.1303a.15, "where it denotes a self-seeking pursuit of political office by unfair means" (BDAG, 392).

τὸν Χριστὸν. Accusative direct object of καταγγέλλουσιν.

καταγγέλλουσιν. Pres act ind 3rd pl καταγγέλλω. Paul has replaced the verb κηρύσσω, which he used in v. 15, with καταγγέλλω ("proclaim, announce" [BDAG, 515]).

οὐχ. Negative particle, which is here used to negate a single word—the adverb ἁγνῶς (Zerwick, §440 n. 2).

ἁγνῶς. Adverb of manner ("purely, sincerely"). A NT *hapax legomenon*. Although the negated adverb (οὐχ ἁγνῶς) is set off by commas in NA[28]/UBS[5] and in SBLGNT, it does not function independently but qualifies, like the PP ἐξ ἐριθείας, the main verb καταγγέλλουσιν. οὐχ ἁγνῶς receives emphasis through right-dislocation (Runge 2010, 317–35).

οἰόμενοι. Pres mid ptc masc nom pl οἴομαι (causal). οἴομαι means "to consider someth[ing] to be true but with a component of tentativeness," "think, suppose, expect" (BDAG, 701). This is the only occurrence of this verb in the letters of Paul. On adverbial participles that follow the main verb, see 1:4 on ποιούμενος.

θλῖψιν. Accusative direct object of ἐγείρειν.

ἐγείρειν. Pres act inf ἐγείρω (indirect discourse). In the current context, ἐγείρω means "to cause to come into existence, raise up, bring into being" (BDAG, 271.5).

τοῖς δεσμοῖς. Dative of respect ("in regard to my imprisonment"). On the plural form of δεσμός ("bond, fetter, chain") as metonymy for imprisonment, see 1:7 on ἔν ... τοῖς δεσμοῖς.

μου. Possessive genitive modifying δεσμοῖς ("my chains").

1:18a Τί γάρ; πλὴν ὅτι παντὶ τρόπῳ, εἴτε προφάσει εἴτε ἀληθείᾳ, Χριστὸς καταγγέλλεται, καὶ ἐν τούτῳ χαίρω.

Τί. Nominative subject in an elliptical construction which, along with the conjunction γάρ, functions as an exclamatory question (lit. "for what?") that can be translated "what does it matter?" or "what difference does it make?" (BDF §299.3).

γάρ. Postpositive conjunction that indicates that the elliptical question Τί γάρ has an explanatory function vis-à-vis the previous verse: "For (even in light of those mentioned in v. 17) what does it matter?" (Fee, 124 n. 35).

πλὴν. Adverb used as a conjunction that serves as a "marker of someth[ing] that is contrastingly added for consideration" (BDAG, 826.1). When followed by ὅτι, as here, πλὴν could be translated as "in any case ..." (BDAG, 826.1.c) or "except that ..." (BDAG, 826.1.d).

ὅτι. Introduces the clausal complement of the elliptical clause, Τί γάρ.

παντὶ τρόπῳ. Dative of manner (Zerwick §60; Robertson, 530).

εἴτε ... εἴτε. Correlative conjunctions ("whether ... or"). εἴτε is a combination of the conditional particle εἰ and the enclitic particle τέ (BDF §454.3; BDAG, 279.6.o).

προφάσει. Dative of manner (Zerwick §60; Robertson, 530). πρόφασις means "pretext, ostensible reason, excuse" (BDAG, 889.2).

ἀληθείᾳ. Dative of manner (Zerwick §60; Robertson, 530). The term ἀλήθεια is here used to describe not the content of Christian preaching but the preachers' motives (Hellerman 2015, 53).

Χριστὸς. Nominative subject of καταγγέλλεται. Fronted for emphasis. Levinsohn explains the absence of the article by the following rule: "If a noun whose referent is known and particular is anarthrous, its referent is salient" (1995, 71). He emphasizes that this principle "cannot be applied when it is not clear that the referent is particular or known" (71–72).

καταγγέλλεται. Pres pass ind 3rd sg καταγγέλλω.

καὶ. Coordinating conjunction.

ἐν τούτῳ. Causal. The near-demonstrative pronoun τούτῳ is anaphoric, referring back to the assertion Χριστὸς καταγγέλλεται.

χαίρω. Pres act ind 1st sg χαίρω. The verb stands in final, emphatic position. This placement is governed by the following functional principle: "When the verb is the most salient constituent of a clause, any non-verbal constituent of the predicate whose referent is 'given' information precedes it" (Levinsohn 1995, 69). Rejoicing is a dominant theme throughout Philippians (see 1:18; 2:17, 18, 28; 3:1; 4:4, 10).

Philippians 1:18b-26

[18b]But I will also continue to rejoice, [19]for I know that this will turn out to me for deliverance through your prayers and the support of the Spirit of Jesus Christ, [20]according to my eager expectation and hope that I will in no way be ashamed, but that with complete boldness, even now as always, Christ will be exalted in my body, whether through life or through death. [21]For to me, to live [is] Christ, and to die [is] gain. [22]But if to live in flesh [is my lot], this [is] fruitful labor for me, and which I shall prefer I do not know. [23]I am hard pressed between the two, having a desire to depart and to be with Christ, for [this is] much better. [24]But to remain in the flesh [is] more necessary for your sake. [25]And because I am convinced of this, I know that I will remain alive and stay on with all of you for your progress and joy in the faith, [26]so that your boasting in Christ Jesus may increase because of me through my return to you.

1:18b Ἀλλὰ καὶ χαρήσομαι,

Ἀλλὰ καὶ. This combination of the marker of contrast (Ἀλλὰ) and the adverbial (adjunctive) use of καὶ functions as the second half of an elliptical οὐ μόνον ... ἀλλὰ καὶ ("not only ... but also") point/counterpoint set. The first half of this formula, which is here elided, is applicable to Paul's assertion ἐν τούτῳ χαίρω at the end of the previous verse: "I [not only] rejoice over this ... but I will also continue to rejoice." The Ἀλλὰ καὶ construction, which is used to open a new section, indicates "that the preceding is to be regarded as a settled matter, thus forming a transition to someth[ing] new" (BDAG, 45.3).

χαρήσομαι. Fut mid ind 1st sg χαίρω. Since in v. 18a Paul used the present-tense χαίρω to describe his feeling of joy concurrent with the writing of this letter, his use of the future-tense χαρήσομαι in v. 18b most likely indicates his expectation of the continuation of this joy into the future (see also 2:17, 18, 28; 3:1; 4:4, 10).

1:19 οἶδα γὰρ ὅτι τοῦτό μοι ἀποβήσεται εἰς σωτηρίαν διὰ τῆς ὑμῶν δεήσεως καὶ ἐπιχορηγίας τοῦ πνεύματος Ἰησοῦ Χριστοῦ

οἶδα. Prf act ind 1st sg οἶδα. The perfect tense has the present meaning, describing "the enduring result rather than the completed act" (Smyth §1946).

γὰρ. Postpositive conjunction that introduces the ground for Paul's rejoicing into the future.

ὅτι. Introduces the clausal complement (indirect discourse) of οἶδα.

τοῦτό μοι ἀποβήσεται εἰς σωτηρίαν. The verbatim parallel to this statement is found in LXX Job 13:16a. Since Paul does not introduce this clause with an explicit citation formula, it is not clear whether it should be regarded as a scriptural quotation or as a scriptural echo that could be recognized only by an informed and attentive reader. In his groundbreaking work on Paul's use of Israel's scripture, Hays argues that the correspondences between Paul and Job "are intimated through the trope of metalepsis. The trope invites the reader to participate in an imaginative act necessary to comprehend the portrayal of Paul's condition offered here" (23).

τοῦτό. Nominative subject of ἀποβήσεται. The demonstrative pronoun τοῦτό, which has a circumflex accent on the penult, acquired an additional accent, the acute, on the ultima from the enclitic μοι (Smyth §183; Carson, 48). τοῦτό refers to Paul's current circumstances.

μοι. Dative of advantage.

ἀποβήσεται. Fut mid ind 3rd sg ἀποβαίνω. The verb ἀποβαίνω (lit. "to get off or depart" [BDAG, 107.1]) is here used figuratively: "to result in a state or condition," "turn out, lead" (BDAG, 107.2).

εἰς σωτηρίαν. Result. While the term σωτηρία could refer to eschatological salvation (BDAG, 986.2; TDNT 7:993; NIDNTT 3:214), it probably refers to Paul's deliverance from prison (Reumann, 210; see 1:26).

διὰ τῆς ... δεήσεως καὶ ἐπιχορηγίας. Means. The PP modifies the clause τοῦτό μοι ἀποβήσεται εἰς σωτηρίαν. Although these two nouns are governed by a single article, the Granville Sharp rule is not applicable because both nouns are impersonal. Even so, they form a TSKS construction that could, as Wallace (1996, 286–90) explains, express five semantic relationships: (1) distinct entities, though united; (2) overlapping entities; (3) first entity subset of second; (4) second entity subset of first; and (5) identical entities. In this case, δέησις ("prayer" [BDAG, 213]) and ἐπιχορηγία ("assistance, support" [BDAG, 387]) represent two distinct entities (the first option), which are "treated as one for the purpose in hand" (Robertson, 787; cf. Zerwick §184). δεήσεως is distributive singular (Fee, 132 n. 26).

ὑμῶν. Subjective genitive modifying δεήσεως. The preposed pronoun is thematically salient (Levinsohn 2000, 64; cf. Fee, 132 n. 26, who says that ὑμῶν is placed before δεήσεως "for clarity and emphasis").

τοῦ πνεύματος. Subjective genitive modifying ἐπιχορηγίας ("the assistance by the Spirit") or objective genitive, conveying the reception of the Spirit ("the provision with the Spirit"; cf. Fee, 133).

Ἰησοῦ Χριστοῦ. Genitive of source modifying πνεύματος ("the Spirit that comes from Jesus Christ"), subjective genitive modifying an implied sending of πνεύματος ("the Spirit sent by Jesus Christ"), or epexegetical genitive (a.k.a. genitive of apposition) explaining πνεύματος ("the Spirit, namely Jesus Christ"). This is the only instance in Paul's letters where πνεῦμα is modified by Ἰησοῦ Χριστοῦ, although similar formulations occur in Gal 4:6 (πνεῦμα τοῦ υἱοῦ αὐτοῦ) and Rom 8:9 (πνεῦμα Χριστοῦ). Given Paul's usual assertions that God the Father gives the Spirit (1 Cor 6:19; 2 Cor 1:21-22; Gal 3:5; 1 Thess 4:8) and his claim that the Lord is the Spirit (2 Cor 3:17-18), it is probably best to understand Ἰησοῦ Χριστοῦ as epexegetical genitive.

1:20 κατὰ τὴν ἀποκαραδοκίαν καὶ ἐλπίδα μου, ὅτι ἐν οὐδενὶ αἰσχυνθήσομαι ἀλλ' ἐν πάσῃ παρρησίᾳ ὡς πάντοτε καὶ νῦν μεγαλυνθήσεται Χριστὸς ἐν τῷ σώματί μου, εἴτε διὰ ζωῆς εἴτε διὰ θανάτου.

κατὰ τὴν ἀποκαραδοκίαν καὶ ἐλπίδα. Standard. The PP modifies τοῦτό μοι ἀποβήσεται εἰς σωτηρίαν. A single article governing two nouns connected with καί creates a TSKS construction (see 1:19 on διὰ τῆς . . . δεήσεως καὶ ἐπιχορηγίας). The terms ἀποκαραδοκία ("eager expectation" [BDAG, 112]) and ἐλπίς ("hope, expectation" [BDAG, 319.1]) are two overlapping entities. Given their semantic similarity, ἀποκαραδοκίαν καὶ ἐλπίδα could be regarded as a hendiadys (e.g., "hope-filled expectation" [Fee, 135]; NET: "confident hope").

μου. Subjective genitive modifying both ἀποκαραδοκίαν and ἐλπίδα.

ὅτι. Introduces a clause that is epexegetical to τὴν ἀποκαραδοκίαν καὶ ἐλπίδα μου, explaining what Paul's eager expectation and hope is. Reumann's (213) suggestion that this ὅτι clause functions as the clausal complement (indirect discourse) of οἶδα, forming a parallel with the ὅτι clause in v. 19, is not persuasive because in such a case the second ὅτι clause would have been preceded by καί (cf. Fee, 129 n. 10).

ἐν οὐδενί. Manner. Fronted for emphasis.

αἰσχυνθήσομαι. Fut pass ind 1st sg αἰσχύνω. The verb means "to experience shame, be put to shame, be disgraced" (BDAG, 30.2). The primary agent of the action is not expressed.

ἀλλ'. Marker of contrast that introduces the second half of the ὅτι clause (ἐν πάσῃ παρρησίᾳ ὡς πάντοτε καὶ νῦν μεγαλυνθήσεται Χριστὸς ἐν τῷ σώματί μου), which forms an antithetical parallel to the first half (ἐν οὐδενὶ αἰσχυνθήσομαι).

ἐν πάσῃ παρρησίᾳ. Manner. The PP modifies μεγαλυνθήσεται.

ὡς. Comparative particle.

πάντοτε. Adverb of time ("always").

καί. Adverbial use, either ascensive ("even") or adjunctive ("also").

νῦν. Adverb of time ("now"). In this context, it designates time shortly after the immediate present (BDAG, 681.1.b).

μεγαλυνθήσεται. Fut pass ind 3rd sg μεγαλύνω. The primary agent of the action is again not expressed. The future tense conveys Paul's expectation that Christ will be exalted in his body. It also indicates that the temporal adverb νῦν does not have to situate the action of the verb in the present.

Χριστός. Nominative subject of μεγαλυνθήσεται.

ἐν τῷ σώματι. Locative ("in my body") or instrumental ("through my body"). The PP modifies μεγαλυνθήσεται. The expression "my body" is a synechdoche for "me/myself."

μου. Possessive genitive modifying σώματι.

εἴτε ... εἴτε. Correlative conjunctions ("whether ... or"); see 1:18.

διὰ ζωῆς. Instrumental. The PP modifies μεγαλυνθήσεται.

διὰ θανάτου. Instrumental. The PP modifies μεγαλυνθήσεται.

1:21 Ἐμοὶ γὰρ τὸ ζῆν Χριστὸς καὶ τὸ ἀποθανεῖν κέρδος.

Ἐμοί. Dative of advantage ("for me") or ethical dative ("as far as I am concerned" or "as I look at it"; cf. Wallace 1996, 147). Fronted for emphasis.

γάρ. Postpositive conjunction that introduces the explanation of two correlative prepositional phrases, εἴτε διὰ ζωῆς εἴτε διὰ θανάτου, at the end of v. 20.

τὸ ζῆν. Pres act inf ζάω. The articular infinitive τὸ ζῆν functions as the subject of an implied ἐστίν. The article distinguishes the subject of the clause from the predicate nominative (Zerwick §173) and functions as an anaphoric reference to the PP διὰ ζωῆς in the previous verse (cf. BDF §399.1). It also nominalizes the infinitive, which is, as Wallace notes, "relatively rare, though more common in the epistles than in narrative literature" (1996, 234). The imperfective aspect of the present infinitive draws attention to the process of living.

Χριστὸς. Predicate nominative in the first verbless clause.

τὸ ἀποθανεῖν. Aor act inf ἀποθνήσκω. The articular infinitive τὸ ἀποθανεῖν functions as the subject of an implied ἐστίν. The article nominalizes the infinitive, marking it as the subject of the clause (Zerwick §173) and serving as an anaphoric reference to the PP διὰ θανάτου in the previous verse (cf. BDF §399.1). Both articular infinitives, τὸ ζῆν and τὸ ἀποθανεῖν, could be translated as gerunds ("living" and "dying"; cf. NRSV; HCSB; NET), but this rendering obscures their aspectual differences. This is especially pertinent to τὸ ἀποθανεῖν, because the aorist infinitive portrays the transition from life to death as a complete event while the gerund "dying" suggests a process.

κέρδος. Predicate nominative in the second verbless clause.

1:22 εἰ δὲ τὸ ζῆν ἐν σαρκί, τοῦτό μοι καρπὸς ἔργου, καὶ τί αἱρήσομαι οὐ γνωρίζω.

εἰ. Introduces the protasis of a first-class condition. This class of conditions assumes that the protasis is true for the sake of the argument and draws the conclusion from that supposition.

δὲ. Marker of development with a contrastive nuance because Paul now considers living, rather than dying, an advantageous option.

τὸ ζῆν. Pres act inf ζάω. Like in v. 21, the articular infinitive τὸ ζῆν functions as the subject of an implied ἐστίν. Unlike v. 21, however, τὸ ζῆν is not linked to an explicit predicate nominative. The context, however, suggests that Paul's elliptical construction refers to the continuation of his physical life: "But if to live in flesh [is my lot] . . ." (DBY). Most English translations obfuscate the Greek syntax by transforming the infinitival phrase to a first-person statement: "If I am to live in the flesh . . ." (NRSV; ESV); "If I am to go on living in the body" (NIV; REB).

ἐν σαρκί. Locative ("in the sphere of flesh"). In this context, the term σάρξ does not have its negative spiritual (e.g., Rom 8:6-8) or ethical (e.g., Gal 5:19-21) implications but refers merely to Paul's physical existence. Thus, it functions as a synechdoche for human life (cf. GW: "if I continue to live in this life").

τοῦτό. Nominative subject of an implied ἐστίν. τοῦτό marks the beginning of the apodosis. The near-demonstrative pronoun refers back to τὸ ζῆν ἐν σαρκί in the protasis (cf. BDAG, 740.1.a.ε).

μοι. Dative of advantage that goes with the implied ἐστίν ("this [is] fruitful labor for me"), rather than dative of possession that goes with καρπὸς ἔργου ("this [is] my fruitful labor"; *pace* Robertson, 537).

καρπὸς. Predicate nominative.

ἔργου. This could be (1) attributed genitive, whose head noun (καρπὸς) functions semantically as an attributive adjective ("fruitful labor"; cf. Wallace 1996, 89–90), (2) epexegetical genitive that clarifies the meaning of καρπὸς ("fruit, which is labor"), or (3) genitive of source that modifies καρπὸς ("fruit from labor"; cf. BDAG, 510.2).

καὶ. Coordinating conjunction that links the apodosis of the conditional clause and the declarative statement that follows.

τί. Accusative direct object of αἱρήσομαι.

αἱρήσομαι. Fut mid ind 1st sg αἱρέω. Although αἱρέω could mean "choose," when it is used with the accusative, as here, it means "prefer" (BDAG, 28.2). αἱρήσομαι is traditionally called "the indirect middle" because it indicates that the subject (Paul) acts for himself and in his own interest (Wallace 1996, 419, 421). NIV renders καὶ τί αἱρήσομαι as a question: "Yet what shall I choose?" My translation follows the punctuation in NA[28]/UBS[5] and in SBLGNT, which regard καὶ τί αἱρήσομαι as an indirect question within a declarative statement. Levinsohn suggests that τί αἱρήσομαι is placed before the negative particle οὐ "because it provides a point of departure for the sentence, as the argument switches from one of the two possibilities that are being contemplated ('to live' over against 'to die') to joint consideration of them both" (2000, 53).

οὐ. Negative particle normally used with indicative verbs.

γνωρίζω. Pres act ind 1st sg γνωρίζω. The regular meaning of γνωρίζω is causative ("to cause information to become known" [BDAG, 203.1]), but in the current context it probably means "to have information or be knowledgeable about someth[ing]," "know" (BDAG, 203.2). The verb stands in final, emphatic position (see 1:18a on χαίρω).

1:23 συνέχομαι δὲ ἐκ τῶν δύο, τὴν ἐπιθυμίαν ἔχων εἰς τὸ ἀναλῦσαι καὶ σὺν Χριστῷ εἶναι, πολλῷ [γὰρ] μᾶλλον κρεῖσσον·

συνέχομαι. Pres pass ind 1st sg συνέχω. In this context, συνέχω (lit. "to be held together from") is used as an idiom, denoting "to be pulled in two directions, to be betwixt and between, to have conflicting thoughts" (LN 30.18) or "to cause distress by force of circumstances" (BDAG, 971.5). The passive voice συνέχομαι expresses Paul's conflicting emotions, which he describes as being torn between two options.

δὲ. Marker of development.

ἐκ τῶν δύο. Source (BDAG, 297.3.g), expressing the idea of "between" (Wallace 1996, 135 n. 170).

τὴν ἐπιθυμίαν. Accusative direct object of ἔχων. Fronted for emphasis. Although in the Pauline corpus (Rom 1:24; 6:12; 7:7-8; 13:14; Gal 5:16; Eph 2:3; Col 3:5; 1 Tim 6:9; 2 Tim 2:22; 3:6) and elsewhere in the NT (Jas 1:14-15; 1 Pet 1:14; 4:2-3; 2 Pet 1:4; 3:3) ἐπιθυμία frequently refers to "a desire for someth[ing] forbidden or simply inordinate," "craving, lust" (BDAG, 372.2), in this context it denotes "desire for good things" (BDAG, 372.1.b).

ἔχων. Pres act ptc masc nom sg ἔχω (causal).

εἰς τὸ ἀναλῦσαι. Aor act inf ἀναλύω (epexegetical to τὴν ἐπιθυμίαν). While εἰς τό + infinitive is typically used to convey purpose or result, the construction εἰς τὸ + the infinitive ἀναλῦσαι is here used to provide the content of Paul's desire. In this context, ἀναλύω (lit. "to depart") is used as a euphemistic expression for death: "to leave this life, to die" (LN 23.101). The perfective aspect of the aorist infinitive is fitting for portraying death as a complete event (cf. τὸ ἀποθανεῖν in 1:21).

καί. Coordinating conjunction, linking two infinitives.

σὺν Χριστῷ. Accompaniment. The PP is oriented toward the future, in contrast to two other occurrences of σὺν Χριστῷ in the Pauline corpus that refer to the past, expressing participation with Christ in his death (Rom 6:8; Col 2:20). σὺν Χριστῷ, which here describes the fellowship with Christ after death, is comparable but not equivalent to the fellowship with Christ at the Parousia described in 1 Thess 4:17 (καὶ οὕτως πάντοτε σὺν κυρίῳ ἐσόμεθα).

εἶναι. Pres act inf εἰμί (epexegetical to τὴν ἐπιθυμίαν). This infinitive is parallel to ἀναλῦσαι (see above).

πολλῷ . . . μᾶλλον. Dative of measure/degree of difference (Wallace 1996, 167) + the comparative adverb of μάλα. πολλῷ indicates "the extent to which the comparison is true" (166): lit. "more by much" = "much more." The construction πολλῷ μᾶλλον is fairly common in Paul (Rom 5:9, 10, 15, 17; 1 Cor 12:22; 2 Cor 3:9, 11; Phil 2:12).

[γάρ]. Postpositive conjunction that introduces the support for the previous statement. It is printed within square brackets because the external evidence for ($\mathfrak{P}^{46}$ ℵ[1] A B C 075 0278 6 33 81 104 326 365 1175 1241 1739 1881 vg[mss] Aug) and against (ℵ* D* D[2] F G K L P Ψ 630 1505 2464 𝔐 lat sy[h]) its inclusion is evenly balanced.

κρεῖσσον. Predicate adjective. κρεῖσσον is the comparative of ἀγαθός. In Hellenistic Greek, the Attic -ττ- consonant combination is frequently replaced by -σσ-, as here (BDF §34.1). Paul uses the Attic form κρεῖττον only in 1 Cor 7:9; elsewhere in the NT, κρεῖττον occurs in Heb

11:40; 12:24; 1 Pet 3:17; 2 Pet 2:21. πολλῷ γὰρ μᾶλλον κρεῖσσον is an elliptical clause (= [τοῦτο] γὰρ [ἐστιν] πολλῷ μᾶλλον κρεῖσσον; "for [this is] much more better"), in which the adjective κρεῖσσον (neut nom sg) functions as the predicate of an implied ἐστίν. The implied subject of the verb (τοῦτο) refers back to ἀναλῦσαι καὶ σὺν Χριστῷ εἶναι.

1:24 τὸ δὲ ἐπιμένειν [ἐν] τῇ σαρκὶ ἀναγκαιότερον δι' ὑμᾶς.

τὸ ... ἐπιμένειν. Pres act inf ἐπιμένω. The articular infinitive serves as the subject of an implied ἐστίν. The article nominalizes the infinitive and functions as an anaphoric reference to 1:22a (BDF §399.1). The imperfective aspect of the present infinitive portrays remaining in the flesh as an ongoing process (cf. τὸ ζῆν in 1:21).

δὲ. Marker of contrast.

[ἐν] τῇ σαρκὶ. Locative ("in the sphere of flesh"). The article is anaphoric, recalling ἐν σαρκί in 1:22 and indicating that the term "flesh" is used again as a synechdoche for human life. The preposition ἐν is placed within square brackets because it is omitted in some important manuscripts (ℵ A C P Ψ 075 6 33 1739 2495 Cl Or), but its attestation is both early and widespread ($\mathfrak{P}^{46}$ B D F G K L 0278 81 104 365 630 1175 1241 1505 1881 2464 𝔐).

ἀναγκαιότερον. Predicate adjective. It is neuter in agreement with the neuter article attached to the infinitive ἐπιμένειν. ἀναγκαιότερον is a comparative of ἀναγκαῖος ("necessary").

δι' ὑμᾶς. Causal.

1:25 καὶ τοῦτο πεποιθὼς οἶδα ὅτι μενῶ καὶ παραμενῶ πᾶσιν ὑμῖν εἰς τὴν ὑμῶν προκοπὴν καὶ χαρὰν τῆς πίστεως,

καὶ. Coordinating conjunction, linking two clauses.

τοῦτο. Accusative direct object of πεποιθὼς. Fronted as a topical frame. The demonstrative pronoun is anaphoric, referring to Paul's assertion in v. 24.

πεποιθὼς. Prf act ptc masc nom sg πείθω (causal). Wallace notes that perfect participles almost always indicate the cause or ground of the action of the main verb and that causal participles typically precede the verb they modify (1996, 631). This word order also indicates that πεποιθὼς provides the background information for οἶδα. This conclusion is based on Runge's observation that the adverbial participles "that precede the main clause share a unified function. The use of the participle represents the choice not to use a finite verb. Since the participle is dependent upon the main verb to supply the information that it does not encode on its own (e.g., mood), the participle does not obtain the same status as a finite verb. This means that the participle plays a supporting role to the main verb, and the role differs depending upon the placement of the participle with respect to the main verb. Those that precede the main verb have the effect of backgrounding the action of the participle, indicating that it is less important than the main verbal action" (Runge 2010, 249; cf. Buth, 277–78, 281 n. 9).

οἶδα. Prf act ind 1st sg οἶδα. The perfect tense has the present meaning, describing "the enduring result rather than the completed act" (Smyth §1946) without any reference to how this knowledge (or lack thereof) emerged. This information is provided by the causal participle πεποιθὼς that precedes οἶδα.

ὅτι. Introduces the clausal complement (indirect discourse) of οἶδα.

μενῶ. Fut act ind 1st sg μένω. The verb μένω means "to continue to exist," "remain, last, persist, continue to live" (BDAG, 631.2).

παραμενῶ. Fut act ind 1st sg παραμένω. This compound verb means "to remain in a state or situation, remain, stay (on)" (BDAG, 769.1). παραμένω is also a common euphemism for "serve" (Moulton and Milligan, 487; cf. BDAG, 769.2). It is debatable to what extent the meanings of μενῶ and παραμενῶ should be distinguished. Given the significant semantic overlap between these two verbs, their consecutive use reinforces Paul's conviction that he will be released from prison and remain with the Philippians (cf. Snyman, 107).

πᾶσιν ὑμῖν. Dative of association.

εἰς τὴν . . . προκοπὴν καὶ χαρὰν. Purpose. A single article governing two nouns connected with καί creates a TSKS construction (see 1:19 on διὰ τῆς . . . δεήσεως καὶ ἐπιχορηγίας) that juxtaposes two distinct entities—προκοπή ("progress") and χαρά ("joy"). Another possibility is to regard προκοπὴν καὶ χαρὰν as a hendiadys ("joyful progress" [Zerwick and Grosvenor, 594]).

ὑμῶν. Subjective genitive modifying προκοπὴν ("the progress that you make"). The placement of the personal pronoun between the article τὴν and the noun προκοπὴν is emphatic (Fee, 153).

τῆς πίστεως. Genitive of reference modifying χαρὰν ("joy with respect to faith" or "joy in faith") or genitive of source qualifying χαρὰν ("joy out of faith" or "joy derived from faith").

1:26 ἵνα τὸ καύχημα ὑμῶν περισσεύῃ ἐν Χριστῷ Ἰησοῦ ἐν ἐμοὶ διὰ τῆς ἐμῆς παρουσίας πάλιν πρὸς ὑμᾶς.

ἵνα. Introduces either a result clause (Porter 1994, 235), a purpose clause (BDAG, 475.1.a.δ), or a purpose-result clause indicating "both the intention and its sure accomplishment" (Wallace 1996, 473).

τὸ καύχημα. Nominative subject of περισσεύῃ. καύχημα denotes "act of taking pride in someth[ing] or that which constitutes a source of pride" (BDAG, 537.1). Fronted as a topical frame.

ὑμῶν. Subjective genitive modifying καύχημα ("what you can be proud of" [BDAG, 537.1]).

περισσεύῃ. Pres act subj 3rd sg περισσεύω. Subjunctive with ἵνα. περισσεύω here means "be present in abundance" (BDAG, 805.1.a.β).

ἐν Χριστῷ Ἰησοῦ. If the PP modifies the verb (περισσεύῃ), ἐν Χριστῷ Ἰησοῦ denotes the sphere in which the Philippians abound, indicating "that the *growing* happens in Christ" (Campbell 2012, 104; cf. O'Brien, 141; Reumann, 230; NASB; HCSB). If the PP modifies the noun (καύχημα), ἐν Χριστῷ Ἰησοῦ denotes the object or the ground for the Philippians' boasting, functioning "as a marker of specification or substance" (Campbell 2012, 104; cf. Fee, 155 n. 21; NRSV; NIV; see also καυχώμενοι ἐν Χριστῷ Ἰησου in 3:3). The first option is supported by the syntax of the clause because the PP follows the verb and not the noun. The second option is supported by the potentially negative connotations of καύχημα (cf. Rom 4:2; 1 Cor 5:6), which are avoided if the boasting is in Christ Jesus, but it is undermined by the awkwardness of the syntax. These difficulties can be resolved if we take ἐν Χριστῷ Ἰησοῦ as a qualifier of both the noun and the verb because growing in Christ "makes sense precisely because he is first of all the grounds for any and all such boasting" (Fee 155 n. 21).

ἐν ἐμοί. Causal (NET: "because of me"; REB: "on my account"). This PP, like the PP ἐν Χριστῷ Ἰησοῦ that comes before it, may go with περισσεύῃ, providing the reason for the increase of the Philippians' pride ("so that your boasting may increase because of me"), or with καύχημα, supplying the reason for the Philippians' boasting ("so that your boasting because of me may increase"). The syntax of the clause favors the first option.

διὰ τῆς ἐμῆς παρουσίας. Means. In this context, παρουσία ("the state of being present at a place" [BDAG, 780.1]) denotes "arrival as the first stage in presence," "coming" (BDAG, 780.2). The possessive adjective stands in the first attributive position (see 1:5 on ἀπὸ τῆς πρώτης ἡμέρας).

πάλιν. Adverb "pert[aining] to return to a position or state." (BDAG, 752.1). In the expression ἡ ἐμὴ παρουσία πάλιν πρὸς ὑμᾶς ("my return to you"), πάλιν is used pleonastically because the term παρουσία ("return") expresses the component "back" (BDAG, 752.1).

πρὸς ὑμᾶς. Locative (motion toward).

Philippians 1:27-30

²⁷Only conduct your lives in a manner worthy of the gospel of Christ, so that, whether I come and see you or am absent, I may hear of your circumstances, [namely] that you are standing firm in one spirit, struggling together with one mind for the faith of the gospel, ²⁸and not being intimidated in any way by your opponents, which is for them a sign of destruction, but of your salvation, and this [is] from God; ²⁹for to you has been graciously granted on behalf of Christ, not only to believe in him but also to suffer on behalf of him, ³⁰having the same struggle, which you saw in me and now hear about me.

1:27 Μόνον ἀξίως τοῦ εὐαγγελίου τοῦ Χριστοῦ πολιτεύεσθε, ἵνα εἴτε ἐλθὼν καὶ ἰδὼν ὑμᾶς εἴτε ἀπὼν ἀκούω τὰ περὶ ὑμῶν, ὅτι στήκετε ἐν ἑνὶ πνεύματι, μιᾷ ψυχῇ συναθλοῦντες τῇ πίστει τοῦ εὐαγγελίου

Μόνον. Adverbial accusative of μόνος, functioning as "a marker of limitation" (BDAG, 659.2). In this verse, Μόνον is used to limit "the action or state to the one designated by the verb" (BDAG, 659.2.a).

ἀξίως. Adverb of manner ("worthily, in a manner worthy of" [BDAG, 94]) modifying πολιτεύεσθε. Fronted for emphasis.

τοῦ εὐαγγελίου. Genitive complement of ἀξίως.

τοῦ Χριστοῦ. Objective genitive modifying εὐαγγελίου ("the gospel about Christ"; cf. BDAG, 403.1.b.β.ℵ) or, less likely, subjective genitive ("the gospel from Christ"; cf. TDNT 2:731 n. 70).

πολιτεύεσθε. Pres mid impv 2nd pl πολιτεύομαι. Elsewhere in the NT, this verb is found only in Acts 23:1. According to BDAG (846), πολιτεύομαι could mean (1) "to be a citizen," (2) "to administer a corporate body," or (3) "to conduct one's life." It is used in the third sense here, but political implications cannot be completely excluded because elsewhere in his letters Paul uses περιπατέω when he speaks about conducting one's life (e.g., Rom 6:4; 8:4; 1 Cor 7:17; 2 Cor 5:7; Gal 5:16; 1 Thess 2:12). It is therefore reasonable to conclude with Hellerman that Paul uses "this politically charged term (subversively, in view of the pride of honors associated with Roman citizenship in the colony) in reference to another citizen body, namely, the Christian community in Philippi. . . .

Paul intentionally marks out the church in the colony as an alternative society vis-à-vis the Roman imperial order" (2015, 78). The imperfective aspect of the present imperative shows that Paul's instruction refers to conduct in life viewed as an ongoing process.

ἵνα. Introduces a purpose clause.

εἴτε ... εἴτε. Correlative conjunctions ("whether ... or"); see 1:18.

ἐλθών. Aor act ptc masc nom sg ἔρχομαι (conditional).

καί. Coordinating conjunction connecting the first pair of participles.

ἰδών. Aor act ptc masc nom sg ὁράω (conditional).

ὑμᾶς. Accusative direct object of ἰδών.

ἀπών. Pres act ptc masc nom sg ἄπειμι (conditional).

ἀκούω. Pres act subj 1st sg ἀκούω. Subjunctive with ἵνα.

τὰ περὶ ὑμῶν. The article functions as a nominalizer, changing the PP περὶ ὑμῶν into the direct object of ἀκούω (lit. "the things concerning you" = "your circumstances"). Paul uses the same formulation in 2:19, 20.

περὶ ὑμῶν. Reference.

ὅτι. Introduces a nominal clause that stands in apposition to τὰ περὶ ὑμῶν.

στήκετε. Pres act ind 2nd pl στήκω. The verb στήκω (lit. "to be in a standing position" [BDAG, 944.1]) is here used figuratively: "to be firmly committed in conviction or belief" (BDAG, 944.2).

ἐν ἑνὶ πνεύματι. Manner. The noun πνεῦμα could refer to the Holy Spirit (NIV: "in the one Spirit") or to human spirit (NRSV: "in one spirit"). The following expression, μιᾷ ψυχῇ, which is parallel to ἐν ἑνὶ πνεύματι, suggests that human spirit ("the anthropological πνεῦμα" [TDNT 6:434–35]) is in view.

μιᾷ ψυχῇ. Dative of means. The expression modifies συναθλοῦντες, but it is placed before it for emphasis. ψυχή denotes "the essence of life in terms of thinking, willing, and feeling," which can be rendered as "inner self, mind, thoughts, feelings, heart, being" (LN 26.4). The adjective μιᾷ stands in the first (anarthrous) attributive position (see 1:4 on ἐν πάσῃ δεήσει).

συναθλοῦντες. Pres act ptc masc nom pl συναθλέω (manner). συναθλέω means to "contend/struggle along with" (BDAG, 964). For a suggestion that the prefix συν does not preclude interpreting συναθλέω as an athletic term that evokes a sense of fellowship among athletes, see Kurek-Chomycz (279–303). The only other occurrence of συναθλέω in Paul's letters (and the NT) is in 4:3. On adverbial participles that follow the main verb, see 1:4 on ποιούμενος.

τῇ πίστει. Dative of advantage.

τοῦ εὐαγγελίου. Objective genitive modifying πίστει ("the faith in the gospel"), genitive of source qualifying πίστει ("the faith that originates from the gospel") or epexegetical genitive explaining πίστει ("the faith that is the gospel").

1:28 καὶ μὴ πτυρόμενοι ἐν μηδενὶ ὑπὸ τῶν ἀντικειμένων, ἥτις ἐστὶν αὐτοῖς ἔνδειξις ἀπωλείας, ὑμῶν δὲ σωτηρίας, καὶ τοῦτο ἀπὸ θεοῦ·

καὶ. Coordinating conjunction.

μὴ. Negative particle normally used with non-indicative verbs.

πτυρόμενοι. Pres pass ptc masc nom pl πτύρω (manner). πτύρω ("to let oneself be intimidated," "be frightened, terrified" [BDAG, 895]) is a NT *hapax legomenon*. This participle is structurally parallel to συναθλοῦντες in v. 27. On adverbial participles that follow the main verb, see 1:4 on ποιούμενος.

ἐν μηδενί. Manner. The two negatives, μὴ . . . μηδενὶ, do not cancel but reinforce each other: lit. "not being intimidated in no way" = "not being intimidated in any way."

ὑπὸ τῶν ἀντικειμένων. Primary (personal) agency.

τῶν ἀντικειμένων. Pres mid ptc masc gen pl ἀντίκειμαι (substantival).

ἥτις. Nominative subject of ἐστίν. The indefinite relative pronoun ὅστις, ἥτις, ὅ τι is used "to emphasize a characteristic quality, by which a preceding statement is to be confirmed" (BDAG, 729.2.b). Zerwick points out that this indefinite relative pronoun "either shares the indeterminate status of its antecedent or, if the antecedent is itself determinate, regards it not as individual but as of such a nature" (§215). In this verse, however, determining the antecedent of ἥτις is very difficult. There are two major alternatives. (1) The first possibility is to take τῇ πίστει at the end of v. 27 as the antecedent of ἥτις (Hawthorne and Martin, 72–73). This reading is supported by the agreement in gender and number between τῇ πίστει and ἥτις, but its drawback is the lengthy participial clause (καὶ μὴ πτυρόμενοι ἐν μηδενὶ ὑπὸ τῶν ἀντικειμένων) that separates them. (2) The second possibility is to regard the entire preceding ὅτι clause (vv. 27b-28a) as the antecedent of ἥτις (Fee, 168 n. 53). The strength of this interpretation is the proximity between the presumed antecedent and the relative pronoun, as well as the ability to explain why Paul chose the indefinite relative pronoun ἥτις (see Zerwick's comments quoted above about the indeterminate status of the antecedent) rather than a regular relative pronoun ἥ, which would have had a specific Greek term as antecedent. A possible weakness of this alternative is the feminine gender of the relative pronoun, which must be explained by its alleged attraction to the predicate nominative ἔνδειξις. This difficulty, however, is solvable because such attractions, although rare, are documented in the NT; see, e.g., Eph 3:13 (ἥτις ἐστὶν δόξα ὑμῶν) and 1 Cor 3:17 (οἵτινές ἐστε ὑμεῖς). It seems, then, that the second alternative is preferable because it offers a better explanation of the syntax of the sentence.

ἐστὶν. Pres act ind 3rd sg εἰμί.

αὐτοῖς. Dative of disadvantage (cf. Wallace 1996, 143–44).

ἔνδειξις. Predicate nominative. ἔνδειξις denotes "someth[ing] that points to or serves as an indicator of someth[ing]," "sign, omen" (BDAG, 332.1).

ἀπωλείας. Objective genitive modifying ἔνδειξις ("pointer to destruction").

ὑμῶν. Possessive genitive modifying σωτηρίας ("your salvation") or objective genitive modifying the verbal idea implicit in σωτηρίας ("salvation of you"). The preposed pronoun is thematically salient (Levinsohn 2000, 64). The genitive ὑμῶν disrupts the parallelism between αὐτοῖς ἔνδειξις ἀπωλείας and ὑμῶν . . . [ἔνδειξις] σωτηρίας. Wallace suggests that the shift from the dative of disadvantage (αὐτοῖς) to the possessive genitive (ὑμῶν) conveys the idea that "the enemies of the gospel do not possess their destruction, but are the unfortunate recipients of it; but believers do possess their salvation" (1996, 144). The variant readings that replace the genitive ὑμῶν, which has strong external support (ℵ A B C² P Ψ 0278 33 81 104 365 1175 1241 et al.), with the dative ὑμῖν (D¹ K L 075 630 𝔐 lat co) or the more inclusive ἡμῖν (C* D* F G b vg^ms) represent scribal modifications seeking to adjust the case of the second- (or first-) person personal pronoun to the dative αὐτοῖς in the previous clause for the sake of parallelism.

δὲ. Marker of development, which here indicates a contrast between the sign of destruction and the sign of salvation.

σωτηρίας. Objective genitive modifying ἔνδειξις ("pointer to salvation"). σωτηρίας is parallel to ἀπωλείας, governed by the same head noun.

καὶ. Coordinating conjunction.

τοῦτο. Nominative subject of an implied ἐστίν. The demonstrative pronoun may refer to σωτηρίας (Fee, 170), to the entire relative clause ἥτις ἐστὶν αὐτοῖς ἔνδειξις ἀπωλείας, ὑμῶν δὲ σωτηρίας (Reumann, 290; Sumney, 37), or "to the whole episode of opposition in its double effect, leading the opponents to destruction and the believers to eternal salvation" (O'Brien, 157).

ἀπὸ θεοῦ. Source.

1:29 ὅτι ὑμῖν ἐχαρίσθη τὸ ὑπὲρ Χριστοῦ, οὐ μόνον τὸ εἰς αὐτὸν πιστεύειν ἀλλὰ καὶ τὸ ὑπὲρ αὐτοῦ πάσχειν,

ὅτι. Introduces a causal clause.

ὑμῖν. Dative indirect object of ἐχαρίσθη. Fronted as a topical frame.

ἐχαρίσθη. Aor pass ind 3rd sg χαρίζομαι. In the current context, χαρίζομαι means "to give freely as a favor," "give graciously" (BDAG, 1078.1). The preceding clause (καὶ τοῦτο ἀπὸ θεοῦ, v. 28) suggests that the implied agent of ἐχαρίσθη is God.

τὸ ὑπὲρ Χριστοῦ. The article functions as a nominalizer, changing the PP ὑπὲρ Χριστοῦ into the subject of ἐχαρίσθη (lit. "the matter on behalf of Christ"). The article is also cataphoric, anticipating two articular infinitives in the οὐ μόνον . . . ἀλλὰ καὶ construction. Wallace (1996, 236) suggests the following literal translation of the verse, which brings out the force of the cataphoric article: "*the* on-behalf-of-Christ thing has been given to you, namely, not only *the* believing in his name, but also *the* suffering for him."

ὑπὲρ Χριστοῦ. Representation.

οὐ μόνον . . . ἀλλὰ καὶ. A point/counterpoint set ("not only . . . but also") that corrects the first assertion (to believe in Christ) by supplementing it with another assertion (to suffer on behalf of Christ). The negative particle οὐ is used rather than μή because it negates the adverb μόνον and not the infinitive τὸ . . . πιστεύειν (Porter 1994, 282). The οὐ μόνον . . . ἀλλὰ καὶ construction confirms Runge's claim that ἀλλά "does more than just indicate contrast. This holds true even if the preceding element is positive rather than negative. It provides a corrective to whatever it stands in contrast with" (2010, 93). Since the οὐ μόνον clause indicates that believing in Christ is not a sufficient description of what is given, the emphasis falls on the ἀλλὰ καὶ clause that affirms the necessity of suffering on behalf of Christ.

τὸ . . . πιστεύειν. Pres act inf πιστεύω. The articular infinitive is appositional to τὸ ὑπὲρ Χριστοῦ (Wallace 1996, 607). The imperfective aspect of the present infinitive portrays believing in Christ as an ongoing process. The verb stands in final, emphatic position (see 1:18a on χαίρω).

εἰς αὐτὸν. Goal of actions or feelings directed toward someone (BDAG, 290.4.c.β). πιστεύω + εἰς means to "to entrust oneself to an entity in complete confidence . . . w[ith] implication of total commitment to the one who is trusted" (BDAG, 817.2). The PP modifies τὸ . . . πιστεύειν. It is placed between the article and the infinitive for clarity (Wallace 1996, 607).

τὸ . . . πάσχειν. Pres act inf πάσχω. The articular infinitive is appositional to τὸ ὑπὲρ Χριστοῦ (Wallace 1996, 607). The imperfective aspect of the present infinitive portrays suffering for the sake of Christ as an ongoing process. The verb stands in final, emphatic position (see 1:18a on χαίρω).

ὑπὲρ αὐτοῦ. Representation. The PP modifies τὸ . . . πάσχειν. It is placed between the article and the infinitive for clarity (Wallace 1996, 607).

1:30 τὸν αὐτὸν ἀγῶνα ἔχοντες, οἷον εἴδετε ἐν ἐμοὶ καὶ νῦν ἀκούετε ἐν ἐμοί.

τὸν αὐτὸν ἀγῶνα. Accusative direct object of ἔχοντες. Fronted for emphasis. Since the intensive pronoun αὐτὸν stands in the first attributive position (see 1:5 on ἀπὸ τῆς πρώτης ἡμέρας), it functions as an identifying adjective that means "the same" (BDAG, 153.3; Wallace 1996, 349). The term ἀγών (lit. "athletic competition") is here used figuratively for a struggle for the gospel (BDAG, 17.2).

ἔχοντες. Pres act ptc masc nom pl ἔχω (manner). O'Brien regards this participle as "an irregular nominative (instead of a dative agreeing with ὑμῖν)" (161; cf. Robertson, 414, 1135; Moule, 31; Porter 1994, 86), but this explanation is based on the questionable assumption, shared by many grammarians, that oblique participles could function adverbially. Culy (2003) has demonstrated that adverbial participles are always in the nominative, except when they modify a genitive subject or an infinitive whose semantic subject is in the accusative. The nominative case of ἔχοντες is therefore not an anomaly but a regular form of an adverbial participle that agrees with the subject of the main verb στήκετε in v. 27. Consequently, the function and form of ἔχοντες are the same as the function and form of συναθλοῦντες (v. 27) and πτυρόμενοι (v. 28). This explanation presumes that vv. 28b-29 (ἥτις ἐστὶν αὐτοῖς ἔνδειξις ἀπωλείας, ὑμῶν δὲ σωτηρίας, καὶ τοῦτο ἀπὸ θεοῦ· ὅτι ὑμῖν ἐχαρίσθη τὸ ὑπὲρ Χριστοῦ, οὐ μόνον τὸ εἰς αὐτὸν πιστεύειν ἀλλὰ καὶ τὸ ὑπὲρ αὐτοῦ πάσχειν) are parenthetical (Hellerman 2015, 87).

οἷον. Direct object of εἴδετε. The relative pronoun οἷος ("of what sort [such]") indicates that something is similar to something else or belongs to a class (BDAG, 701). Since the antecedent of οἷον is ἀγῶνα, the use of this relative pronoun suggests that the struggles of the Philippians were of the same kind as those experienced by Paul.

εἴδετε. Aor act ind 2nd pl ὁράω. The aorist tense refers to the past, describing what the Philippians saw when Paul was with them.

ἐν ἐμοί. Locative ("which you saw in my case"; BDAG, 329.8) or agency ("which you saw me engaged in"; LN 90.6).

καὶ. Coordinating conjunction.

νῦν. Temporal adverb, with "focus on the immediate present, designating both a point of time as well as its extent" (BDAG, 681.1.a). Fronted as a temporal frame.

ἀκούετε. Pres act ind 2nd pl ἀκούω. The temporal marker νῦν indicates that the present tense describes the current experience of the Philippians, i.e., what they presently hear about Paul's struggle.

ἐν ἐμοί. See above.

Philippians 2:1-4

¹Therefore, if [there is] any encouragement in Christ, if any consolation of love, if any fellowship of the Spirit, if any affection and compassion, ²complete my joy, that you think the same thing, having the same love, [being] united in spirit, thinking the one thing, ³[doing] nothing according to selfish ambition or according to empty conceit, but in humility considering one another as surpassing yourselves, ⁴each looking out not for your own interests, but each [looking out] also for the interests of others.

2:1 Εἴ τις οὖν παράκλησις ἐν Χριστῷ, εἴ τι παραμύθιον ἀγάπης, εἴ τις κοινωνία πνεύματος, εἴ τις σπλάγχνα καὶ οἰκτιρμοί,

Εἴ. Introduces the first protasis of a first-class condition. This conditional clause consists of a fourfold protasis, each of which is introduced by a conditional particle followed by an indefinite pronoun and a noun. The first-class condition assumes that the protasis is true for the sake of the argument and draws the conclusion from that supposition. Although the particle εἰ is a proclitic, it is accented because it acquired an acute accent from the enclitic τις (Carson, 49).

τις . . . παράκλησις. Nominative subject of an implied ἐστίν. The term παράκλησις could denote either an "act of emboldening another in belief or course of action" (BDAG, 766.1) or the "lifting of another's spirits" (BDAG, 766.3). If the former, παράκλησις ("encouragement, exhortation") refers to Paul's exhortation to the Philippians. If the latter, παράκλησις ("comfort, consolation") refers to the comfort that comes from God. While there are good reasons for each option (see Hellerman 2015, 93–94), the inferential conjunction οὖν, which links this verse to Paul's description of the Philippians' suffering on behalf of Christ in 1:29-30, tips the scales in favor of the second alternative (cf. Fee, 179–80). Like most English translators, I have used the term "encouragement" because this rendering of παράκλησις, while conveying solace, retains some ambiguity of the Greek term. The indefinite pronoun τις functions as an adjective, modifying παράκλησις ("any encouragement").

οὖν. Postpositive inferential conjunction. οὖν usually takes second position in its clause, but here it is placed third because the conditional particle Εἴ and the indefinite pronoun τις form one syntactic unit, or even one word (BDF §475.2), whose fourfold repetition (Εἴ τις . . . εἴ τι . . . εἴ τις . . . εἴ τις) is used for rhetorical effect.

ἐν Χριστῷ. Cause or reason ("because of Christ" or "on account of Christ"; cf. BDAG, 329.9). This function of ἐν Χριστῷ is parallel to the functions of the two genitives ἀγάπης and πνεύματος (Campbell 2012, 105, 111).

εἴ. Introduces the second protasis of a first-class condition. Although the particle εἰ is a proclitic, it is accented because it acquired an acute accent from the enclitic τι (Carson, 49).

τι παραμύθιον. Nominative subject of an implied ἐστίν. παραμύθιον ("consolation, means of consolation, alleviation" [BDAG, 769]) is a NT *hapax legomenon* whose semantic range partially overlaps with παράκλησις. The indefinite pronoun τι functions as an adjective, modifying παραμύθιον ("any consolation").

ἀγάπης. Genitive of source modifying παραμύθιον ("consolation that arises from love").

εἴ. Introduces the third protasis of a first-class condition. Although the particle εἰ is a proclitic, it is accented because it acquired an acute accent from the enclitic τις (Carson, 49).

τις κοινωνία. Nominative subject of an implied ἐστίν. In this context, κοινωνία means either "association, communion, fellowship, close relationship" (BDAG, 552.1) or "participation, sharing" (BDAG, 553.4). The indefinite pronoun τις functions as an adjective, modifying κοινωνία ("any fellowship").

πνεύματος. The function of this genitive depends on the sense of the head noun κοινωνία. If κοινωνία means "communion, fellowship," πνεύματος could be either genitive of source ("fellowship that is issued from the Spirit"; cf. Campbell 2012, 104) or genitive of association ("fellowship with the Spirit"; cf. BDAG, 552.1). If κοινωνία means "participation, sharing," πνεύματος is an objective genitive ("participation in the Spirit" or "sharing in the Spirit"; cf. O'Brien, 174; Fee, 181 n. 40). Although the noun πνεύματος is anarthrous, it most likely refers to the Holy Spirit (cf. ἡ κοινωνία τοῦ ἁγίου πνεύματος in 2 Cor 13:13; Fee, 181).

εἴ. Introduces the fourth protasis of a first-class condition. Although the particle εἰ is a proclitic, it is accented because it acquired an acute accent from the enclitic τις (Carson, 49).

τις σπλάγχνα καὶ οἰκτιρμοί. Compound nominative subject of an implied ἐστίν or εἰσίν. On the meaning of σπλάγχνα, see 1:8 on ἐν σπλάγχνοις. In the NT, the noun σπλάγχνον always occurs in the plural (Luke 1:78; 2 Cor 6:12; 7:15; Col 3:12; Phlm 7, 12, 20; 1 John 3:17), as here. The noun οἰκτιρμός, which likewise typically occurs in the plural (Rom 12:1; 2 Cor 1:3; Heb 10:28), as here, means "pity, mercy, compassion" (BDAG, 700). The combination σπλάγχνα καὶ οἰκτιρμοί could be regarded as a hendiadys ("compassionate mercy"; cf. σπλάγχνα οἰκτιρμοῦ in Col 3:12; Silva, 90–91; BDAG, 700; TDNT 5:161), but since the meanings of these terms do not completely overlap (σπλάγχνα denoting "the abode of tender feelings" and οἰκτιρμοί denoting "the manifestation of these in compassionate yearnings and actions" [Lightfoot, 108]), they should probably be regarded as two distinct qualities (Fee, 182 n. 41). The indefinite pronoun τις functions as an adjective, modifying σπλάγχνα καὶ οἰκτιρμοί. The incongruity between the singular masc/fem pronoun and two plural nouns is an example of solecism (BDF §137.2; Robertson, 130; MHT 3:316). BDF (§137.2) suggests that the neuter plural "τινα is avoided for rhythmical considerations." Robertson (410) ponders that a scribe replaced an original τινα with τις because of its use in the previous examples or because a scribe mistakenly regarded σπλάγχνα as singular. Given the lack of any evidence for τινα in the Greek manuscript tradition, however, this scenario is not very likely.

2:2 πληρώσατέ μου τὴν χαρὰν ἵνα τὸ αὐτὸ φρονῆτε, τὴν αὐτὴν ἀγάπην ἔχοντες, σύμψυχοι, τὸ ἓν φρονοῦντες,

πληρώσατέ μου τὴν χαρὰν. The main clause of the apodosis functions as a metacomment, "serving to highlight the key proposition that follows: thinking the same thing" (Runge 2010, 278).

πληρώσατέ. Aor act impv 2nd pl πληρόω. The verb marks the beginning of the apodosis, which extends to the end of v. 4. πληρώσατέ, which has an acute accent on the antepenult, acquired an additional accent, the acute, on the ultima from the enclitic μου (Smyth §183; Carson 1985, 48). In this verse dominated by the verbs in the present tense, the perfective aspect of πληρώσατέ stands out, calling attention to the completion of Paul's joy, which is presented in a summary fashion. According to Fanning "[t]he focus is on the end-point of the action even though the command is a general precept" (369).

μου. Possessive genitive modifying χαρὰν. The preposed pronoun (lit. "my the joy") is thematically salient (Levinsohn 2000, 64). Fee calls the pronoun μου, which is placed before its head noun, "a rare example of 'vernacular possessive'" (184 n. 52).

τὴν χαρὰν. Accusative direct object of πληρώσατέ.

ἵνα. Introduces an epexegetical clause that explains the clause πληρώσατέ μου τὴν χαρὰν (Wallace 1996, 476; Zerwick §410; Moule 145 n. 3, and Porter 1994, 239, call it "the content clause") or, less likely, a clause that functions as a direct object of an implied verb, such as παρακαλῶ (BDF §392.1c).

τὸ αὐτὸ. Accusative direct object of φρονῆτε. Fronted for emphasis. The article functions as a nominalizer and αὐτὸ as an identical adjective ("the same [thing]").

φρονῆτε. Pres act subj 2nd pl φρονέω. Subjunctive with ἵνα. The sense of φρονέω in this verse is similar to the sense the verb has in 1:7 ("to have an opinion with regard to someth[ing]" [BDAG, 1065.1]).

τὴν αὐτὴν ἀγάπην. Accusative direct object of ἔχοντες. Fronted for emphasis. Since the intensive pronoun αὐτὴν is in the first attributive position (see 1:5 on ἀπὸ τῆς πρώτης ἡμέρας), it functions as an identifying adjective that means "the same" (BDAG, 153.3; Wallace 1996, 349–50).

ἔχοντες. Pres act ptc masc nom pl ἔχω (manner or means). The postposed participle provides an elaboration of the main clause, πληρώσατέ μου τὴν χαρὰν ἵνα τὸ αὐτὸ φρονῆτε. Runge notes that "[t]he use of finite verb forms in lieu of participles would have resulted in a series of exhortations rather than one exhortation with additional elaborative detail" (2016, 263). On adverbial participles that follow the main verb, see 1:4 on ποιούμενος.

σύμψυχοι. This adjective (lit. "one-souled"; a NT *hapax legomenon*) could be taken as a modifier of the participial clause that follows (τὸ ἓν φρονοῦντες) or as an independent qualification of the main clause. Fee, who prefers the first option, suggests that σύμψυχοι describes "*how* ('together in soul') they are to 'set their minds on the one thing' mentioned in the primary clause" (183 n. 47), but he does not explain which specific function—attributive or predicative—this adjective would have in relation to the adverbial participle φρονοῦντες. The second option is suggested by the punctuation adopted in NA[28]/UBS[5] and SBLGNT, which separates σύμψυχοι with two commas from the surrounding participial clauses. On this reading, σύμψυχοι functions as a predicate adjective in an elliptical participial construction (σύμψυχοι [ὄντες]), which is parallel in function to the τὴν αὐτὴν ἀγάπην ἔχοντες that comes before it and to the τὸ ἓν φρονοῦντες that comes after it. The second option is, in my view, preferable because it better explains the syntax of the Greek text in this verse.

τὸ ἕν. The article functions as a nominalizer, changing the numerical adjective ἕν into the direct object of φρονοῦντες. Fronted for emphasis. Zerwick argues that the article, which is not necessary to express unity of thought, indicates that "Paul is thinking of some definite 'one thing' known to him and to the Philippians" (§170). The variant τὸ αὐτὸ, attested in some manuscripts (ℵ* A C I Ψ 33 81 1241 2464 f vg), is most likely a scribal assimilation of τὸ ἕν φρονοῦντες to the expression τὸ αὐτὸ φρονῆτε in the first part of the verse.

φρονοῦντες. Pres act ptc masc nom pl φρονέω (manner or means). The postposed participle provides an elaboration of the main clause, πληρώσατέ μου τὴν χαρὰν ἵνα τὸ αὐτὸ φρονῆτε (see ἔχοντες above). On adverbial participles that follow the main verb, see 1:4 on ποιούμενος.

2:3 μηδὲν κατ' ἐριθείαν μηδὲ κατὰ κενοδοξίαν ἀλλὰ τῇ ταπεινοφροσύνῃ ἀλλήλους ἡγούμενοι ὑπερέχοντας ἑαυτῶν,

μηδὲν . . . μηδὲ . . . ἀλλὰ. A point/counterpoint set that negates two wrong motivations for action (selfish ambition or empty conceit) and replaces them with the right attitude (in humility reckoning others better than yourselves). The negative substantive μηδὲν serves as the accusative direct object of an implied πράσσοντες (Lightfoot, 108) or ποιοῦντες (Hellerman 2015, 99). μηδὲ is a negative particle that indicates development.

κατ' ἐριθείαν. Standard. This PP is frequently used as a periphrasis of the adverb (BDAG, 513.5.b.β); lit. "according to selfish ambition" = "selfishly."

κατὰ κενοδοξίαν. Standard. κενοδοξία ("empty conceit" [BDAG, 538]) is a NT *hapax legomenon*.

τῇ ταπεινοφροσύνῃ. Dative of manner. The noun ταπεινοφροσύνη means "humility, modesty" (BDAG, 989). Zerwick (§170) suggests that the article indicates a specific type of humility—"that humility proper to Christians which Paul has so often inculcated and on which he is about to insist once more" in the Christ hymn. Levinsohn, conversely, explains the presence of the article by the placement of ταπεινοφροσύνη it the clause, marking it as "the point of departure for what follows" (1995, 72) rather than pointing to a particular type of humility.

ἀλλήλους. Accusative direct object of ἡγούμενοι. Fronted for emphasis.

ἡγούμενοι. Pres mid ptc masc nom pl ἡγέομαι (manner). ἡγέομαι here means "to think, consider, regard" (BDAG, 434.2). This postposed participle provides an elaboration of the main clause, πληρώσατέ μου τὴν χαρὰν ἵνα τὸ αὐτὸ φρονῆτε (see ἔχοντες in 2:2), explicating either the main verb πληρώσατέ (Reumann, 307) or φρονῆτε in the ἵνα clause (Fee, 189). On adverbial participles that follow the main verb, see 1:4 on ποιούμενος. For other occurrences of ἡγέομαι in Philippians, see 2:6, 25; 3:7, 8.

ὑπερέχοντας. Pres act ptc masc acc pl ὑπερέχω (indirect discourse). This participle is a good illustration of the principle that "an anarthrous participle in the *accusative* case, in conjunction with an accusative noun or pronoun, sometimes indicates indirect discourse after a verb of perception or communication" (Wallace 1996, 645; Robertson, 1123). In this context, ὑπερέχω means "to be in a controlling position," "have power over, be in authority (over), be highly placed" (BDAG, 1033.2), rather than "to surpass in quality or value," "be better than, surpass, excel" (*pace* BDAG, 1033.3; O'Brien, 182–83). This meaning makes better sense in light of the next verse, which shows that "it is not so much that others in the community are to be thought of as 'better than I am,' but as those whose needs and concerns 'surpass' my own" (Fee, 189).

ἑαυτῶν. Genitive of comparison.

2:4 μὴ τὰ ἑαυτῶν ἕκαστος σκοποῦντες ἀλλὰ [καὶ] τὰ ἑτέρων ἕκαστοι.

μὴ . . . ἀλλὰ [καὶ]. A point/counterpoint set ("not this . . . but also that") that corrects the first appeal (looking out for one's own interest) by supplementing it with the second appeal (looking out for the interests of others). The paired set of clauses is not completely balanced because the counterpoint clause (μὴ τὰ ἑαυτῶν ἕκαστος σκοποῦντες) does not include the adverb μόνον (for a parallel point/counterpoint set of this type, see 1:29). Since, however, the point clause (ἀλλὰ [καὶ] τὰ ἑτέρων ἕκαστοι) contains the adjunctive καί, which has a strong early and widespread attestation ($\mathfrak{P}^{46}$ ℵ A B C D¹ L P Ψ 075 0278 33 81 104 365 630 1175 1241 1505 1739 1881 2464 𝔐 vg$^{st.ww}$ sy Cass), although it is omitted in some Western witnesses (D*·c F G L it vg^{cl}) because it was perceived as awkward without μόνον (Fee, 175 n. 8), the sense of μόνον in the first clause is most likely implied. This means, as Runge notes, that "Paul is not asking his readers to forsake their own interests altogether, but rather to not limit their concern to theirs alone. The emphasis of the verse is placed on the point, insuring that the counterintuitive 'valuing other people' receives primary attention" (2010, 96; cf. O'Brien, 185; *pace* NRSV; NIV; for the view that the μὴ . . . ἀλλὰ καί construction is here used to emphasize the contrast with the preceding clause ["not this . . . but rather that"], see Ehorn and Lee, 9–16).

τὰ ἑαυτῶν. The article nominalizes the genitive of the reflexive pronoun ἑαυτῶν (lit. "the things of yourselves" = "your own interests"), changing it into the accusative direct object of σκοποῦντες. Fronted for emphasis.

ἕκαστος. Nominative subject of σκοποῦντες. The singular ἕκαστος is used with the plural participle because ἕκαστος carries a distributive sense (BDAG, 298.b). Given its strong external attestation ($\mathfrak{P}^{46}$ ℵ C D K L P 075 104 365 630 1241 1505 1739 1881 2464 $\mathfrak{M}$ sy$^{(p)}$ Hil Ambst Aug), this is the preferred reading. The plural ἕκαστοι (A B F G Ψ 0278 33 81 1175 lat) is most likely a scribal adjustment to other plurals in this verse (Metzger, 545).

σκοποῦντες. Pres act ptc masc nom pl σκοπέω (manner). This participle of manner is here used in the imperatival sense (Lightfoot, 110). As a postposed participle, it provides an elaboration of the main clause, πληρώσατέ μου τὴν χαρὰν ἵνα τὸ αὐτὸ φρονῆτε (see ἔχοντες in 2:2). On adverbial participles that follow the main verb, see 1:4 on ποιούμενος. The verb σκοπέω means to "look (out) for, notice," and it is used with the accusative of person or thing (BDAG, 931; see τὰ ἑαυτῶν above and τὰ ἑτέρων below).

τὰ ἑτέρων. The article nominalizes the genitive of the substantival adjective ἑτέρων (lit. "the things of others" = "the interests of others"), changing it into the accusative direct object of an implied σκοποῦντες (cf. Porter, 283). Fronted for emphasis.

ἕκαστοι. Nominative subject of an implied σκοποῦντες. The use of the plural form ἕκαστοι is extremely rare. Much more common is the singular ἕκαστος with a plural verb (see above). In this case, however, ἕκαστοι is the preferred reading because it has a stronger textual support ($\mathfrak{P}^{46}$ ℵ A B D P Ψ 075 33 81 104 365 1175 1241 1739 et al.) than ἕκαστος (K L 0278 630 1505 $\mathfrak{M}$ et al.) and represents the *lectio difficilior*. O'Brien suggests that the unusual plural is here used for the sake of emphasis, "perhaps even as denoting an earnest repetition, giving the meaning 'each and all'" (185).

Philippians 2:5-11

⁵Have this mind among yourselves, which [was] also in Christ Jesus, ⁶who, although he was in the form of God, did not regard being equal to God as something to be grasped, ⁷but emptied himself by taking on the form of a slave, coming into existence in the likeness of human beings. And when he was found in appearance as a human being, ⁸he humiliated himself by becoming obedient to the point of death, that is, death on a cross. ⁹For this reason also God exalted him and granted him the name that is above every name, ¹⁰so that at the name of Jesus every knee should bend—of those in heaven and of those on earth and of those

under the earth—[11]and every tongue should confess that Jesus Christ is Lord, to the glory of God the Father.

2:5 Τοῦτο φρονεῖτε ἐν ὑμῖν ὃ καὶ ἐν Χριστῷ Ἰησοῦ,

Τοῦτο. Accusative direct object of φρονεῖτε. The demonstrative pronoun is anaphoric, pointing back to the attitude described in vv. 1-4 (O'Brien, 205; Fee, 199; Reumann, 340). The postpositive conjunction γάρ, attested in a number of manuscripts ($\mathfrak{P}^{46}$ ℵ² D F G K L P 075 0278 104 365 630 1175 1505 1739 1881 𝔐 lat sy^h), is probably a scribal addition because, as Metzger explains, "if γάρ were present originally, no good reason can be found for its deletion, whereas the anacoluthon involved in τοῦτο standing alone seems to cry out for a connective" (545).

φρονεῖτε. Pres act impv 2nd pl φρονέω. φρονέω here means "to have an attitude, to think in a particular manner" (LN 26.16). The imperfective aspect of the present imperative indicates that Paul's instruction refers to an ongoing disposition of mind or a "kind of thinking" (BDAG, 1066.3).

ἐν ὑμῖν. Locative. Paul's focus on the mutual relations of the Philippians in vv. 1-4 shows that the sense of ἐν ὑμῖν is corporate ("among you") rather than distributive ("in you").

ὅ. Nominative subject of an implied ἦν (if ἐν Χριστῷ Ἰησοῦ has locative function, referring to Christ's mind-set expressed through his self-humiliation and obedience) or accusative direct object of an implied indicative φρονεῖτε (if ἐν Χριστῷ Ἰησοῦ describes the believer's relationship to Christ). The antecedent of the relative pronoun is Τοῦτο. Robertson (703) calls the demonstrative before the relative (Τοῦτο - ὅ) "the normal correlative" but notes that this sequence is not common in the NT.

καί. Adverbial use (adjunctive).

ἐν Χριστῷ Ἰησοῦ. If the function of ἐν Χριστῷ Ἰησοῦ is parallel to the function of ἐν ὑμῖν, its sense is locative. On this reading, ἐν Χριστῷ Ἰησοῦ refers "to the person of Jesus in whom this attitude of humility is found" (O'Brien, 205; cf. Campbell 2012, 106). If ἐν Χριστῷ Ἰησοῦ refers to the believer's union with Christ, the Philippians are asked to have the same thoughts among themselves as they have in their communion with Christ Jesus (cf. BDAG, 1066.3). The main weakness of this interpretation is its questionable assumption "that believers could adopt one attitude in their mutual relations and another as incorporated in Christ" (O'Brien, 257). The first interpretation is therefore preferable because it invites the Philippians to emulate Christ's attitude of humility. This reading is also more compatible with the anaphoric Τοῦτο and the adjunctive καί, which reinforces the parallelism between ἐν ὑμῖν and ἐν Χριστῷ Ἰησοῦ (cf. Levinsohn 2000, 106).

2:6 ὃς ἐν μορφῇ θεοῦ ὑπάρχων οὐχ ἁρπαγμὸν ἡγήσατο τὸ εἶναι ἴσα θεῷ

ὅς. Nominative subject of ἡγήσατο and all other verbs in vv. 6-8. The antecedent of the relative pronoun is Χριστῷ Ἰησοῦ in v. 5.

ἐν μορφῇ. State or condition. The meaning of the term μορφή, which in the NT appears only here and in the next verse, is controversial. According to LN, μορφή means "the nature or character of something with emphasis upon both the internal and external form–'nature, character'" (58.2), while according to BDAG, it denotes "form, outward appearance, shape" (659), i.e., that "which may be perceived by the senses" (TDNT 4:745). A significant overlap between these two meanings is evident in the semantic range of the μορφ- word-group (μόρφωσις [Rom 2:20; 2 Tim 3:5], μορφόω [Gal 4:19], μεταμορφόω [Rom 12:2; 2 Cor 3:18], συμμορφίζω [Phil 3:10], and σύμμορφος [Phil 3:21]), which "describes not simply external appearances or behaviour but also that which inwardly corresponds (or is expected to correspond) to the outward" (O'Brien, 207). Traditionally, the correspondence between external appearance and internal reality has been interpreted in terms of Christ's preexistent ontological status, i.e., in terms of his deity, but it is probably better to understand it in terms of rank and social status that was publicly displayed by Christ's preincarnate glory (O'Brien, 211; Hellerman 2009, 779-97). For the view that μορφή corresponds to εἰκών, alluding to the creation of the first human being κατ'εἰκόνα θεοῦ (LXX Gen 1:27), see Dunn (1989, 114-21; 1998, 282-88); for a critique, see Wallace (1966, 19-25) and Jowers (745-46).

θεοῦ. Possessive genitive qualifying μορφῇ.

ὑπάρχων. Pres act ptc masc nom sg ὑπάρχω (concessive). In Hellenistic Greek, ὑπάρχω ("to be in a state or circumstance") was widely used as a substitute for εἶναι, although it is also possible to understand it to mean "be inherently (so)" or "be really" (BDAG, 1029.2).

οὐχ. Negative particle in the first component (the counterpoint) of a point/counterpoint set ("not this . . . but that"), which negates the incorrect statement (v. 6: Christ Jesus regarded being equal to God as something to be grasped) and replaces it with the correct assertion (v. 7: he emptied himself, taking the form of a slave).

ἁρπαγμόν. Complement to the infinitival phrase, τὸ εἶναι ἴσα θεῷ, in a double accusative object-complement construction (Wallace 1996, 186). ἁρπαγμόν is fronted for emphasis, but its anarthrous form indicates that it serves as the complement in an object-complement construction and not as the direct object of ἡγήσατο (602). The noun ἁρπαγμός is a NT *hapax legomenon*, which most likely denotes "someth[ing] to which one can claim or assert title by gripping or grasping" (BDAG, 133.2). What is less clear, however, is whether the term refers to "holding fast to someth[ing] already obtained" (*res rapta*) or to "the appropriation to oneself of someth[ing] that is sought after" (*res rapienda*) (BDAG, 133.2.a). Another possibility is to understand ἁρπαγμός as "a piece of good fortune, windfall, prize, gain," but "again it remains an open question whether the windfall has already been seized and is waiting to be used, or whether it has not yet been appropriated" (BDAG, 133.2.b). For a recent suggestion that ἁρπαγμός means "rape and robbery" rather than "something to be exploited or grasped," see Shaner (342–63).

ἡγήσατο. Aor mid ind 3rd sg ἡγέομαι. The verb means to "think, consider, regard" (BDAG, 434.2). For other occurrences of ἡγέομαι in Philippians, see 2:3, 25; 3:7, 8.

τὸ εἶναι. Pres act inf εἰμί. The infinitival phrase τὸ εἶναι ἴσα θεῷ serves as the direct object of ἡγήσατο in a double accusative object-complement construction (Wallace 1996, 220, 602; Robertson, 1059). The article nominalizes the infinitive, marking it as the object of the verb and distinguishing it from the complement (see ἁρπαγμὸν above), but it probably also serves as an anaphoric reference to μορφῇ θεοῦ (BDF §399.1; Wright 1986, 344; O'Brien, 216; Fee, 207 n. 62; for a dissenting view, see Wallace 1996, 220).

ἴσα. Predicate adverb (MHT 3:226). ἴσα is the accusative neuter plural of the adjective ἴσος ("equal"), which is here used as an adverb rather than as an adjective (BDAG, 481; BDF §434.1). Because of its adverbial function, the plural ἴσα differs little from the singular ἴσον (Robertson, 407; *pace* Lightfoot, 112).

θεῷ. Dative complement of ἴσα (Wallace 1996, 174).

2:7 ἀλλ' ἑαυτὸν ἐκένωσεν μορφὴν δούλου λαβών, ἐν ὁμοιώματι ἀνθρώπων γενόμενος· καὶ σχήματι εὑρεθεὶς ὡς ἄνθρωπος

ἀλλ'. Marker of contrast in the second component (the point) of the point/counterpoint set, which started in the previous verse (see οὐχ in v. 6).

ἑαυτὸν. Accusative direct object of ἐκένωσεν.

ἐκένωσεν. Aor act ind 3rd sg κενόω. In the current context, κενόω means "to empty" (BDAG, 539.1). In the NT this verb occurs four more times, exclusively in the letters of Paul (Rom 4:14; 1 Cor 1:17; 9:15; 2 Cor 9:3), with the meaning "destroy, render void or of no effect"

(BDAG, 539.2). The assumption that κενόω requires a genitive qualifier that, although not stated, must be understood—i.e., that Christ emptied himself "of something"—has generated intense scholarly debate. If ἐν μορφῇ θεοῦ ὑπάρχων in v. 6 is understood in terms of rank and social status, then κενόω probably means, as LN (87.70) proposes, "to completely remove or eliminate elements of high status or rank by eliminating all privileges or prerogatives associated with such status and rank." Paul's simple statement, however, shows that no genitive of content is needed: "Christ did not empty himself *of* anything; he simply 'emptied *himself*,' poured himself out" (Fee, 210). The perfective aspect of the aorist verb tense indicates that this action is portrayed as a complete event.

μορφὴν. Accusative direct object of λαβών (on the meaning of this term, see 2:6 on ἐν μορφῇ). μορφὴν δούλου is fronted for emphasis.

δούλου. Possessive genitive qualifying μορφὴν.

λαβών. Aor act ptc masc nom sg λαμβάνω (manner or means). Although the aorist participle "usually denotes *antecedent* time to that of the controlling verb" (Wallace 1996, 614), BDF (§339) emphasizes that "[t]he notion of relative past time . . . is not at all necessarily inherent in the aorist participle." In this clause, the aorist participle λαβών, which explains how Christ emptied himself, describes an action that is simultaneous with ἐκένωσεν.

ἐν ὁμοιώματι. State or condition. The term ὁμοίωμα ("similarity, likeness" [LN 64.3]) "denies nothing of the content of μορφή but of itself indicates simply that in every respect he was like a man" (Zerwick and Grosvenor, 596). ἐν ὁμοιώματι ἀνθρώπων is fronted for emphasis.

ἀνθρώπων. Attributive genitive modifying ὁμοιώματι ("human likeness"). The use of the plural draws attention to Jesus' similarity to all human beings, i.e., to the entire human race, rather than to a specific person. The singular ἀνθρώπου, found in some early manuscripts ($\mathfrak{P}^{46}$ t vg^{mss} Mcion^T Cyp), is most likely a scribal adjustment of the original ἀνθρώπων to the preceding singular δούλου and the following singular ἄνθρωπος (Metzger, 545–46).

γενόμενος. Aor mid ptc masc nom sg γίνομαι (manner or means). Formally, this participle modifies the preceding participle λαβών, explaining how Christ took on the form of a slave (Fee, 196; Silva 106). Semantically, both participles explain the main verb ἐκένωσεν. In terms of relative time, γενόμενος describes an action that is coincident with the action of λαβών and, thus, with ἐκένωσεν. There is a notable contrast between ὃς ἐν μορφῇ θεοῦ ὑπάρχων (v. 6) and ἐν ὁμοιώματι ἀνθρώπων γενόμενος (v. 7), the former describing Christ's existence from the beginning and the latter describing his coming into existence as a human being.

καί. Coordinating conjunction. It marks the beginning of a new sentence. Some English translations (KJV; RSV; NIV; ESV; NASB) follow the verse division in the Textus Receptus, which places καὶ σχήματι εὑρεθεὶς ὡς ἄνθρωπος at the beginning of v. 8.

σχήματι. Dative of respect (BDF §197; Wallace 1996, 146; Zerwick §53) or, less likely, locative dative (Robertson, 523) or instrumental dative (O'Brien, 227). The noun σχῆμα denotes "the generally recognized state or form in which someth[ing] appears," "outward appearance, form, shape" (BDAG, 981.1).

εὑρεθείς. Aor pass ptc masc nom sg εὑρίσκω (temporal). The participle modifies ἐταπείνωσεν in v. 8. Both the aorist tense of the participle and its placement before the main verb suggest that it describes an event that is antecedent to the main verb (cf. Porter 1994, 188). On the function of adverbial participles that precede the main verb, see 1:25 on πεποιθώς. In this context, εὑρίσκω has a figurative sense, "to discover intellectually through reflection, observation, examination, or investigation" (BDAG, 412.2). The primary agent of the passive participle εὑρεθείς is not expressed, but the context implies that the discovery of Christ's humanity was made by others. While ἐν ὁμοιώματι ἀνθρώπων γενόμενος conveys the reality of Christ's human nature, σχήματι εὑρεθεὶς ὡς ἄνθρωπος describes who Christ was "in the eyes of those who saw His incarnate life" (Martin, 207).

ὡς ἄνθρωπος. In this formulation, ὡς functions as a "marker introducing the perspective from which a pers[on], thing, or activity is viewed or understood as to character, function, or role" (BDAG, 1104.3). The singular ἄνθρωπος does not point to Jesus' gender ("man") but to his humanity ("human being"). The expression "as a human being" specifies the "mode of existence" for Jesus' actions described in the next verse (Fee, 215).

2:8 ἐταπείνωσεν ἑαυτὸν γενόμενος ὑπήκοος μέχρι θανάτου, θανάτου δὲ σταυροῦ.

ἐταπείνωσεν. Aor act ind 3rd sg ταπεινόω. The verb ταπεινόω here means "to cause someone to lose prestige or status" (BDAG, 990.2). The reflexive pronoun ἑαυτόν, which serves as the direct object of the verb (see below), shows that the focus falls on Christ's voluntary reversal of his status. The aorist tense is past-referring, while its perfective aspect portrays Christ's act as a complete event. The verb ἐταπείνωσεν echoes the noun ταπεινοφροσύνη in 2:3. To call attention to this connection and to highlight the social implications of Christ's self-imposed action, I have followed Hellerman's (2015, 116) suggestion and translated ἐταπείνωσεν as "humiliated" rather than "humbled."

ἑαυτὸν. Accusative direct object of ἐταπείνωσεν.

γενόμενος. Aor mid ptc masc nom sg γίνομαι (manner). The adverbial participle modifies ἐταπείνωσεν, explaining how Christ humiliated himself. On adverbial participles that follow the main verb, see 1:4 on ποιούμενος.

ὑπήκοος. Predicate adjective.

μέχρι θανάτου. Degree ("to the point of death") or temporal ("until [the time of] death"). μέχρι is an improper preposition (see 1:5 on ἄχρι τοῦ νῦν). In this PP, the term θανάτου refers to death in general (BDAG, 443.1.b.β).

θανάτου. Genitive in apposition to θανάτου from the preceding PP. The genitive modifier σταυροῦ indicates that the term now has a specific meaning, referring to death on a cross.

δὲ. Marker of development. It is used here to insert an explanation ("that is") of the previous, more general formulation (BDAG, 213.2).

σταυροῦ. Genitive of place ("death on a cross"), genitive of production ("death produced by a cross"; cf. Wallace 1996, 105), or genitive of means modifying θανάτου ("death by [means of] a cross").

2:9 διὸ καὶ ὁ θεὸς αὐτὸν ὑπερύψωσεν καὶ ἐχαρίσατο αὐτῷ τὸ ὄνομα τὸ ὑπὲρ πᾶν ὄνομα,

διὸ. Inferential conjunction that marks a transition to a new section. While in the first part of the hymn "Christ Jesus is the acting subject all the way through," in the second half "it is God who acts and Christ is the object of the divine action" (Beare, 85).

καὶ. Adverbial use (adjunctive). Levinsohn says that this "καί is to be interpreted as a marker of *confirmation*. In particular, God's act of highly exalting Jesus confirms what Jesus did in obedience" (2000, 104).

ὁ θεὸς. Nominative subject of ὑπερύψωσεν and ἐχαρίσατο. It is fronted as a new point of departure (topical frame), because now the attention shifts from Jesus to God (Levinsohn 2000, 104).

αὐτὸν. Accusative direct object of ὑπερύψωσεν.

ὑπερύψωσεν. Aor act ind 3rd sg ὑπερυψόω. A NT *hapax legomenon* that means "to raise to a high point of honor," "raise, exalt" (BDAG, 1034). This compound verb (ὑπέρ + ὑψόω) anticipates ὑπὲρ πᾶν ὄνομα at the end of the verse. In the clause διὸ καὶ ὁ θεὸς αὐτὸν ὑπερύψωσεν, the verb stands in final, emphatic position (Levinsohn 1995, 70).

καὶ. Coordinating conjunction.

ἐχαρίσατο. Aor mid ind 3rd sg χαρίζομαι. On the meaning of the verb, see 1:29 on ἐχαρίσθη. ἐχαρίσατο shows that what follows is not a reward for Christ's actions but God's free gift, i.e., "the divine vindication of Christ's emptying himself and humbling himself in obedience by dying on a cross" (Fee, 220).

αὐτῷ. Dative indirect object of ἐχαρίσατο.

τὸ ὄνομα. Accusative direct object of ἐχαρίσατο. Although the article is absent in some uncials and many minuscules (D F G K L P Ψ 075 0278 81 104 365 630 1175ᶜ 1241 1505 1881 2464 𝔐 et al.), the external evidence for its inclusion is very strong (𝔓⁴⁶ ℵ A B C 33 629 1175* 1739). Metzger conjectures that "the last syllable of ἐχαρίσατο somehow led to the omission of the article" (546). It is generally assumed that ὄνομα does not denote Jesus' proper name (Ἰησοῦς), which he already possesses, but the name "Lord" (κύριος; see v. 11), which the LXX uses as the equivalent of Yahweh. In that case, τὸ functions as a par excellence article, pointing out "*the* name" as the only name worth mentioning (Wallace 1996, 222–23), which "probably reflects an OT phenomenon where 'the name' was a periphrasis for Yahweh" (Fee, 221 n. 20; cf. Exod 9:16; 2 Sam 7:22-23; Isa 12:4; 26:8; 63:12-14).

τὸ ὑπὲρ πᾶν ὄνομα. The article functions as an adjectivizer, changing the prepositional phrase ὑπὲρ πᾶν ὄνομα into an attributive modifier of ὄνομα and placing it in the second attributive position (see 1:1 on τοῖς οὖσιν).

ὑπὲρ πᾶν ὄνομα. The basic spatial sense of the preposition ὑπέρ ("location above") is extended metaphorically, so that it serves as a "marker of a degree beyond that of a compared scale of extent, in the sense of excelling, surpassing" (BDAG, 1031.B).

2:10 ἵνα ἐν τῷ ὀνόματι Ἰησοῦ πᾶν γόνυ κάμψῃ ἐπουρανίων καὶ ἐπιγείων καὶ καταχθονίων

ἵνα. Introduces either a purpose clause (most interpreters), a result clause (Fee, 223), or a purpose-result clause (Wallace 1996, 473).

ἐν τῷ ὀνόματι Ἰησοῦ πᾶν γόνυ κάμψῃ. An allusion to LXX Isa 45:23c (ἐμοὶ κάμψει πᾶν γόνυ).

ἐν τῷ ὀνόματι. Temporal ("when the name of Jesus is mentioned" [BDAG, 713.1.d.γ.ℶ]; cf. Moule, 78) or causal (O'Brien, 240).

Ἰησοῦ. Possessive genitive modifying ὀνόματι ("the name that belongs to Jesus") rather than epexegetical genitive clarifying ὀνόματι ("the name which is Jesus").

πᾶν γόνυ. Nominative subject of κάμψῃ. Fronted for emphasis. The adjective πᾶν stands in the first (anarthrous) attributive position (see 1:4 on ἐν πάσῃ δεήσει).

κάμψῃ. Aor act subj 3rd sg κάμπτω. Subjunctive with ἵνα. κάμπτω is used here as an intransitive verb that means "to assume a bending posture" (BDAG, 507.2).

ἐπουρανίων καὶ ἐπιγείων καὶ καταχθονίων. These are adjectives used as substantives, which are either masculine or neuter genitive plural. If they are masculine, they function as possessive genitives modifying πᾶν γόνυ ("every knee of those in heaven and of those on earth and of those under the earth"). If they are neuter, they function as genitives of place modifying πᾶν γόνυ ("every knee in the heavenly and earthly and subterranean places"; cf. Wallace 1996, 125 n. 142). ἐπουρανίων "pert[ains] to being associated with a locale for transcendent things and beings," "heavenly, in heaven" (BDAG, 388.2); ἐπιγείων "pert[ains] to what is characteristic of the earth as opposed to heavenly," "earthly" (BDAG, 368.1); and καταχθονίων (a NT *hapax legomenon*) means "under the earth, subterranean" (BDAG, 530). All three substantival adjectives are anarthrous because no specific identities and locales are in view.

2:11 καὶ πᾶσα γλῶσσα ἐξομολογήσηται ὅτι κύριος Ἰησοῦς Χριστὸς εἰς δόξαν θεοῦ πατρός.

καὶ πᾶσα γλῶσσα ἐξομολογήσηται ὅτι κύριος Ἰησοῦς Χριστὸς εἰς δόξαν θεοῦ πατρός. An allusion to LXX Isa 45:23d (καὶ ἐξομολογήσεται πᾶσα γλῶσσα τῷ θεῷ).

καὶ. Coordinating conjunction.

πᾶσα γλῶσσα. Nominative subject of ἐξομολογήσηται. Fronted for emphasis. The adjective πᾶσα stands in the first (anarthrous) attributive position (see 1:4 on ἐν πάσῃ δεήσει). In this context, the noun γλῶσσα denotes either "the organ of speech" (BDAG, 201.1) or "a body of words and systems that makes up a distinctive language" (BDAG, 201.2). The first option highlights the parallelism between πᾶν γόνυ and πᾶσα γλῶσσα (Fee, 225 n. 36). The second option presumes that "*every language* = every person, regardless of the language that pers[on] speaks" (BDAG, 201.2).

ἐξομολογήσηται. Aor mid subj 3rd sg ἐξομολογέω. Subjunctive with ἵνα. ἐξομολογέω means "to declare openly in acknowledgment" (BDAG, 351.3). The variant reading ἐξομολογήσεται (A C D F* G K L P Ψ^{vid} 075 0278 6 33 81 104 365 630* 1175 et al.) could be an assimilation to the future indicative ἐξομολογήσεται in Isa 45:23, or, conversely, the subjunctive ἐξομολογήσηται could be an assimilation to the subjunctive κάμψῃ governed by ἵνα in v. 10. On internal grounds, then, the decision is difficult. The external evidence for ἐξομολογήσηται ($\mathfrak{P}^{46}$ ℵ B F^c 323

630ᶜ 2495 et al.), however, slightly tips the scales in favor of the aorist subjunctive (Metzger, 546).

ὅτι. Introduces the clausal complement (indirect discourse [most English translations] or direct discourse [Fee, 225 n. 37]) of ἐξομολογήσηται.

κύριος. Predicate nominative. Fronted for emphasis. Since this clause does not have a copula, κύριος cannot be properly called preverbal. Its placement before the subject of the clause, however, indicates that it has the same semantic value as the preverbal predicate nominative (Wallace 1996, 269). Although κύριος is anarthrous, it is probably definite because, according to Collwell's rule, the definiteness of a preverbal anarthrous predicate nominative cannot be excluded (Wallace 1996, 262, 270).

Ἰησοῦς Χριστός. Nominative subject of an implied ἐστίν.

εἰς δόξαν. Purpose (see 1:11 on εἰς δόξαν καὶ ἔπαινον).

θεοῦ. Objective genitive modifying δόξαν.

πατρός. Genitive in apposition to θεοῦ.

Philippians 2:12-18

¹²Therefore, my beloved, just as you have always obeyed, not only in view of my [anticipated] presence but now much more in my absence, work out your own salvation with fear and trembling, ¹³for the one who produces in you both the willing and the working for his good pleasure is God. ¹⁴Do all things without grumbling and disputing, ¹⁵in order that you may become blameless and innocent, faultless children of God in the midst of a crooked and perverted generation, among whom you shine like luminaries in the world, ¹⁶holding firmly to the word of life, in order that I may be proud on the day of Christ that I did not run in vain or labor in vain. ¹⁷But even if I am being poured out as a drink offering on the sacrifice and service of your faith, I am glad and rejoice with all of you. ¹⁸And in the same way you also should be glad and rejoice with me.

2:12 Ὥστε, ἀγαπητοί μου, καθὼς πάντοτε ὑπηκούσατε, μὴ ὡς ἐν τῇ παρουσίᾳ μου μόνον ἀλλὰ νῦν πολλῷ μᾶλλον ἐν τῇ ἀπουσίᾳ μου, μετὰ φόβου καὶ τρόμου τὴν ἑαυτῶν σωτηρίαν κατεργάζεσθε·

Ὥστε. An inferential conjunction ("for this reason, therefore, so" [BDAG, 1107.1]) that introduces the conclusion drawn from the preceding hymn and marks the beginning of a new unit.

ἀγαπητοί. Vocative of direct address. The adjective ἀγαπητοί is here used as a substantive.

μου. Subjective genitive modifying ἀγαπητοί ("beloved by me").

καθώς. Introduces a comparative clause that establishes analogy between the past and present experience of the audience.

πάντοτε. Adverb of time ("always"). Fronted for emphasis.

ὑπηκούσατε. Aor act ind 2nd pl ὑπακούω. The temporal adverb πάντοτε indicates that obeying, which is portrayed as a whole (perfective aspect), represents an ongoing or repeated action. The direct object of ὑπηκούσατε is not expressed.

μὴ ... μόνον ἀλλὰ ... πολλῷ μᾶλλον. A point/counterpoint set ("not only ... but much more") that corrects the first assertion (to work out their own salvation in anticipation of Paul's presence) by supplementing it with another assertion (to work out their own salvation in Paul's absence). On the point/counterpoint set of this type, see 1:29 on οὐ μόνον ... ἀλλὰ καί. In this verse, the adjunctive καί is replaced by the phrase πολλῷ μᾶλλον, which consists of the dative of measure / degree of difference and the comparative adverb of μάλα (see 1:23). The negative particle μὴ is here used rather than οὐ because it goes with the imperative κατεργάζεσθε.

ὡς. Temporal conjunction (BDAG, 1105.8.b; BDF §455.2). Since the presence of ὡς in the text appears superfluous, its omission by some copyists (B 33 1241 vg[mss] Ambst) may have been deliberate (Metzger, 546).

ἐν τῇ παρουσίᾳ. Temporal. If the PP modifies ὑπηκούσατε, ἐν τῇ παρουσίᾳ refers to Paul's earlier visit to Philippi (cf. Reumann, 385). If the PP modifies κατεργάζεσθε, ἐν τῇ παρουσίᾳ refers to Paul's anticipated visit to Philippi (see 1:27; cf. O'Brien, 276, 281). Three observations support the second option: (1) the term παρουσία is used in this sense in 1:26; (2) the negative particle μὴ, which is typically used with non-indicative moods, suggests that both prepositional phrases within the μὴ ... μόνον ἀλλὰ ... πολλῷ μᾶλλον point/counterpoint set (ἐν τῇ παρουσίᾳ μου and ἐν τῇ ἀπουσίᾳ μου) modify the following imperative rather than the preceding indicative (Robertson, 1162); and (3) the use of ὡς as a temporal conjunction ("in light of" or "in view of"; cf. O'Brien, 281).

μου. Possessive genitive (cf. the use of the possessive adjective in τῆς ἐμῆς παρουσίας at 1:26) or subjective genitive modifying παρουσίᾳ.

νῦν. Adverb of time ("now"). Fronted as a temporal frame.

ἐν τῇ ἀπουσίᾳ. Temporal. The noun ἀπουσία ("absence") is a NT *hapax legomenon*.

μου. Subjective genitive modifying ἀπουσίᾳ.

μετὰ φόβου καὶ τρόμου. Manner. Fronted for emphasis. This PP occurs two more times in the Pauline corpus (2 Cor 7:15; Eph 6:5; see also ἐν φόβῳ καὶ ἐν τρόμῳ in 1 Cor 2:3). In the LXX, φόβος and τρόμος frequently appear together in various stereotypical expressions (φόβος καὶ τρόμος [Exod 15:16; Ps 54:6; Jdt 2:28]; ἐν φόβῳ καὶ ἐν τρόμῳ [Isa 19:16]; ὁ τρόμος ὑμῶν καὶ ὁ φόβος [Gen 9:2]; τὸν τρόμον σου καὶ τὸν φόβον σου [Deut 2:25]; τὸν τρόμον ὑμῶν καὶ τὸν φόβον ὑμῶν [Deut 11:25]). In this context, μετὰ φόβου καὶ τρόμου refers to "a sense of awe and reverence in the presence of God" (O'Brien, 284).

τὴν . . . σωτηρίαν. Accusative direct object of κατεργάζεσθε. In the current context, the term σωτηρία most likely denotes eschatological salvation.

ἑαυτῶν. Possessive genitive modifying σωτηρίαν ("your own salvation").

κατεργάζεσθε. Pres mid impv 2nd pl κατεργάζομαι. The compound verb (κατά + ἔργάζομαι) "accents the carrying of the work through" (Robertson, 564). The imperfective aspect of the present imperative portrays "the *present* 'outworking' of their *eschatological salvation*" (Fee, 235) until it is brought to completion.

2:13 θεὸς γάρ ἐστιν ὁ ἐνεργῶν ἐν ὑμῖν καὶ τὸ θέλειν καὶ τὸ ἐνεργεῖν ὑπὲρ τῆς εὐδοκίας.

θεὸς. The absence of the article indicates that in this clause θεὸς functions as the predicate nominative (*pace* Runge 2010, 198). It is placed in a preverbal position for emphasis (Wallace 1996, 46). Since the definiteness of a preverbal anarthrous predicate nominative cannot be excluded (Wallace 1996, 264), θεὸς is either definite, accentuating that "it is God himself who is at work in you" (O'Brien, 286), or qualitative, emphasizing "what God does in the believer rather than who it is that does it" (Wallace 1996, 264).

γάρ. Postpositive conjunction that introduces the reason for the exhortation in v. 12.

ἐστιν. Pres act ind 3rd sg εἰμί.

ὁ ἐνεργῶν. Pres act ptc masc nom sg ἐνεργέω (substantival). Nominative subject of ἐστιν (*pace* Sumney, 53). Two articular infinitives that follow suggest that ἐνεργέω is here used as a transitive verb (cf. 1 Cor 12:6, 11; Gal 3:5). When a participle is used as a substantive, as here, "the participle adds the semantic features of its respective verb tense-forms, which must be considered in appreciating the full force of the phrase or clause" (Porter 1994, 183). In this case, the imperfective aspect of the present participle ἐνεργῶν calls attention to God's continuous working in believers (O'Brien, 286).

ἐν ὑμῖν. Locative. The PP could be understood individually ("in you"), collectively ("among you"), or both ("not only in you individually but among you collectively" [Bruce, 57]).

καὶ ... καί. "Both ... and."
τὸ θέλειν. Pres act inf θέλω. The articular infinitive τὸ θέλειν functions as the first direct object of ἐνεργῶν (Wallace 1996, 603). The article nominalizes the infinitive and serves as anaphoric reference to κατεργάζεσθε in v. 12 (BDF §399.1). Both the willing (τὸ θέλειν) and the working (τὸ ἐνεργεῖν) are portrayed as actions in progress (imperfective aspect).
τὸ ἐνεργεῖν. Pres act inf ἐνεργέω. The articular infinitive τὸ ἐνεργεῖν functions as the second direct object of ἐνεργῶν (Wallace 1996, 603). The article nominalizes the infinitive and serves as anaphoric reference to κατεργάζεσθε in v. 12 (BDF §399.1).
ὑπὲρ τῆς εὐδοκίας. Cause or reason (BDAG, 1031.A.2) or advantage (Moule, 65). Although the term εὐδοκία could refer to human benevolent disposition, as in 1:15 (Hawthorne and Martin, 143), in the current context, which lays emphasis on God's activity, εὐδοκία almost certainly refers to God's good pleasure. The article τῆς probably serves as a possessive pronoun, referring back to θεός (Fee, 239 n. 39).

2:14 Πάντα ποιεῖτε χωρὶς γογγυσμῶν καὶ διαλογισμῶν,

Πάντα. Accusative direct object of ποιεῖτε. Fronted for emphasis. This verse is connected to the previous one by asyndeton.
ποιεῖτε. Pres act impv 2nd pl ποιέω.
χωρὶς γογγυσμῶν καὶ διαλογισμῶν. Separation. χωρίς ("without") is an improper preposition (see 1:5 on ἄχρι τοῦ νῦν). γογγυσμῶν (from γογγυσμός) is an onomatopoetic noun that denotes "utterance made in a low tone of voice." When such utterance has negative aspect, as here, γογγυσμός means "complaint, displeasure, expressed in murmuring" (BDAG, 204). In this context, the noun διαλογισμῶν (from διαλογισμός) also has a negative sense, denoting "verbal exchange that takes place when conflicting ideas are expressed" (BDAG, 232.3).

2:15 ἵνα γένησθε ἄμεμπτοι καὶ ἀκέραιοι, τέκνα θεοῦ ἄμωμα μέσον γενεᾶς σκολιᾶς καὶ διεστραμμένης, ἐν οἷς φαίνεσθε ὡς φωστῆρες ἐν κόσμῳ,

ἵνα. Introduces a purpose clause.
γένησθε. Aor mid subj 2nd pl γίνομαι. Subjunctive with ἵνα. γίνομαι here means "to experience a change in nature and so indicate entry into a new condition, become someth[ing]" (BDAG, 198.5).
ἄμεμπτοι. Predicate adjective. ἄμεμπτοι ("blameless, faultless" [BDAG, 52]) is the first of three semantically related alpha-privative

adjectives—ἄμεμπτοι, ἀκέραιοι, and ἄμωμα—which Paul uses to describe the public testimony of the Christian community in Philippi.

καί. Coordinating conjunction, linking two predicate adjectives.

ἀκέραιοι. Predicate adjective. ἀκέραιοι is another alpha-privative adjective (lit. "unmixed"), which is here used figuratively: "pure, innocent" (BDAG, 35).

τέκνα . . . ἄμωμα. Nominative in apposition to ἄμεμπτοι καὶ ἀκέραιοι. The alpha-privative adjective ἄμωμα ("without fault," "blameless" [BDAG, 56.2]) modifies τέκνα, standing in the fourth attributive position (see 1:6 on ἔργον ἀγαθὸν).

θεοῦ. Genitive of relationship modifying τέκνα.

μέσον γενεᾶς σκολιᾶς καὶ διεστραμμένης. Locative. μέσον is the adverbial accusative of μέσος, which is here used as an improper preposition (see 1:5 on ἄχρι τοῦ νῦν) with the genitive γενεᾶς (BDAG, 635.1.c; Porter 1994, 180). The adjective σκολιᾶς ("crooked") and the attributive participle διεστραμμένης ("perverted") modify γενεᾶς, standing in the fourth attributive position (see 1:6 on ἔργον ἀγαθὸν).

διεστραμμένης. Prf pass ptc fem gen sg διαστρέφω (attributive). διαστρέφω here means "to cause to depart from an accepted standard of oral or spiritual values," "make crooked, pervert" (BDAG, 237.2). The stative aspect of the perfect participle gives prominence to the current state of moral corruption. On the relation of this participle to the noun it modifies, see above.

ἐν οἷς. Locative. The dative masculine plural relative pronoun οἷς is a *constructio ad sensum*, because its antecedent, γενεᾶς σκολιᾶς καὶ διεστραμμένης, is a collective noun (BDF §296).

φαίνεσθε. Pres mid ind 2nd pl φαίνω.

ὡς. Comparative particle.

φωστῆρες. Nominative subject of an implied φαίνονται. This noun is part of the elided comparative structure that presumes the repetition of the appropriate form of the main verb: ὡς φωστῆρες [φαίνονται] ἐν κόσμῳ = "like lights [shine] in the world." The noun φωστήρ denotes "any light-producing object in the sky, such as the sun, moon, and other planets and stars—'light, luminary, star'" (LN 1.27).

ἐν κόσμῳ. Locative (lit. "in the universe").

2:16 λόγον ζωῆς ἐπέχοντες, εἰς καύχημα ἐμοὶ εἰς ἡμέραν Χριστοῦ, ὅτι οὐκ εἰς κενὸν ἔδραμον οὐδὲ εἰς κενὸν ἐκοπίασα.

λόγον. Accusative direct object of ἐπέχοντες.

ζωῆς. Objective genitive ("the word about life"), genitive of product ("the word that creates life"; *pace* O'Brien, 298, who calls it the genitive of origin), or epexegetical genitive that explains λόγον ("the word that is life"). λόγον ζωῆς is fronted for emphasis.

ἐπέχοντες. Pres act ptc masc nom pl ἐπέχω (manner, means, or causal). On adverbial participles that follow the main verb, see 1:4 on ποιούμενος. ἐπέχω could mean "to hold forth" (KJV; ASV; GNT), referring to missionary activity of the Philippians (Fee, 247–48), or "hold fast" (BDAG, 362.1), referring to their steadfastness in faith (LN 31.47; cf. O'Brien, 297; Reumann, 394). Although Paul's statement in the previous verse (ἐν οἷς φαίνεσθε ὡς φωστῆρες ἐν κόσμῳ) may support the former, the eschatological focus of the current verse favors the latter. The imperfective aspect of the present participle lends further support for this reading, calling attention to the Philippians' continuous endurance in faith.

εἰς καύχημα. Purpose. καύχημα denotes either the "act of taking pride" or "that which constitutes a source of pride" (BDAG, 537.1).

ἐμοὶ. Dative of advantage. Like most English versions, I have rendered the phrase εἰς καύχημα ἐμοὶ (lit. "for a pride to me" or "for a source of pride to me") as a full clause, translating ἐμοὶ as the subject and the verbal noun καύχημα as a verb ("in order that I may be proud").

εἰς ἡμέραν. Temporal ("in/on the day of Christ") or purpose ("for the day of Christ").

Χριστοῦ. Aporetic genitive (cf. Wallace 1996, 81 n. 26) modifying ἡμέραν ("the day of Christ" = "the day when Christ comes"); see 1:6 on Χριστοῦ Ἰησοῦ.

ὅτι. If καύχημα denotes the "act of taking pride" (see above), ὅτι introduces the clausal complement (indirect discourse) of the verbal idea contained in καύχημα, which functions as a *nomen actionis* (Hellerman 2015, 138–39). If καύχημα denotes "that which constitutes a source of pride" (see above), ὅτι introduces a clause that is epexegetical to καύχημα (cf. Zerwick and Grosvenor, 597). Some English translations (NASB; NJB; NCV) regard ὅτι as causal ("because"), but this sense is less likely in the current context.

οὐκ ... οὐδὲ. "Neither ... nor." οὐδὲ is a combination of the negative particle οὐ and the marker of narrative development δέ. οὐκ negates ἔδραμον, while οὐδὲ negates ἐκοπίασα.

εἰς κενὸν. Purpose ("to no purpose") or manner ("vainly"; cf. Robertson, 550). Fronted for emphasis.

ἔδραμον. Aor act ind 1st sg τρέχω. The verb (lit. "run") is here used figuratively: "to make an effort to advance spiritually or intellectually," "exert oneself" (BDAG, 1015.2). For other examples of the metaphorical use of this athletic metaphor in Paul's letters, see Rom 9:16; 1 Cor 9:24, 26; Gal 2:2; 5:7.

εἰς κενόν. See above.

ἐκοπίασα. Aor act ind 1st sg κοπιάω. Paul frequently uses κοπιάω ("work hard, toil, strive, struggle" [BDAG, 558.2]) to describe physical, mental, or spiritual exertion in ministry (Rom 16:12; 1 Cor 15:10; 2 Cor 10:15; Gal 4:11; 1 Thess 5:12).

2:17 Ἀλλ' εἰ καὶ σπένδομαι ἐπὶ τῇ θυσίᾳ καὶ λειτουργίᾳ τῆς πίστεως ὑμῶν, χαίρω καὶ συγχαίρω πᾶσιν ὑμῖν·

Ἀλλ'. Marker of contrast.

εἰ. Introduces the protasis of a first-class condition. This class of conditions assumes that the protasis (Ἀλλ' εἰ καὶ σπένδομαι ἐπὶ τῇ θυσίᾳ καὶ λειτουργίᾳ τῆς πίστεως ὑμῶν) is true for the sake of the argument and draws the conclusion from that supposition (χαίρω καὶ συγχαίρω πᾶσιν ὑμῖν).

καὶ. Adverbial use (ascensive). εἰ καὶ = "even if" (BDAG, 278.6.e).

σπένδομαι. Pres pass ind 1st sg σπένδω. In the only two occurrences of this verb in the NT (here and in 2 Tim 4:6), σπένδω (lit. "offer a libation/drink-offering" [BDAG, 937]) is used figuratively ("to be offered up") to describe the apostle's shedding of his blood as a sacrifice, i.e., his potential martyrdom. The imperfective aspect of the verb form portrays this act as a process.

ἐπὶ τῇ θυσίᾳ καὶ λειτουργίᾳ. Locative. The locative sense of the preposition ἐπὶ requires understanding θυσία not as the "act of offering" (BDAG, 462.1) but as "that which is offered as a sacrifice" (BDAG, 462.2). λειτουργία denotes "service of a formal or public type" (BDAG, 591.1). A single article governing θυσίᾳ καὶ λειτουργίᾳ creates a TSKS construction (see 1:19 on διὰ τῆς ... δεήσεως καὶ ἐπιχορηγίας) that juxtaposes two distinct yet correlated entities associated with priestly functions and ritual—sacrifice and service. Another possibility, preferred by some interpreters, is to regard θυσίᾳ καὶ λειτουργίᾳ as a hendiadys, i.e., two coordinated entities that form one conception: "sacrificial service" (BDAG, 591.1.b; Zerwick §184; O'Brien, 309; Reumann, 401).

τῆς πίστεως. Genitive of source/origin modifying θυσίᾳ καὶ λειτουργίᾳ ("sacrifice and service coming from your faith" [NIV]) or epexegetical genitive clarifying θυσίᾳ καὶ λειτουργίᾳ ("sacrifice and service, that is, your faith"; cf. O'Brien, 310).

ὑμῶν. Subjective genitive modifying πίστεως. Since the genitive phrase τῆς πίστεως ὑμῶν functions as a qualifier of the PP ἐπὶ τῇ θυσίᾳ καὶ λειτουργίᾳ, which in turn modifies σπένδομαι, "Paul is asserting that he is willing for the sacrifice of his own life to be that libation which will complete the Philippians' offering to God, making it perfectly acceptable" (O'Brien, 306).

χαίρω. Pres act ind 1st sg χαίρω. The verb marks the beginning of the apodosis of a first-class condition. Paul portrays both his own feeling of joy and his sharing of joy with the Philippians (συγχαίρω) as an ongoing process (imperfective aspect). Rejoicing is a dominant theme throughout Philippians (see 1:18; 2:18, 28; 3:1; 4:4, 10).

συγχαίρω. Pres act ind 1st sg συγχαίρω.

πᾶσιν ὑμῖν. Dative of association.

2:18 τὸ δὲ αὐτὸ καὶ ὑμεῖς χαίρετε καὶ συγχαίρετέ μοι.

τὸ ... αὐτό. Adverbial accusative. The article functions as a nominalizer and αὐτό as an identical adjective ("in the same way"; cf. Moule, 34).

δέ. Marker of development.

καί. Adverbial use (adjunctive).

ὑμεῖς. Nominative subject of χαίρετε and συγχαίρετέ. The personal pronoun is emphatic.

χαίρετε. Pres act impv 2nd pl χαίρω. χαίρετε is parallel to χαίρω in v. 17.

καί. Coordinating conjunction.

συγχαίρετέ. Pres act impv 2nd pl συγχαίρω. συγχαίρετέ is parallel to συγχαίρω in v. 17. συγχαίρετέ, which has an acute accent on the antepenult, acquired an additional accent, the acute, on the ultima from the enclitic μοι (Smyth §183; Carson, 48).

μοι. Dative of association.

Philippians 2:19-24

[19]Now I hope in the Lord Jesus to send Timothy to you soon, so that I also may be encouraged when I learn about your circumstances. [20]For I have no one like-minded who will genuinely be concerned about your circumstances, [21]for they all seek their own interests, not those of Jesus Christ. [22]But you know his proven character, how, as a child [serves] a father, he has served with me in [the furtherance of] the gospel. [23]Therefore, I hope to send him immediately, as soon as I determine my circumstances. [24]And I am convinced in the Lord that I myself will also come soon.

2:19 Ἐλπίζω δὲ ἐν κυρίῳ Ἰησοῦ Τιμόθεον ταχέως πέμψαι ὑμῖν, ἵνα κἀγὼ εὐψυχῶ γνοὺς τὰ περὶ ὑμῶν.

Ἐλπίζω. Pres act ind 1st sg ἐλπίζω. The verb begins a new section, giving support to Levinsohn's contention that "it is incorrect to suggest that, whenever a sentence begins with a verb or participle, rather than with a nonverbal constituent, *complete* continuity with the last events described is indicated" (2000, 15).

δὲ. Marker of development.

ἐν κυρίῳ Ἰησοῦ. Locative, expressing the ground of Paul's hope (Harris, 130) or, more broadly, "the sphere in which his hope moves" (O'Brien, 317). The repetition of ἐν κυρίῳ in 2:24 forms an *inclusio* that marks the beginning and the ending of this section.

Τιμόθεον. Accusative direct object of πέμψαι. Fronted for emphasis.

ταχέως. Adverb of time, "with focus on brevity of interval rather than on speed of activity" (BDAG, 992.2).

πέμψαι. Aor act inf πέμπω (complementary to Ἐλπίζω).

ὑμῖν. Dative indirect object of πέμψαι.

ἵνα. Introduces a purpose clause.

κἀγώ. Formed by crasis from καὶ ἐγώ. καὶ is adjunctive ("also"); ἐγώ is the nominative subject of εὐψυχῶ. Fronted as a topical frame.

εὐψυχῶ. Pres act subj 1st sg εὐψυχέω. Subjunctive with ἵνα. εὐψυχέω ("to be heartened, be glad, have courage" [BDAG, 417]) is a NT *hapax legomenon*.

γνούς. Aor act ptc masc nom sg γινώσκω (temporal).

τὰ περὶ ὑμῶν. The article functions as a nominalizer, changing the PP περὶ ὑμῶν into the direct object of γνούς (lit. "the things concerning you" = "your circumstances"). Paul uses the same formulation in 1:27 and 2:20.

περὶ ὑμῶν. Reference. Porter explains that "[t]his metaphorical extension of the basic meaning appears derived from the sense that if one thing surrounds another it has this other thing as its concern or is restricted to it" (1994, 169).

2:20 οὐδένα γὰρ ἔχω ἰσόψυχον, ὅστις γνησίως τὰ περὶ ὑμῶν μεριμνήσει

οὐδένα. Accusative direct object of ἔχω in a double accusative object-complement construction. Fronted for emphasis.

γάρ. Postpositive conjunction that introduces the explanation of Paul's decision to send Timothy to the Philippians.

ἔχω. Pres act ind 1st sg ἔχω. In this context, ἔχω means "to have at hand, have at one's disposal" (BDAG, 420.1.c).

ἰσόψυχον. Complement to οὐδένα in a double accusative object-complement construction. ἰσόψυχον ("of like soul/mind" [BDAG, 481]) is a NT *hapax legomenon*.

ὅστις. Nominative subject of μεριμνήσει. The antecedent of this indefinite relative pronoun is οὐδένα.

γνησίως. Adverb of manner ("sincerely, genuinely" [BDAG, 202]). This is another NT *hapax legomenon*.

τὰ περὶ ὑμῶν. The article functions as a nominalizer, changing the PP περὶ ὑμῶν into the direct object of μεριμνήσει (see 2:19).

περὶ ὑμῶν. Reference (see 2:19).

μεριμνήσει. Fut act ind 3rd sg μεριμνάω. μεριμνάω ("care for, be concerned about" [BDAG, 632.2]) is here used as a transitive verb.

2:21 οἱ πάντες γὰρ τὰ ἑαυτῶν ζητοῦσιν, οὐ τὰ Ἰησοῦ Χριστοῦ.

οἱ πάντες. Nominative subject of ζητοῦσιν. The adjective πάντες functions as a substantive ("all [of them] [in contrast to a part]" [BDAG, 784.4.d]).

γὰρ. Postpositive conjunction that introduces an explanation of why Paul has no one except Timothy who will be genuinely concerned about the affairs of the Philippians. γάρ usually takes a second position but may come "third, fourth or fifth in the clause . . . partly because of necessity . . . and partly by the choice of the author" (BDF §475.2). In this clause, it is pushed into a third position after οἱ πάντες, which is fronted as a new topical frame.

τὰ ἑαυτῶν. The article nominalizes the genitive of the reflexive pronoun ἑαυτῶν (lit. "the things of themselves" = "their own interests"), turning it into the direct object of ζητοῦσιν. Fronted for emphasis.

ζητοῦσιν. Pres act ind 3rd pl ζητέω. In this context, ζητέω means to "strive for one's own advantage" (BDAG, 428.3.b).

οὐ. Negative particle normally used with indicative verbs. Here the particle negates the entire phrase τὰ Ἰησοῦ Χριστοῦ.

τὰ Ἰησοῦ Χριστοῦ. The article functions as a nominalizer, turning the genitive phrase Ἰησοῦ Χριστοῦ into the direct object of ζητοῦσιν (lit. "the things of Jesus Christ" = "the things concerning Jesus Christ").

2:22 τὴν δὲ δοκιμὴν αὐτοῦ γινώσκετε, ὅτι ὡς πατρὶ τέκνον σὺν ἐμοὶ ἐδούλευσεν εἰς τὸ εὐαγγέλιον.

τὴν . . . δοκιμὴν. Accusative direct object of γινώσκετε. The noun δοκιμή denotes "the experience of going through a test with special ref. to the result" (BDAG, 256.2). τὴν . . . δοκιμὴν is fronted as a topical frame, providing "the point of departure for the communication about Timothy's character" (Levinsohn 1995, 62).

δὲ. Marker of development.

αὐτοῦ. Objective genitive modifying δοκιμὴν.

γινώσκετε. Pres act ind 2nd pl γινώσκω.

ὅτι. Introduces either (1) a clause that is epexegetical to δοκιμὴν ("But you know his proven character, how . . ."; cf. NRSV; ESV); (2) the clausal complement (indirect discourse) of γινώσκετε ("But you know his proven character, that . . ."; NASB; LEB); or (3) a causal clause that provides a reason for τὴν δὲ δοκιμὴν αὐτοῦ γινώσκετε ("But you know his proven character, because . . ."; cf. NIV; HCSB). My translation reflects the first option.

ὡς. Comparative particle.

πατρὶ. Dative complement of an implied δούλευει (cf. BDAG, 259.2.a.α).

τέκνον. Nominative subject of an implied δούλευει. This noun is part of the elided comparative structure that presumes the repetition of the appropriate form of the main verb: ὡς πατρὶ τέκνον [δούλευει] = "as a child [serves] a father." The simile ὡς πατρὶ τέκνον is not symmetrical to the clause σὺν ἐμοὶ ἐδούλευσεν; the former presumes a child's subordination to a father, whereas the latter presumes that Timothy served together with Paul (Hellerman 2015, 150).

σὺν ἐμοὶ. Accompaniment.

ἐδούλευσεν. Aor act ind 3rd sg δουλεύω.

εἰς τὸ εὐαγγέλιον. Reference/respect (see 1:5).

2:23 τοῦτον μὲν οὖν ἐλπίζω πέμψαι ὡς ἂν ἀφίδω τὰ περὶ ἐμὲ ἐξαυτῆς·

τοῦτον. Accusative direct object πέμψαι. The demonstrative pronoun is anaphoric, referring back to Timothy. Fronted for emphasis.

μὲν. The first element of a point/counterpoint set that correlates a clause introduced by μέν with a clause introduced by δέ (v. 24). On the downgrading effect of the presence of μέν, see 1:15 on μὲν . . . δὲ.

οὖν. Postpositive inferential conjunction. It has a resumptive function, signaling the continuation of the main theme of sending Timothy in 2:19 (Runge 2016, 231).

ἐλπίζω. Pres act ind 1st sg ἐλπίζω.

πέμψαι. Aor act inf πέμπω (complementary to ἐλπίζω).

ὡς ἂν. A combination of the temporal conjunction ὡς and a marker of contingency ἄν, which means "as soon as" (BDAG, 57.I.c.δ).

ἀφίδω. Aor act subj 1st sg ἀφοράω. Subjunctive with ἄν. ἀφοράω (lit. "to direct one's attention without distraction" [BDAG, 158.1]) here means "to develop more precise knowledge about someth[ing] in the offing," "determine, see" (BDAG, 158.2).

τὰ περὶ ἐμὲ. The article functions as a nominalizer, changing the PP περὶ ἐμὲ into the direct object of ἀφίδω (lit. "the things concerning me" = "my circumstances"). This PP conveys the same idea as τὰ περὶ ὑμῶν in 1:27; 2:19, 20.

περὶ ἐμὲ. Reference.

ἐξαυτῆς. Adverb of time (ἐξαυτῆς = ἐξ αὐτῆς τῆς ὥρας) that means "at once, immediately, soon thereafter" (BDAG, 346). The word order, in which the adverb ἐξαυτῆς follows the indefinite temporal clause ὡς ἂν ἀφίδω τὰ περὶ ἐμὲ, indicates that Paul plans to send Timothy immediately after he determines his own circumstances.

2:24 πέποιθα δὲ ἐν κυρίῳ ὅτι καὶ αὐτὸς ταχέως ἐλεύσομαι.

πέποιθα. Perf act ind 1st sg πείθω. The perfect tense of πείθω ("to come to believe the certainty of something on the basis of being convinced" [LN 31.46]) has the sense of a present: "I have been persuaded and therefore am convinced" (see 1:6). The change from ἐλπίζω, pertaining to sending Timothy (vv. 19, 23), to πέποιθα, pertaining to Paul's travel plans (here), may suggest that Paul was more certain about his own arrival than about the arrival of Timothy (Reumann, 423; O'Brien, 327).

δὲ. The second element of a point/counterpoint set that correlates a clause introduced by μέν (v. 23) with a clause introduced by δέ (here).

ἐν κυρίῳ. Locative, expressing the ground of Paul's confidence or, more broadly, the sphere in which his confidence operates (see 2:19). ἐν κυρίῳ in this verse forms an *inclusio* with ἐν κυρίῳ Ἰησοῦ in 2:19, marking the end of this section.

ὅτι. Introduces the clausal complement (indirect discourse) of πέποιθα.

καὶ. Adverbial use (adjunctive).

αὐτὸς. Intensive pronoun that reinforces the implied subject of ἐλεύσομαι ("I myself"). The collocation καὶ αὐτὸς is fronted for emphasis, providing a new point of departure and calling attention to Paul's own travel plans (Levinsohn 2000, 105).

ταχέως. Adverb of time, "with focus on brevity of interval rather than on speed of activity" (BDAG, 992.2).

ἐλεύσομαι. Fut mid ind 1st sg ἔρχομαι.

Philippians 2:25-30

²⁵But I considered [it] necessary to send Epaphroditus—my brother and fellow-worker and fellow-soldier, but your messenger and servant of my need—to you, ²⁶since he was longing for all of you and was distressed because you heard that he was sick. ²⁷For indeed he was sick, coming near to death, but God had mercy on him—and not only on him, but also on me—so that I would not have sorrow upon sorrow. ²⁸Therefore I am sending him with special urgency so that, when you see him, you may rejoice again, and I may be less anxious. ²⁹Therefore welcome him in the Lord with all joy and hold such people in esteem, ³⁰because for the work of Christ he came near to the point of death, risking his life in order that he might make up for what was lacking in your service to me.

2:25 Ἀναγκαῖον δὲ ἡγησάμην Ἐπαφρόδιτον τὸν ἀδελφὸν καὶ συνεργὸν καὶ συστρατιώτην μου, ὑμῶν δὲ ἀπόστολον καὶ λειτουργὸν τῆς χρείας μου, πέμψαι πρὸς ὑμᾶς,

Ἀναγκαῖον. Complement to the infinitival phrase, Ἐπαφρόδιτον . . . πέμψαι πρὸς ὑμᾶς, in a double accusative object-complement construction (lit. "I considered sending Epaphroditus to you necessary"). Fronted for emphasis. To keep the adjective "necessary" in its preposed position without sacrificing the principles of good English syntax, I have, like most English versions, included a nonexistant direct object ("it") into my translation.

δὲ. Marker of development, signaling a change of topic from the anticipated visits by Timothy and Paul to the visit by Epaphroditus.

ἡγησάμην. Aor mid ind 1st sg ἡγέομαι. ἡγέομαι usually takes double accusative (cf. Acts 26:2; 1 Tim 1:12; 6:1; Heb 10:29; 11:11, 26; 2 Pet 2:13; 3:15) or is combined with an infinitive and an accusative adjective, as in 2:6 and here (BDAG, 434.2; cf. 2 Cor 9:5; 2 Pet 1:13). ἡγησάμην is frequently viewed as an epistolary aorist, denoting the time from the standpoint of the audience (BDF §334; Sumney, 63; Hellerman 2015, 155). Porter, however, rightly objects that "this is not a necessary assumption if tense forms are not temporally based. Instead what appears to occur is that the author composes the letter within his own coding time, and at junctures he may refer to coincidental processes using the Aorist. . . . The reader then interprets the letter from the same perspective as the author, beginning from an understanding of the coding-time implicatures implied by the author's use of temporal deictic indicators" (1989, 228). In this verse, ἡγησάμην may refer to Paul's view on the sending of Epaphroditus that was already past from the standpoint of his letter writing.

Ἐπαφρόδιτον. Accusative direct object of the infinitive πέμψαι. Fronted for emphasis.

τὸν ἀδελφὸν καὶ συνεργὸν καὶ συστρατιώτην. Accusatives in apposition to Ἐπαφρόδιτον. A single article governing three substantives linked by καί, none of which is impersonal, plural, and a proper name, creates a TSKS personal construction that fits the requirements for the Granville Sharp rule, which posits that all three substantives have the same referent, here Epaphroditus (Wallace 1996, 270–72, 275).

μου. Genitive of relationship modifying all three nouns in the TSKS construction (see above). The presence of the genitive pronoun does not invalidate the Granville Sharp rule (Wallace 1996, 275).

ὑμῶν. Genitive of relationship modifying both ἀπόστολον and λειτουργὸν. The preposed pronoun is thematically salient (Levinsohn 2000, 64).

δὲ. Marker of development, distinguishing the first three epithets of Epaphroditus, which express his relationship to Paul (see μου above), from the next two epithets, which express his relationship to the Philippians (see ὑμῶν above).

ἀπόστολον καὶ λειτουργὸν. Accusatives in apposition to Ἐπαφρόδιτον. In this context, the term ἀπόστολος has a nontechnical sense of "delegate, envoy, messenger" (BDAG, 122.1). The term λειτουργός may denote "one engaged in administrative or cultic service" (BDAG, 591.1) or "one engaged in personal service" (BDAG, 592.2). In the current context, the latter is more likely.

τῆς χρείας. Objective genitive modifying λειτουργὸν.

μου. Possessive genitive modifying χρείας.

πέμψαι. Aor act inf πέμπω. The infinitival phrase Ἐπαφρόδιτον . . . πέμψαι πρὸς ὑμᾶς serves as the direct object of ἡγήσατο in a double accusative object-complement construction (see Ἀναγκαῖον above).

πρὸς ὑμᾶς. Locative (motion toward).

2:26 ἐπειδὴ ἐπιποθῶν ἦν πάντας ὑμᾶς καὶ ἀδημονῶν, διότι ἠκούσατε ὅτι ἠσθένησεν.

ἐπειδὴ. Causal conjunction introducing the reason for Paul's decision to send Epaphroditus to the Philippians. This is the only occurrence of this conjunction in Philippians.

ἐπιποθῶν. Pres act ptc masc nom sg ἐπιποθέω (imperfect periphrastic). Fronted for emphasis. ἐπιποθέω means "to have a strong desire for someth[ing], with implication of need" (BDAG, 377). Paul used the same verb in 1:8 to express his own longing to see the Philippians.

ἦν. Impf act ind 3rd sg εἰμί.

πάντας ὑμᾶς. Accusative direct object of ἐπιποθῶν. In a number of manuscripts πάντας ὑμᾶς is followed by the infinitive ἰδεῖν (א* A C D I^vid 0278 33 81 104 326 365 1175 1241 2495 sy bo). Since, however, many witnesses do not include the infinitive (א² F G K L P Ψ 630 1505 1739 1881 2464 𝔐 lat sa), a decision based on external evidence is difficult. On the basis of internal criteria, however, the shorter text is preferable because "scribes were more likely to add the infinitive, in accordance with the expression ἐπιποθεῖν ἰδεῖν in Ro 1.11; 1 Th 3.6; 2 Tm 1.4, than to delete it" (Metzger, 547).

καί. Coordinating conjunction, linking two periphrastic participles.

ἀδημονῶν. Pres act ptc masc nom sg ἀδημονέω (imperfect periphrastic). This participle continues the periphrastic construction with ἦν. ἀδημονέω means to "be in anxiety, be distressed, troubled" (BDAG, 19).

διότι. Causal conjunction (δι' ὅτι), introducing an explanation of ἀδημονῶν. This is the only occurrence of this conjunction in Philippians.

ἠκούσατε. Aor act ind 2nd pl ἀκούω.

ὅτι. Introduces the clausal complement (indirect discourse) of ἠκούσατε.

ἠσθένησεν. Aor act ind 3rd sg ἀσθενέω. The verb here means "to suffer a debilitating illness," "be sick" (BDAG, 142.1).

2:27 καὶ γὰρ ἠσθένησεν παραπλήσιον θανάτῳ· ἀλλ' ὁ θεὸς ἠλέησεν αὐτόν, οὐκ αὐτὸν δὲ μόνον ἀλλὰ καὶ ἐμέ, ἵνα μὴ λύπην ἐπὶ λύπην σχῶ.

καὶ γάρ. A combination of the ascensive καί ("even") and the explanatory γάρ ("for"), "in which each particle retains its own force" (BDF §452.3).

ἠσθένησεν. Aor act ind 3rd sg ἀσθενέω.

παραπλήσιον θανάτῳ. Locative. παραπλήσιον (a NT *hapax legomenon*) is adverbial accusative, which is here used as an improper preposition (see 1:5 on ἄχρι τοῦ νῦν) with the dative θανάτῳ (BDF §184; Harris 239, 249). Lit. "near to death" = "he nearly died" (BDAG, 770).

ἀλλ'. Marker of contrast, highlighting a difference between Epaphroditus' life-threatening illness and his recovery because of God's mercy.

ὁ θεός. Nominative subject of ἠλέησεν.

ἠλέησεν. Aor act ind 3rd sg ἐλεέω. This is the only instance in Paul's letters in which he uses ἐλεέω ("have compassion/mercy/pity" [BDAG, 315]) to describe physical healing.

αὐτόν. Accusative direct object of ἠλέησεν.

οὐκ ... μόνον ἀλλὰ καί. A point/counterpoint set ("not only ... but also") that corrects the assertion that God had mercy on Epaphroditus by supplementing it with the assertion that God had mercy also on Paul. On the point/counterpoint set of this type, see 1:29 on οὐ μόνον ... ἀλλὰ καί.

αὐτόν. Accusative direct object of ἠλέησεν.

δέ. Marker of development.

ἐμέ. Accusative direct object of ἠλέησεν.

ἵνα. Introduces a purpose-result clause (O'Brien, 337 n. 52; Reumann, 429).

μή. Negative particle normally used with non-indicative verbs.

λύπην. Accusative direct object of σχῶ. Fronted for emphasis.

ἐπὶ λύπην. Addition (Harris, 138; BDAG, 365.7). Fronted for emphasis.

σχῶ. Aor act subj 1st sg ἔχω. Subjunctive with ἵνα.

2:28 σπουδαιοτέρως οὖν ἔπεμψα αὐτόν, ἵνα ἰδόντες αὐτὸν πάλιν χαρῆτε κἀγὼ ἀλυπότερος ὦ.

σπουδαιοτέρως. Comparative of the adverb σπουδαίως. Fronted for emphasis. If the adverb refers to time (BDAG, 939.1), σπουδαιοτέρως means "with special urgency" (BDAG, 939.1) or "as quickly as possible" (O'Brien, 328). If the adverb refers to manner (BDAG, 939.2), σπουδαιοτέρως means "more eagerly" (NASB; NKJV) or "more diligently" (ASV).

οὖν. Postpositive inferential conjunction.

ἔπεμψα. Aor act ind 1st sg πέμπω. ἔπεμψα is usually regarded as an epistolary aorist because it refers to the sending of Epaphroditus, who would carry Paul's letter to the Philippians, which has not yet occurred from the standpoint of the letter writing (cf. Wallace 1996, 563; for Porter's critique, see 2:25 on ἡγησάμην). The perfective aspect of the verb form portrays this action as a complete event.

αὐτόν. Accusative direct object of ἔπεμψα. The antecedent of the personal pronoun is Epaphroditus.

ἵνα. Introduces a purpose clause.

ἰδόντες. Aor act ptc masc nom pl ὁράω (temporal).

αὐτόν. Accusative direct object of ἰδόντες. The antecedent is still Epaphroditus.

πάλιν. Adverb "pert[aining] to repetition in the same (or similar) manner" (BDAG, 752.2). Most English translations presume that πάλιν modifies ἰδόντες (e.g., NRSV: "at seeing him again"; NIV: "when you see him again"). However, in light of Paul's custom of placing the adverb before the verb (Rom 15:10, 12; 2 Cor 5:12; 11:16; 12:21; Gal 1:9, 17; 2:1,

18; 4;19; Phil 4:4), it is more likely that πάλιν modifies χαρῆτε (Lightfoot, 124; O'Brien, 339; Reumann, 430; Fee, 280).

χαρῆτε. Aor act subj 2nd pl χαίρω. Subjunctive with ἵνα.

κἀγώ. Formed by crasis from καὶ ἐγώ. καὶ is a coordinating conjunction; ἐγώ is the nominative subject of ὦ. Fronted as a topical frame.

ἀλυπότερος. Predicate adjective. ἀλυπότερος is a comparative of the alpha-privative adjective ἄλυπος ("free from anxiety" [BDAG, 48]). ἀλυπότερος could be translated "less anxious" (NRSV; LEB; HCSB; ESV), "less concerned" (NASB), or "less sorrowful" (ASV; NKJV). A NT *hapax legomenon*. Fronted for emphasis.

ὦ. Pres act subj 1st sg εἰμί. Subjunctive with ἵνα.

2:29 προσδέχεσθε οὖν αὐτὸν ἐν κυρίῳ μετὰ πάσης χαρᾶς καὶ τοὺς τοιούτους ἐντίμους ἔχετε,

προσδέχεσθε. Pres mid impv 2nd pl προσδέχομαι. With the accusative of person (see αὐτὸν below), προσδέχομαι means "receive in a friendly manner" (BDAG, 877.1.a). The significance of the imperfective aspect of the present imperative probably lies not in portraying an action in progress but in giving prominence to Paul's request to welcome Epaphroditus wholeheartedly upon his arrival to Philippi (cf. Hellerman 2015, 162).

οὖν. Postpositive inferential conjunction.

αὐτὸν. Accusative direct object of προσδέχεσθε. The antecedent of the pronoun continues to be Epaphroditus.

ἐν κυρίῳ. Locative ("in the sphere of Christ's lordship"; Reumann, 431), manner (taking ἐν κυρίῳ as an equivalent to the adjective χριστιανός; cf. Harris, 130), or causal ("because of the Lord"; cf. Campbell 2012, 154). The PP modifies the imperative προσδέχεσθε, indicating "that Epaphroditus is to be received as a fellow member of the believing community" (O'Brien, 340–41).

μετὰ πάσης χαρᾶς. Manner. This PP also modifies the imperative προσδέχεσθε.

καὶ. Coordinating conjunction.

τοὺς τοιούτους. Accusative direct object of ἔχετε in a double accusative object-complement construction. Fronted as a topical frame. The nominalized adjective τοιούτους means "of such a kind, such as this, like such" (BDAG, 1009).

ἐντίμους. Complement to τοὺς τοιούτους in a double accusative object-complement construction. Fronted for emphasis. ἐντίμους (from ἔντιμος) means "honored, respected" (BDAG, 340.1).

ἔχετε. Pres act impv 2nd pl ἔχω.

2:30 ὅτι διὰ τὸ ἔργον Χριστοῦ μέχρι θανάτου ἤγγισεν παραβολευσάμενος τῇ ψυχῇ, ἵνα ἀναπληρώσῃ τὸ ὑμῶν ὑστέρημα τῆς πρός με λειτουργίας.

ὅτι. Introduces a causal clause.
διὰ τὸ ἔργον. Causal. Fronted as a topical frame. ἔργον denotes "that which one does as regular activity," "work, occupation, task" (BDAG, 391.2).
Χριστοῦ. According to BDAG (391.2), this genitive indicates "the one who assigns the task." In that sense it can probably be classified as a subjective genitive. Two other possibilities are genitive of purpose ("the work for Christ") and possessive genitive ("Christ's work"). Ephraemi Rescriptus (C) does not have any genitive modifier, while some manuscripts have κυρίου (ℵ A P Ψ 075 33 81 104 365 1241 1505 sy^h bo) or the articular τοῦ Χριστοῦ (D K L 630 𝔐). The UBS Committee preferred the anarthrous Χριστοῦ (attested in 𝔓^46 B F G 0278 6 1175 1739 1881 2464 sa), deeming the omission in C an accidental oversight and the variant κυρίου a scribal adaptation to the common Pauline expression τὸ ἔργον τοῦ κυρίου (1 Cor 15:58 and 16:10; cf. Metzger, 547).
μέχρι θανάτου. Degree ("to the point of death"). Fronted for emphasis. μέχρι is an improper preposition (see 1:5 on ἄχρι τοῦ νῦν). In the NT, the PP μέχρι θανάτου occurs only here and in 2:8.
ἤγγισεν. Aor act ind 3rd sg ἐγγίζω. In this clause, ἐγγίζω means "to draw near in a temporal sense" (BDAG, 270.2).
παραβολευσάμενος. Aor mid ptc masc nom sg παραβολεύομαι (causal or manner). παραβολεύομαι ("expose to danger" [BDAG, 759]) is a NT *hapax legomenon*. On adverbial participles that follow the main verb, see 1:4 on ποιούμενος.
τῇ ψυχῇ. Dative of respect (Zerwick §53).
ἵνα. Introduces a purpose clause.
ἀναπληρώσῃ. Aor act subj 3rd sg ἀναπληρόω. Subjunctive with ἵνα. ἀναπληρόω means "to supply what is lacking" (BDAG, 70.3).
τὸ ὑμῶν ὑστέρημα τῆς πρός με λειτουργίας. A cumbersome construction consisting of two genitives (ὑμῶν and τῆς πρός με λειτουργίας) that are dependent on the same noun standing between them (τὸ . . . ὑστέρημα; cf. BDF §168.1).
τὸ . . . ὑστέρημα. Accusative direct object of ἀναπληρώσῃ. ὑστέρημα denotes "need, want, deficiency" (BDAG, 1044).
ὑμῶν. Subjective genitive modifying ὑστέρημα (BDF §168.1; MHT 3:218).
τῆς . . . λειτουργίας. Objective genitive modifying ὑστέρημα (BDF §168.1; MHT 3:218).

πρός με. Locative (motion toward). The PP modifies λειτουργίας, standing in the first attributive position (see 1:5 on ἀπὸ τῆς πρώτης ἡμέρας).

Philippians 3:1-11

¹Henceforth, my brothers [and sisters], rejoice in the Lord. To write the same things to you [is] not troublesome for me, and it [is] safe for you. ²Beware of the dogs, beware of the evil workers, beware of the mutilation. ³For we are the circumcision, the ones who worship by the Spirit of God and boast in Christ Jesus and do not put confidence in the flesh—⁴although I have grounds for confidence even in the flesh. If anyone else thinks to have reason to be confident in the flesh, I [can do so] even more. ⁵[I am], with respect to circumcision, an eight-day-er; from the race of Israel; of the tribe of Benjamin; a Hebrew [born] from Hebrews; according to the law, a Pharisee; ⁶according to zeal, a persecutor of the church; according to the righteousness that is in the law, proven to be blameless. ⁷Nevertheless, whatever things were gain to me—these things I consider loss because of Christ. ⁸More than that, I also continue to consider all things to be loss because of the surpassing greatness of the knowledge of Christ Jesus my Lord, for the sake of whom I have suffered the loss of all things and continue to consider [them] garbage, in order that I may gain Christ ⁹and may be found in him, not having a righteousness of my own that [is] from the law but [one] that [is] through faith in Christ—the righteousness from God based on faith, ¹⁰so that I may know him and the power of his resurrection and the participation in his sufferings by being conformed to his death, ¹¹if somehow I may attain to the resurrection from the dead.

Verses 5-6 consist of seven paratactic autobiographical descriptions of Paul, which are best understood as predicates of an implied εἰμί. For the sake of clarity, I have separated them with semicolons, although they all belong to one large sentence that presumes εἰμί at the beginning.

3:1 Τὸ λοιπόν, ἀδελφοί μου, χαίρετε ἐν κυρίῳ. τὰ αὐτὰ γράφειν ὑμῖν ἐμοὶ μὲν οὐκ ὀκνηρόν, ὑμῖν δὲ ἀσφαλές.

Τὸ λοιπόν. Adverbial accusative of time (BDAG, 602.3.a.α; Wallace 1996, 201). Wallace (293) notes that "this idiomatic adverbial use is frequently, if not normally, articular," as here. Here Τὸ λοιπόν has "a connective sense" (Porter 1994, 122; cf. 1 Cor 7:29; 1 Thess 4:1; 2 Thess 3:1), marking a transition to a new topic (O'Brien, 348; Alexander, 96–97). Since, however, the term could also signal the end of the letter, as in 4:8 and 2 Cor 13:11, some scholars argue that it functions in this way also here, marking the conclusion of an earlier letter that is now incorporated into the canonical form of Philippians (Reumann, 452; Beare, 100; cf. GNT: "in conclusion").

ἀδελφοί. Vocative of direct address (see 1:12).

μου. Genitive of relationship modifying ἀδελφοί.

χαίρετε. Pres act impv 2nd pl χαίρω. If the verb has its normal sense, it means "to be in a state of happiness and well-being" (BDAG, 1074.1). If Τὸ λοιπόν marks the ending of an earlier letter (see above), χαίρετε may be understood as a formalized greeting, such as "farewell" (BDAG, 1075.2.a; TDNT 9:367; Beare, 100; Reumann, 452). Making a sharp distinction between the two possible senses of χαίρω, however, is not justified because rejoicing is a dominant theme throughout Philippians (1:18; 2:17, 18, 28; 3:1; 4:4, 10), so that the basic sense of the verb—"rejoice, be glad"—is recognizable even in its uses in stereotyped greetings (cf. O'Brien, 348–49; Silva, 144 n. 3; Reumann, 452).

ἐν κυρίῳ. Causal, expressing the ground for the Philippians' joy (Campbell 2012, 161; O'Brien, 350; Reumann, 452), close association, depicting the Philippians' union with Christ (BDAG, 327.4.c; O'Brien, 350), or locative, describing the sphere within which the Philippians rejoice (O'Brien, 350; Reumann, 452).

τὰ αὐτὰ. Accusative direct object of γράφειν. Fronted for emphasis. The article functions as a nominalizer and αὐτὰ as an identical adjective ("the same things").

γράφειν. Pres act inf γράφω. The infinitival phrase τὰ αὐτὰ γράφειν ὑμῖν functions as the subject of an implied ἐστίν. The use of γράφειν here also shows that the infinitive does not have to be articular to function as a subject of a clause (Wallace 1996, 601).

ὑμῖν. Dative indirect object of γράφειν.

ἐμοὶ. Dative of advantage (BDF §188).

μὲν. The first element of a point/counterpoint set that correlates a clause introduced by μέν with a clause introduced by δέ (see 2:23).

οὐκ. Negative particle normally used with indicative verbs.

ὀκνηρόν. Predicate adjective. It is neuter singular in agreement with the infinitive subject phrase. In this context, ὀκνηρόν ("causing hesitation, reluctance") can be translated "troublesome" (BDAG, 702.2). Reed (1996, 63–90) argues that γράφειν . . . οὐκ ὀκνηρόν represents an adaptation of the so-called hesitation formula that is commonly used in Hellenistic letters with the sense "do not hesitate to write."

ὑμῖν. Dative of advantage.

δέ. The second element of a point/counterpoint set that correlates a clause introduced by μέν (see above).

ἀσφαλές. Predicate adjective. It is again neuter singular in agreement with the infinitive subject phrase. Here ἀσφαλές (from ἀσφαλής) "pert[ains] to a state of safety and security, and hence free from danger—'safe, safely, secure, securely'" (LN 21.10).

3:2 Βλέπετε τοὺς κύνας, βλέπετε τοὺς κακοὺς ἐργάτας, βλέπετε τὴν κατατομήν.

Βλέπετε τοὺς κύνας, βλέπετε τοὺς κακοὺς ἐργάτας, βλέπετε τὴν κατατομήν. This is an example of alliteration—the repetition of words that start with the same letters of the alphabet: β (Βλέπετε ... βλέπετε ... βλέπετε), τ (τοὺς ... τοὺς ... τὴν), and κ (κυνάς ... κακούς ... κατατομήν).

Βλέπετε ... βλέπετε ... βλέπετε. Pres act impv 2nd pl βλέπω. The syntax (βλέπω + accusative) may suggest that the verb means "direct one's attention to someth[ing], consider, note" (BDAG, 179.6; cf. Kilpatrick, 146–48; Hawthorne and Martin, 174). However, the threefold repetition of the imperative, the use of asyndeton, and the polemical tone vv. 2-3 indicate that the verb functions as a warning, "watch, look to, beware of" (BDAG, 179. 5; cf. LN 27.58), even though it is not followed by the particle μή ("lest") or the preposition ἀπό (Fee, 293 n. 36; O'Brien, 354; Reumann, 461; Hellerman 2015, 170).

τοὺς κύνας. Accusative direct object of the first Βλέπετε. The noun κύνας (from κύων = "dog") is here used as a figurative extension of an invective, denoting "an infamous pers[on]" (BDAG, 579.3), "a particularly bad person, perhaps specifically one who ridicules what is holy" (LN 88.122).

τοὺς κακοὺς ἐργάτας. Accusative direct object of the second βλέπετε. The adjective κακοὺς stands in the first attributive position (see 1:5 on ἀπὸ τῆς πρώτης ἡμέρας). According to Robertson, in this construction "the adjective receives greater emphasis than the substantive" (776).

τὴν κατατομήν. Accusative direct object of the third βλέπετε. A NT *hapax legomenon*. Paul's use of the noun κατατομή ("mutilation, cutting in pieces") is a wordplay (paronomasia) on περιτομή ("circumcision"; see v. 3) "prob[ably] to denote those for whom circumcision results in (spiritual) destruction" (BDAG, 528; cf. LN 19.22).

3:3 ἡμεῖς γάρ ἐσμεν ἡ περιτομή, οἱ πνεύματι θεοῦ λατρεύοντες καὶ καυχώμενοι ἐν Χριστῷ Ἰησοῦ καὶ οὐκ ἐν σαρκὶ πεποιθότες,

ἡμεῖς. Nominative subject of ἐσμεν. Fronted for emphasis. The sense of the personal pronoun is inclusive, referring to all believers regardless of their ethnic origin (O'Brien, 359; Reumann, 474; Fee, 298).

γάρ. Postpositive conjunction that introduces the explanation of βλέπετε τὴν κατατομήν in v. 2.

ἐσμεν. Pres act ind 1st pl εἰμί.

ἡ περιτομή. Predicate nominative. The abstract noun περιτομή ("circumcision") is here used, via metonymy, as a reference to "believers in Jesus Christ (as truly circumcised people of the promise)" (BDAG, 807.2.b). Elsewhere in Paul's letters, this term is used for Jews or Jewish Christians (Rom 3:30; 4:9; Gal 2:7, 12).

οἱ ... λατρεύοντες καὶ καυχώμενοι ... καὶ ... πεποιθότες. Nominatives in apposition to ἡμεῖς. A single article governing three substantival participles connected with καί creates a TSKS plural construction (see Wallace 1996, 278–83). Semantically, the groups in such a construction could be (1) distinct entities, though united; (2) overlapping entities; (3) first entity subset of second; (4) second entity subset of first; and (5) identical entities. The participles in this verse represent the fifth option: λατρεύοντες = καυχώμενοι = πεποιθότες (cf. Wallace 1996, 283).

λατρεύοντες. Pres act ptc masc nom pl λατρεύω (substantival). Since λατρεύω ("to serve") is used in the LXX (Exod 23:25; Deut 6:13; 10:12, 20; Josh 22:28) and in the NT (Matt 4:10; Luke 1:74; Acts 7:7, 42; 26:7; Rom 1:9; 2 Tim 1:3; Heb 9:9, 14; Rev 7:15) to denote "the carrying out of religious duties, esp. of a cultic nature, by human beings" (BDAG, 587), it can be translated as "to worship."

πνεύματι. The placement of this dative between οἱ and λατρεύοντες indicates that it modifies the first participle in the TSKS construction. Because λατρεύω is usually complemented by the dative, it is possible to regard πνεύματι as the dative direct object of λατρεύοντες. Since, however, "the Spirit is seldom the object of worship," as Reumann (464) notes, a better solution is to take πνεύματι as the instrumental dative (Moule, 46; Robertson, 540) or, perhaps, the dative of sphere ("in the Spirit" [NRSV; NASB]), with no direct object of λατρεύοντες expressed.

θεοῦ. Genitive of source modifying πνεύματι. The variant reading θεῷ (א[2] D* P Ψ 075 365 1175 lat sy Chr) is most likely a scribal modification seeking to supply the object of λατρεύοντες and to avoid the possibility that the dative πνεύματι could mean worshipping the Spirit (Metzger, 547; O'Brien, 346).

καυχώμενοι. Pres mid ptc masc nom pl καυχάομαι (substantival). On the function of this participle, see οἱ... λατρεύοντες καὶ καυχώμενοι... καὶ... πεποιθότες above. καυχάομαι here means "to take pride in someth[ing]" (BDAG, 536.1).

ἐν Χριστῷ Ἰησοῦ. Causal ("on account of Christ"), expressing the cause or ground of Paul's boasting (Campbell 2012, 99–100).

οὐκ. Negative particle normally used with indicative verbs. This form of the particle shows that οὐκ negates not the participle πεποιθότες but the PP ἐν σαρκὶ.

ἐν σαρκὶ. Locative ("in the sphere of flesh"). Unlike the neutral use of this PP in 1:22, 24, the sense of ἐν σαρκὶ πεποιθότες here is negative, denoting "plac[ing] one's trust in earthly things or physical advantages" (BDAG, 916.5).

πεποιθότες. Prf act ptc masc nom pl πείθω (substantival). On the function of this participle, see οἱ... λατρεύοντες καὶ καυχώμενοι... καὶ... πεποιθότες above. The perfect tense of πείθω ("to come to believe the certainty of something on the basis of being convinced" [LN 31.46]) has the present sense (see 1:6).

3:4 καίπερ ἐγὼ ἔχων πεποίθησιν καὶ ἐν σαρκί. Εἴ τις δοκεῖ ἄλλος πεποιθέναι ἐν σαρκί, ἐγὼ μᾶλλον·

καίπερ. Concessive conjunction ("although"), which clarifies the concessive sense of the participle (MHT 1:230; BDF §425.1). The participial clause introduced by καίπερ is not an independent sentence but a dependent clause that qualifies the main clause in v. 3.

ἐγὼ. Nominative subject of the participle ἔχων. The first-person personal pronoun is expressed because there is a switch from the plural subject (ἡμεῖς) in the previous verse to the singular subject in this verse. It is fronted as a topical frame, marking a new point of departure (Levinsohn 1995, 63).

ἔχων. Pres act ptc masc nom sg ἔχω (concessive).

πεποίθησιν. Accusative direct object of ἔχων. πεποίθησις means "a state of certainty about someth[ing], to the extent of placing reliance on," "trust, confidence" (BDAG, 796.1). If, in terms of relative time, the present tense of the participle ἔχων describes an action that is concurrent with the action of the main verb ἐσμεν (v. 3), πεποίθησις denotes ground or reason for confidence rather than confidence itself (cf. Reumann, 466; O'Brien, 366–67; Hellerman 2015, 175). If, however, the participle ἔχων describes an action that took place before the action of the main verb ἐσμεν, πεποίθησις denotes confidence Paul once had in the flesh (cf. HCSB). My translation reflects the first option.

καὶ. Adverbial use (ascensive or adjunctive). This καὶ modifies the PP ἐν σαρκί and not the participle ἔχων (*pace* KJV: "Though I might also have confidence in the flesh"). My translation "even in the flesh" presumes ascensive sense, but adjunctive meaning is also possible (cf. HCSB: "although I once had confidence in the flesh too").

ἐν σαρκί. Locative (see 3:3).

Εἴ. Introduces the protasis of a first-class condition. The indefinite pronoun τις indicates that this is an example of a general first-class condition (Wallace 1996, 706). It is connected to the previous sentence by asyndeton. Although the particle εἰ is a proclitic, it is accented because it acquired an acute accent from the enclitic τις (Carson, 49).

τις ... ἄλλος. Nominative subject of δοκεῖ. Fronted for emphasis. In this construction, the indefinite pronoun τις functions as a substantive. It is modified by the adjective ἄλλος, which stands in the fourth attributive position (see 1:6 on ἔργον ἀγαθὸν).

δοκεῖ. Pres act ind 3rd sg δοκέω.

πεποιθέναι. Prf act inf πείθω (indirect discourse). The subject of the infinitive is not expressed because it is the same as the subject of δοκεῖ (BDF §396).

ἐγὼ μᾶλλον. An elliptical clause (= ἐγὼ μᾶλλον [δοκῶ πεποιθέναι ἐν σαρκί]; cf. O'Brien, 368) that serves as the apodosis of a first-class condition.

ἐγώ. Nominative subject of a verbless clause.

μᾶλλον. Comparative of the adverb μάλα ("to a greater or higher degree," "more" [BDAG, 613.1]).

3:5 περιτομῇ ὀκταήμερος, ἐκ γένους Ἰσραήλ, φυλῆς Βενιαμίν, Ἑβραῖος ἐξ Ἑβραίων, κατὰ νόμον Φαρισαῖος,

περιτομῇ. Dative of respect (BDF §197).

ὀκταήμερος. Predicate nominative with an implied εἰμί. ὀκταήμερος is a NT *hapax legomenon* ("on the eight day"), which is here used as a substantive (lit. "a person-of-eight-days" [BDAG, 702] or "an eight-day-er" [Hellerman 2015, 176]). In contrast to most English translations, which render περιτομῇ ὀκταήμερος with a paraphrase "circumcised on the eight day," I have translated it literally: "with respect to circumcision, an eight-day-er."

ἐκ γένους. Source or origin. Since γένος here denotes "a relatively large group of persons regarded as being biologically related" (LN 10.1), it is more accurate to render it as "race" than as "people" (NRSV; NIV; ESV) or "nation" (LEB; HCSB; NASB) because the last two designations include proselytes, who do not belong to γένος (O'Brien, 370).

Ἰσραήλ. Epexegetical genitive explaining γένους. This indeclinable noun here probably functions as a religious designation of the elect who are in a covenantal relationship with God.

φυλῆς. Genitive of source/origin or, alternatively, a genitive object of an implied ἐκ, forming a prepositional phrase that also conveys source or origin (cf. Sumney, 75). φυλή denotes "a subgroup of a nation characterized by a distinctive blood line," "tribe" (BDAG, 1069.1).

Βενιαμίν. Epexegetical genitive explaining φυλῆς.

Ἑβραῖος. Predicate nominative with an implied εἰμί. Ἑβραῖος is here used either as an "ethnic name for an Israelite" (BDAG, 270.1) or as a designation for "Hebrew-/Aramaic-speaking Israelite in contrast to a Gk.-speaking Israelite" (BDAG, 270.2). The latter is more likely because Paul has already mentioned his credentials based on his ethnicity.

ἐξ Ἑβραίων. Source or origin (Robertson, 598). ἐξ Ἑβραίων is not "the genitive in relationship to a *par excellence* noun" (*pace* Wallace 1996, 103 n. 84), such as "a real Hebrew if there ever was one!" (NLT), but a prepositional phrase that denotes Paul's origin, i.e., his parents ("a Hebrew [born] from Hebrews").

κατὰ νόμον. Reference.

Φαρισαῖος. Predicate nominative with an implied εἰμί. This is the only occurrence of this noun in the NT outside the Gospels and Acts.

3:6 κατὰ ζῆλος διώκων τὴν ἐκκλησίαν, κατὰ δικαιοσύνην τὴν ἐν νόμῳ γενόμενος ἄμεμπτος.

κατὰ ζῆλος. Reference. The noun ζῆλος, which is usually masculine (John 2:17; Rom 10:2; 2 Cor 7:7, 11; 11:2), is neuter here (also in 2 Cor 9:2). It is therefore not surprising that many copyists corrected or changed the neuter accusative ζῆλος to the masculine accusative ζῆλον (ℵ² D¹ K L P Ψ 075 33 81 104 365 630 𝔐 et al.). ζῆλος is used here as a positive term ("zeal, ardor, marked by a sense of dedication" [BDAG, 427.1]).

διώκων. Pres act ptc masc nom sg διώκω (substantival or attributive). If διώκων is an anarthrous substantive (MHT 3:151; Zerwick §371; NRSV; NASB; ESV), it functions as the predicate nominative with an implied εἰμί (see v. 5). If it is attributive (LEB; NIV; HCSB), it functions as the predicate adjective. In this context, διώκω means "to harass someone, esp. because of beliefs," "persecute" (BDAG, 254.2).

τὴν ἐκκλησίαν. Accusative direct object of διώκων. The term ἐκκλησία here denotes "the global community of Christians" (BDAG, 304.3.c) rather than a local Christian community (BDAG, 303.3.b). Elsewhere in Paul's letters, διώκω + τὴν ἐκκλησίαν occurs in Gal 1:13 (καθ' ὑπερβολὴν ἐδίωκον τὴν ἐκκλησίαν τοῦ θεου) and 1 Cor 15:9 (ἐδίωξα τὴν ἐκκλησίαν τοῦ θεου).

κατὰ δικαιοσύνην. Reference. In this context, δικαιοσύνη means "the quality or characteristic of upright behavior" (BDAG, 248.3), denoting "uprightness as determined by divine/legal standards" (BDAG, 248.3.c).

τὴν ἐν νόμῳ. The article functions as an adjectivizer, changing the PP ἐν νόμῳ into an attributive modifier of δικαιοσύνην and placing it in the second attributive position (see 1:1 on τοῖς οὖσιν and 2:9 on τὸ ὑπὲρ πᾶν ὄνομα).

ἐν νόμῳ. Locative ("rooted in the law"; cf. Hawthorne and Martin, 187; O'Brien, 379) or, less likely, instrumental ("by means of the law"; cf. Beker, 260; Sanders, 23).

γενόμενος. Aor mid ptc masc nom sg γίνομαι (attributive). Predicate adjective with an implied εἰμί (see v. 5). In terms of relative time, the aorist participle γενόμενος ("to come into a certain state or possess certain characteristics," "to be, prove to be, turn out to be" [BDAG, 199.7]) describes Paul's status that he achieved before his current situation.

ἄμεμπτος. Predicate adjective with γενόμενος. ἄμεμπτος means "blameless, faultless of the Mosaic covenant" (BDAG, 52). For γίνομαι + ἄμεμπτος, see LXX Gen 17:1 (γίνου ἄμεμπτος).

3:7 [Ἀλλ'] ἅτινα ἦν μοι κέρδη, ταῦτα ἥγημαι διὰ τὸν Χριστὸν ζημίαν.

[Ἀλλ']. Marker of contrast, "signaling that what follows replaces his potential reason for boasting" (Runge 2010, 99). Ἀλλ' is printed within square brackets because it is missing in some important early manuscripts ($\mathfrak{P}^{46.61vid}$ ℵ* A G 0282 33 81 1241 b d Lcf Ambst), but the external evidence for its inclusion is quite strong (ℵ² B D F K L P Ψ 075 104 365 630 1175 1505 1739 1881 2464 𝔐 lat sy co). Since "the context cries out for such a contrastive particle" (Fee, 311 n. 1), the shorter reading is clearly the more difficult reading, which might tip the scales in its favor. However, the decision is still difficult because the omission of an original Ἀλλ' could have happened because both words ἀλλά and ἅτινα begin and end with the letter alpha (homoeoteleuton). My translation follows the NA²⁸/UBS⁵ text.

ἅτινα. Introduces a relative clause in a left-dislocation (Runge 2010, 287–313), resumed by ταῦτα. This structure is usually called a pendent construction because it functions as "the logical (not grammatical) subject at the beginning of the sentence, followed by a sentence in which that subject is taken up by a pronoun in the case required by the syntax" (Zerwick §25). In discourse analysis, the placement of a pendent construction at the beginning of the clause, which is then resumed by a pronominal trace in the main clause, is called "left-dislocation" (Runge 2010, 289). Left-dislocations "have the effect of either announcing or shifting the topic of the clause that follows. This attracts more attention to the topic than it would have otherwise received with one of the more conventional methods" (290). In this verse, placing the relative clause ἅτινα ἦν μοι κέρδη in a left-dislocation serves as a thematic highlighter, drawing attention to the fact that in the past, Paul considered his aforementioned characteristics as gain. Within the relative clause, ἅτινα functions as the nominative subject of ἦν. ἅτινα is a combination of the relative pronoun ἅ and the indefinite pronoun τινα, which here probably stands for ἅ because its antecedent—the list of seven accomplishments described in vv. 5-6—is determinate (cf. BDF §293; Reumann, 488).

ἦν. Impf act ind 3rd sg εἰμί. Neuter plural subjects typically take singular verbs (BDF §133).

μοι. Dative of advantage.

κέρδη. Predicate nominative. κέρδη is plural (from κέρδος = "gain") in agreement with the plural subject ἅτινα.

ταῦτα. Accusative direct object of ἥγημαι in a double accusative object-complement construction. The demonstrative pronoun resumes the pendent clause in a left-dislocation, ἅτινα ἦν μοι κέρδη. Fronted as a topical frame. Runge (2010, 297) explains that placing the resumptive pronoun in a marked position at the beginning of the clause makes it easier for the reader to recognize where the left-dislocation (ἅτινα ἦν μοι κέρδη) ends and the main clause (ταῦτα ἥγημαι διὰ τὸν Χριστὸν ζημίαν) begins.

ἥγημαι. Prf mid ind 1st sg ἡγέομαι. The perfect tense of ἡγέομαι expresses Paul's current view of his past privileges (*pace* Gnilka, 191, who suggests that ἡγέομαι refers to Paul's Damascus road experience). ἥγημαι is contrasted with ἦν in the pendent relative clause, calling attention to Paul's changed perspective on the very things that were gain for him in the past (cf. O'Brien, 383). For other occurrences of ἡγέομαι in Philippians, see 2:3, 6, 25; 3:8.

διὰ τὸν Χριστὸν. Cause ("because of"; cf. BDAG, 225.B.2.a; Robertson, 583–84; Fee, 315 n. 8) or purpose ("for the sake of"; cf. Silva, 168; O'Brien, 385).

ζημίαν. Complement to ταῦτα in a double accusative object-complement construction. The singular ζημίαν is a *constructio ad sensum* because the term ζημία ("damage, disadvantage, loss, forfeit" [BDAG, 428]) is understood collectively.

3:8 ἀλλὰ μενοῦνγε καὶ ἡγοῦμαι πάντα ζημίαν εἶναι διὰ τὸ ὑπερέχον τῆς γνώσεως Χριστοῦ Ἰησοῦ τοῦ κυρίου μου, δι' ὃν τὰ πάντα ἐζημιώθην, καὶ ἡγοῦμαι σκύβαλα, ἵνα Χριστὸν κερδήσω

ἀλλὰ μενοῦνγε. This combination of particles can be translated "yet indeed" (NKJV), "more than that" (BDAG, 630; NRSV; NASB; LEB; HCSB; REB), or "what is more" (NIV).

ἀλλὰ. Adversative particle, which here marks not so much a contrast but "a shift from counting just his potential list as loss to counting all things as loss" (Runge 2010, 99).

μενοῦνγε. Emphatic compound conjunction consisting of three particles: μέν, οὖν, and γε. Runge argues that each particle in this collocation plays a specific role in the current context: "[T]he οὖν of the compound μενοῦνγε instructs the reader to view v. 8 as an inferential development closely connected to v. 7. The μέν has the normal forward-pointing constraint, signaling a counterpoint correlation with some related element that follows (v. 8d). The combination of an ascensive καί with γε strengthens the connection with v. 7 by creating this additional thematic link" (2010, 99).

καὶ. Adverbial use (adjunctive or ascensive).

ἡγοῦμαι. Pres mid ind 1st sg ἡγέομαι. For other occurrences of ἡγέομαι in Philippians, see 2:3, 6, 25; 3:7. The difference between the perfect-tense ἥγημαι in v. 7 and the present-tense ἡγοῦμαι in this verse is not temporal but aspectual. While ἥγημαι describes Paul's current view of his past privileges (stative aspect), ἡγοῦμαι expresses his ongoing view of all things (imperfective aspect). To indicate this difference, ἡγοῦμαι can be translated "I continue to consider" (cf. O'Brien, 381, 386).

πάντα. Accusative direct object of ἡγοῦμαι *and* accusative subject of the infinitive εἶναι.

ζημίαν. Predicate accusative. ζημίαν stands in a predicate relationship to πάντα, with which it is connected by the infinitive εἶναι. Fronted for emphasis.

εἶναι. Pres act inf εἰμί (indirect discourse).

διὰ τὸ ὑπερέχον. Cause or purpose (see 3:7 on διὰ τὸν Χριστὸν).

τὸ ὑπερέχον. Pres act ptc neut acc sg ὑπερέχω (substantival). On the function of this participle, see διὰ τὸ ὑπερέχον above. ὑπερέχω here means "to surpass in quality or value," "be better than, surpass, excel" (BDAG, 1033.3). τὸ ὑπερέχον = "the surpassing greatness" (BDAG, 1033.3.b).

τῆς γνώσεως. Attributed genitive modifying ὑπερέχον (Wallace 1996, 90). In this construction, the head substantive τὸ ὑπερέχον functions as an attributive adjective to the genitive γνώσεως ("the surpassing greatness of the knowledge" = "the surpassing knowledge"). Alternatively, τῆς γνώσεως could be regarded as an epexegetical genitive that explains ὑπερέχον ("the surpassing greatness, which is knowledge"; cf. Sumney, 78; O'Brien, 387). This is the only occurrence of the expression γνῶσις Χριστοῦ Ἰησοῦ in the letters of Paul. It is generally assumed that in this formulation the term γνῶσις refers to the act of knowing Jesus (see v. 10) rather than to the body of data about Jesus (Fee, 317 n. 20; O'Brien, 388; Reumann, 490); cf. 2 Cor 5:16 (εἰ καὶ ἐγνώκαμεν κατὰ σάρκα Χριστόν).

Χριστοῦ Ἰησοῦ. Objective genitive modifying γνώσεως ("the knowledge of Christ Jesus" = "knowing Christ Jesus").

τοῦ κυρίου. Genitive in apposition to Χριστοῦ Ἰησοῦ.

μου. Genitive of subordination modifying κυρίου ("the Lord over me") or possessive genitive ("my Lord"; cf. Sumney, 78; O'Brien, 387).

δι' ὅν. Cause or purpose. The antecedent of the accusative relative pronoun is Χριστοῦ Ἰησοῦ.

τὰ πάντα. Accusative of respect. Fronted for emphasis.

ἐζημιώθην. Aor mid ind 1st sg ζημιόω. The verb means "to suffer the loss of something which one has previously possessed, with the implication that the loss involves considerable hardship or suffering" (LN 57.69). ζημιόω with acc. τὶ = "to suffer loss w[ith] respect to someth[ing]" (BDAG, 428.1). Although ἐζημιώθην could be interpreted as true passive, with the sense that Paul suffered "loss at the hand of an external agent" (Hellerman 2015, 184; cf. Porter 1994, 66: "I was made to suffer loss"), it is better to regard it as θη-middle, with the sense that Paul voluntarily renounced his former privileges (cf. BDAG, 428.1: "permit oneself... to sustain loss"). On the voice, see "Deponency" in the Series Introduction.

καὶ. Coordinating conjunction that adds the correlating clause (ἡγοῦμαι [τὰ πάντα] σκύβαλα) to the anticipatory clause at the beginning of the verse (ἡγοῦμαι πάντα ζημίαν εἶναι), which was signaled by the particle μέν within μενοῦνγε (Runge 2010, 99).

ἡγοῦμαι. Pres mid ind 1st sg ἡγέομαι. On the aspectual force of this verb, see the first occurrence of ἡγοῦμαι in this verse. The implied direct object of the verb is τὰ πάντα in a double accusative object-complement construction.

σκύβαλα. Complement to the implied τὰ πάντα in a double accusative object-complement construction. σκύβαλα (from σκύβαλον) is a NT *hapax legomenon*. According to LSJ, the term means "dung, excrement" or "refuse, offal." In the current context, the second meaning is more suitable. BDAG (932) explains that the term denotes "useless or undesirable material that is subject to disposal," which can be rendered "refuse, garbage."

ἵνα. Introduces a purpose clause.

Χριστόν. Accusative direct object of κερδήσω. Fronted for emphasis.

κερδήσω. Aor act subj 1st sg κερδαίνω. Subjunctive with ἵνα. κερδαίνω means "to acquire by effort or investment," "to gain" (BDAG, 541.1).

3:9 καὶ εὑρεθῶ ἐν αὐτῷ, μὴ ἔχων ἐμὴν δικαιοσύνην τὴν ἐκ νόμου ἀλλὰ τὴν διὰ πίστεως Χριστοῦ, τὴν ἐκ θεοῦ δικαιοσύνην ἐπὶ τῇ πίστει,

καί. Coordinating conjunction, linking two verbs—κερδήσω and εὑρεθῶ—that belong to the ἵνα clause that began at the end of v. 8. Some scholars call this conjunction an epexegetic καί because "Paul is about to explain what it means to gain Christ" (Silva, 159; cf. Reumann, 519). It should be noted, however, that epexegetic function is not a semantic quality of καί but a conclusion based on the sense of the clauses connected by καί. As a conjunction, καί "connects two items of equal status, constraining them to be closely related to one another" (Runge 2010, 24). Explanation, contrast, or any other function traditionally associated with καί are qualities that are dependent on the semantics of the context rather than specific semantic qualities of καί.

εὑρεθῶ. Aor pass subj 1st sg εὑρίσκω. Subjunctive with ἵνα. The primary agent of the action is not expressed.

ἐν αὐτῷ. Locative (Paul's incorporation in Christ) or close association (Paul's union with Christ). Campbell notes that the locative function is inferred from the use of the verb εὑρεθῶ, which "naturally suggests a *place* in which that occurs." Close association, however, is more plausible "because of the personal nature of gaining Christ; Paul does not merely refer to his 'location' within the sphere of Christ's rule but regards his situation as one of personal connection such that he 'obtains' Christ somehow and is found in him" (Campbell 2012, 187).

μὴ . . . ἀλλά. A point/counterpoint set ("not this . . . but that") that negates the notion that Paul has a righteousness on his own that comes from the law (ἐμὴν δικαιοσύνην τὴν ἐκ νόμου) and replaces it with the notion that he has the righteousness that comes through faith in Christ (τὴν διὰ πίστεως Χριστοῦ).

ἔχων. Pres act ptc masc nom sg ἔχω (concessive, causal, or manner). On adverbial participles that follow the main verb, see 1:4 on ποιούμενος.

ἐμὴν δικαιοσύνην. Accusative direct object of ἔχων. Fronted for emphasis. The possessive adjective ἐμήν is used predicatively (ἐμὴν δικαιοσύνην = "righteousness which is my own"; cf. MHT 3:191; BDF §285.2), standing in the first (anarthrous) predicate position (Wallace 1996, 310). The absence of the definite article is unusual because ἐμός, ή, όν typically occurs with the article. Zerwick (§180) suggests that "the absence of the article with ἐμὴν δικαιοσύνην insists strongly on the quality of the righteousness, so that one might almost render 'not having a righteousness of my own'" (cf. O'Brien, 394).

τὴν ἐκ νόμου. The article functions as an adjectivizer, changing the PP ἐκ νόμου into an attributive modifier of δικαιοσύνην and placing it in the second attributive position (see 1:1 on τοῖς οὖσιν and 2:9 on τὸ ὑπὲρ πᾶν ὄνομα). Turner notes that "we hardly ever find a prepositional clause used as attribute to an anarthrous noun" (MHT 3:221). The construction ἐμὴν δικαιοσύνην τὴν ἐκ νόμου is one of several exceptions to this rule (cf. Acts 15:23; 26:18, 22; Rom 9:30; 1 Tim 1:4; 2 Tim 1:13). The attributive PP τὴν ἐκ νόμου receives emphasis through right-dislocation (Runge 2010, 317-35).

ἐκ νόμου. Source or origin (BDAG, 296.3.c; Reumann, 494).

τὴν διὰ πίστεως. The article functions as an adjectivizer, changing the PP διὰ πίστεως into an attributive modifier of an implied δικαιοσύνην (see τὴν ἐκ νόμου above).

διὰ πίστεως. Means (if Χριστοῦ is an objective genitive) or cause/ground (if Χριστοῦ is a subjective genitive). If the former, the term πίστεως (from πίστις) has the active sense, denoting "state of believing on the basis of the reliability of the one trusted" (BDAG, 818.2). If the latter, πίστις denotes "that which evokes trust and faith," "faithfulness, reliability, fidelity, commitment" (BDAG, 818.1.a).

Χριστοῦ. Objective genitive, functioning semantically as the direct object of the verbal idea implicit in πίστεως ("faith in Christ"; cf. BDAG, 819.2.b.β; NRSV; REB; ASV; HCSB; ESV; LEB; NASB; NIV; TDNT 6:210 n. 267), or subjective genitive, functioning semantically as the subject of the verbal idea implicit in πίστεως ("Christ's faithfulness" or "Christ's faith"; cf. CEB; KJV; RHE; Wallace 1996, 114-16; O'Brien, 398-400; Sumney, 80). The meaning of πίστις Χριστοῦ, which has been the subject of fierce scholarly debate, cannot be resolved through grammatical arguments (*pace* Dunn 1991, 732-34, who maintains that πίστις takes an objective genitive when both nouns are anarthrous and a subjective genitive when both nouns are articular) because both alternatives are grammatically feasible. Rather, each usage should be assessed in the light of theological and contextual factors. In my view, understanding Χριστοῦ as the objective genitive allows for a coherent interpretation of both occurrences of πίστις in this verse (see comments on ἐπὶ τῇ πίστει below) and is consistent with other references to the Philippians' faith (1:25, 27; 2:17) and believing (1:29) in this letter.

τὴν ... δικαιοσύνην. Accusative in apposition to the implied δικαιοσύνην. The entire formulation τὴν ἐκ θεοῦ δικαιοσύνην ἐπὶ τῇ πίστει receives more prominence through right-dislocation. Runge (2010, 322–24, 329) calls this effect of right-dislocation "thematic highlighting" because its purpose is to highlight the specific quality of righteousness that comes from God and is based on faith.

ἐκ θεοῦ. Source or origin. The PP ἐκ θεοῦ functions as an attributive modifier of δικαιοσύνην, which is placed in the first attributive position (see 1:5 on ἀπὸ τῆς πρώτης ἡμέρας).

ἐπὶ τῇ πίστει. Cause, expressing the "basis for a state of being, action, or result" (BDAG, 364.6). ἐπὶ τῇ πίστει provides additional elaboration of the meaning of the nominal phrase τὴν ἐκ θεοῦ δικαιοσύνην. Since πίστει is not accompanied by a genitive qualifier, it probably refers to the believer's faith in Christ rather than to Christ's faithfulness. If that is the case, and if Χριστοῦ is understood as the objective genitive, τῇ could be regarded as an anaphoric article, referring back to the anarthrous πίστεως in the previous clause (Fee, 325 n. 45; Hansen, 242). The view that Χριστοῦ is a subjective genitive presumes that there is a shift in the meaning of πίστις from Christ's faithfulness to human response to Christ's faithfulness (O'Brien, 400). On this reading, the article τῇ may function, as Sumney suggests, to "distinguish this use of the word from the immediately preceding use" (81).

3:10 τοῦ γνῶναι αὐτὸν καὶ τὴν δύναμιν τῆς ἀναστάσεως αὐτοῦ καὶ [τὴν] κοινωνίαν [τῶν] παθημάτων αὐτοῦ, συμμορφιζόμενος τῷ θανάτῳ αὐτοῦ,

τοῦ γνῶναι. Aor act inf γινώσκω. This genitive articular infinitive could denote purpose (BDAG, 688.2.d.β.ℷ; BDF §400.5; Moule 128–29; MHT 3:141–42; Haubeck and von Siebenthal, 1076–77) or result (Moule 128–29; MHT 3:136, 141–42) of the righteousness from God based on faith (τὴν ἐκ θεοῦ δικαιοσύνην ἐπὶ τῇ πίστει), or it could be epexegetical to the entire ἵνα clause in vv. 8-9 (Moule, 128–29; Collange, 131). The implied subject of the infinitive is Paul ("so that I may know ...").

αὐτόν. Accusative direct object of γνῶναι (the first of three). The next two direct objects indicate that the antecedent of the personal pronoun αὐτόν is Christ rather than God.

καὶ ... καί. Coordinating conjunctions linking three direct objects of γνῶναι. Some interpreters argue that the first καί functions epexegetically because "Paul appears to define *knowing Christ* as the believer's experiencing of Christ's own death and resurrection" (Silva, 163; cf. Hellerman 2015, 189; Sumney, 81; Fee, 328). Since, however, epexegetic function is not a semantic quality of καί (see 3:9), it is better to regard both instances of καί as conjunctions that connect three items of equal status (Runge 2010, 24) and make conclusions about their relationship in this clause on the basis of their conceptual and theological relationships in Paul's overall thought.

τὴν δύναμιν. Accusative direct object of γνῶναι (the second of three). δύναμις here denotes "potential for functioning in some way," "power, might, strength, force, capability" (BDAG, 262.1).

τῆς ἀναστάσεως. Genitive of source modifying δύναμιν ("the power derived from the resurrection") or descriptive genitive qualifying δύναμιν ("the power that characterized his resurrection"; Hellerman 2015, 190).

αὐτοῦ. Objective genitive modifying ἀναστάσεως ("resurrecting him"); cf. NCV: "the power that raised him from the dead."

[τὴν] κοινωνίαν. Accusative direct object of γνῶναι (the third of three). In this context, the term κοινωνία means "participation, sharing" (BDAG, 553.4). The article is placed within square brackets because the external evidence for its exclusion ($\mathfrak{P}^{46}$ ℵ* A B 1241 2464) and inclusion (ℵ² D F G K L P Ψ 075 33 81 104 365 630 1175 1505 1739 1881 𝔐) is evenly balanced. If the shorter reading, which is attested in the earliest manuscript tradition and appears to be "more difficult on grounds of symmetry and parallelism" (O'Brien, 382), is prioritized, the second and third direct objects of γνῶναι form a TSKS (article-substantive-καί-substantive) construction: τὴν δύναμιν... καὶ κοινωνίαν (see 1:7 on ἐν τῇ ἀπολογίᾳ καὶ βεβαιώσει). Since, however, δύναμις and κοινωνία are impersonal nouns, they do not fulfill the conditions for the application of the Granville Sharp rule. As elements of an impersonal TSKS construction, they could be (1) distinct entities, though united; (2) overlapping entities; (3) first entity subset of second; (4) second entity subset of first; and (5) identical entities (Wallace 1996, 278, 286–88). It is therefore questionable whether one could conclude, merely on the basis of the single article governing δύναμιν... καὶ κοινωνίαν, "that the power of the resurrected Christ and the fellowship of his suffering are to be thought of not as two totally separate experiences but as alternate aspects of the same experience" (Hawthorne and Martin, 197). Such a conclusion can be made even if the longer reading is accepted because it does not depend on grammar but on a reconstruction of Paul's theology.

[τῶν] παθημάτων. Objective genitive modifying κοινωνίαν ("participation in his sufferings" or "sharing his sufferings"). The article is absent in some of the earliest manuscripts ($\mathfrak{P}^{46}$ ℵ* B), but its attestation is quite strong (ℵ² A D F G K L P Ψ 075 33 81 104 365 630 1175 1241 1505 1739 1881 2464 𝔐).

αὐτοῦ. Subjective genitive qualifying παθημάτων ("his sufferings"). The personal pronoun refers to Christ.

συμμορφιζόμενος. Pres pass ptc masc nom sg συμμορφίζω (manner or means). If the participle modifies the preceding expression, [τὴν] κοινωνίαν [τῶν] παθημάτων αὐτοῦ, as it is generally assumed, it explains how Paul participates in Christ's suffering. If, however, the participle modifies the entire preceding clause, τοῦ γνῶναι αὐτὸν καὶ τὴν δύναμιν τῆς ἀναστάσεως αὐτοῦ καὶ [τὴν] κοινωνίαν [τῶν] παθημάτων αὐτοῦ, as O'Brien suggests, "it is not in the fellowship of Christ's sufferings as such that Paul is conformed to Christ's death; rather, it is by participating in those sufferings (which he experiences in the course of his apostolic labours) *and* as strengthened to do so in the power of his resurrection that he is continually being conformed to Christ's death" (407). The verb συμμορφίζω ("to cause to be similar in form or style to someth[ing] else" [BDAG, 958]) is a NT *hapax legomenon*, although its cognate adjective σύμμορφος occurs in 3:21 and Rom 8:29. The imperfective aspect of the present participle portrays Paul's experience of being conformed to Christ's death as an ongoing process. The nominative case of συμμορφιζόμενος is a *constructio ad sensum* because the participle should have been in the accusative in agreement with the semantic subject of the infinitive γνῶναι (Reumann, 502).

τῷ θανάτῳ. Dative complement of συμμορφιζόμενος.

αὐτοῦ. Subjective genitive modifying θανάτῳ ("his death"). The personal pronoun refers to Christ.

3:11 εἴ πως καταντήσω εἰς τὴν ἐξανάστασιν τὴν ἐκ νεκρῶν.

εἴ. Introduces the protasis of a third-class condition. This class of conditional clauses typically has ἐάν + subjunctive, but it can occasionally have εἰ + subjunctive, as here (Robertson, 1017). It can be described as "underdetermined, but with prospect of determination. This class uses in the condition clause the mode of expectation (*Erwartung*), the subj. It is not determined as is true of the first and second class conditions. But the subj. mode brings the expectation within the horizon of a lively hope in spite of the cloud of hovering doubt" (1016). Since Paul makes this statement at the end of a long series of declarations about his relationship with Christ, it is best to regard it as "an expression of expectation" (BDF §375), which is based on his desire to know the power of Christ's resurrection (v. 10) and "contingent upon . . . his being conformed to

Christ's death" (O'Brien, 412; cf. Fee, 335–36). Although the particle εἰ is a proclitic, it is accented because it acquired an acute accent from the enclitic πως (Carson, 49).

πως. An enclitic particle used as a "marker of undesignated means or manner" (BDAG, 901.1). A combination of εἰ and πως could be translated "if perhaps" or "if somehow" (BDAG, 279.6.n). Elsewhere in the NT, εἴ πως occurs in Acts 27:12; Rom 1:10; 11:14.

καταντήσω. Aor act subj 1st sg καταντάω. Subjunctive with εἴ πως in a third-class condition. The meaning of καταντάω, "to reach a condition or goal" (BDAG, 523.2), is a figurative extension of the verb's literal meaning, "to get to a geographical destination" (BDAG, 523.1).

εἰς τὴν ἐξανάστασιν. Goal. The prefixed ἀνάστασις (ἐξανάστασις = ἐκ+ ἀνάστασις) is a NT *hapax legomenon*. BDAG (345) suggests that "the compound in contrast to the simplex ἀνάστασις that precedes connotes a coming to fullness of life, as vss. 12–21 indicate."

τὴν ἐκ νεκρῶν. The article functions as an adjectivizer, changing the PP ἐκ νεκρῶν into an attributive modifier of ἐξανάστασιν and placing it in the second attributive position (see 1:1 on τοῖς οὖσιν and 2:9 on τὸ ὑπὲρ πᾶν ὄνομα).

ἐκ νεκρῶν. Source. The repetition of the preposition ἐκ (ἐξανάστασιν ... ἐκ νεκρῶν) and the use of ἀνάστασις + ἐκ νεκρῶν elsewhere in the NT (Luke 20:35; Acts 4:2; 1 Pet 1:3) indicate that this PP refers to a partial resurrection ("from among the dead" or "out of the dead") rather than to a general resurrection of the dead. This meaning is even more appropriate in the current context, in which Paul speaks about his own resurrection from the dead.

Philippians 3:12-16

[12]Not that I have already obtained [this] or have already been brought to completion, but I press on [to see] whether I may also take hold [of that] for which I also have been taken hold by Christ Jesus. [13]Brothers [and sisters], I do not consider that I have taken hold [of it]. But one thing [I do]: forgetting the things behind and reaching forward to the things ahead, [14]I press on toward the goal for the prize [announced] by the upward call of God in Christ Jesus. [15]Therefore, as many as [are] mature, let us hold this opinion. And if you think anything differently, God will reveal also this to you. [16]In any case, unto that to which we have attained—let us behave in conformity to the same [standard].

3:12 Οὐχ ὅτι ἤδη ἔλαβον ἢ ἤδη τετελείωμαι, διώκω δὲ εἰ καὶ καταλάβω, ἐφ' ᾧ καὶ κατελήμφθην ὑπὸ Χριστοῦ ['Ιησοῦ].

Οὐχ ὅτι. An ellipsis for οὐ λέγω ὅτι (BDF §480.5). Paul frequently uses this formulaic expression (2 Cor 1:24; 3:5; 7:9; Phil 3:12; 4:11, 17; 2 Thess 3:9) to qualify something in the preceding material to avoid misunderstanding.

Οὐχ. Negative particle normally used with indicative verbs.

ὅτι. Introduces the clausal complement (indirect discourse) of an implied λέγω (see Οὐχ ὅτι above).

ἤδη. Temporal adverb ("already").

ἔλαβον. Aor act ind 1st sg λαμβάνω. The aorist ἔλαβον portrays Paul's experience, both past and present, as a whole (imperfective aspect). This transitive verb does not have an expressed object because "[i]n keeping with its economical nature, Greek regularly implies an object that was already mentioned in the preceding context, rather than restating it" (Wallace 1996, 409). Grammatically, the implied direct object of ἔλαβον is τὴν ἐξανάστασιν τὴν ἐκ νεκρῶν mentioned at the end of the preceding verse, but semantically, it is the full knowledge of Christ that will be attained at the resurrection of the dead (Fee, 343; O'Brien, 421–22). In some manuscripts, ἔλαβον is followed by ἢ ἤδη δεδικαίωμαι (𝔓⁴⁶ D*.c [F G] ar [b Ir^lat] Ambst). While the internal arguments for (cf. 417–18) and against (cf. Fee, 337 n. 1) the originality of this clause are inconclusive, its presence in the text is doubtful given the strong external support for a shorter text (Metzger, 547–48).

ἢ. Marker of an alternative/disjunctive particle (BDAG, 432.1).

ἤδη. Temporal adverb (see above).

τετελείωμαι. Perf pass ind 1st sg τελειόω. This is the only occurrence of this verb in Paul. In this context, τελειόω most likely means to "bring to an end, bring to its goal/accomplishment" (BDAG, 996.2), "to be completely successful, to succeed fully" (LN 68.31), although "consecrate, initiate" (BDAG, 996.3; cf. LN 53.50) as a technical term in mystery religions is also possible if Paul was using the verb to correct the views of his opponents (O'Brien, 423; Reumann, 553). The perfect-tense verb form is frontgrounded, calling attention to Paul's current state of not yet having arrived at the final goal (stative aspect).

διώκω. Pres act ind 1st sg διώκω. Unlike 3:6, where διώκω refers to Paul's persecution of the church, here and in 3:14 διώκω means "to move rapidly and decisively toward an objective," "hasten, run, press on" (BDAG, 254.1). The imperfective aspect of the present tense portrays Paul's pursuit of his eschatological objective as an ongoing process.

δὲ. Marker of development.

εἰ. Introduces an indirect question (BDAG, 278.5.b.β; BDF §368; Robertson, 916) that functions as "an expression of expectation" (BDF §375). Technically, this is a type of a third-class condition (Robertson, 1024), like the one in 3:11. Since the use of εἰ in an indirect question is elliptical, it requires some kind of introduction for the sake of clarity, such as "(to see) whether . . ." (BDAG, 278.5.b.β; Robertson, 1024).

καί. Adverbial use (adjunctive).

καταλάβω. Aor act subj 1st sg καταλαμβάνω. Subjunctive with εἰ in an indirect question. The compound verb (κατά + λαμβάνω) is a strengthened version of the simple verb form (TDNT 4:9) and means "to make someth[ing] one's own," "win, attain" (BDAG, 519.1). The implied direct object of the verb is probably τὴν ἐξανάστασιν τὴν ἐκ νεκρῶν from the end of v. 11 or, more broadly, the full knowledge of Christ (see ἔλαβον above).

ἐφ᾽ ᾧ. Cause or purpose. Causal function is based on the idiomatic use of the PP ἐφ᾽ ᾧ in Rom 5:12 and 2 Cor 5:4, where it stands for ἐπὶ τούτῳ ὅτι, "for this reason that, because" (BDAG, 365.6.c; cf. BDF §235; Wallace 1996, 342; O'Brien, 425). The idea that ἐφ᾽ ᾧ indicates the purpose for which Christ took hold of Paul is based on the supposition that καταλάβω implies a direct object, which serves as an understood antecedent of the relative pronoun ᾧ (cf. Fee, 346 n. 31; Robertson, 605). This reading is also supported by the use of ἐφ᾽ ᾧ in 4:10. My translation reflects the second option.

καί. Adverbial use (adjunctive).

κατελήμφθην. Aor pass ind 1st sg καταλαμβάνω.

ὑπὸ Χριστοῦ [Ἰησοῦ]. Primary (personal) agency. The name Ἰησοῦ is printed within square brackets because it is omitted in some important witnesses (B D F G 33 b Tert Cl Ambst), although its attestation is both early and widespread ($\mathfrak{P}^{46.61vid}$ ℵ A K L P Ψ 075 81 104 365 630 1175 1241 1505 1739 1881 2464 𝔐 ar vg sy).

3:13 ἀδελφοί, ἐγὼ ἐμαυτὸν οὐ λογίζομαι κατειληφέναι· ἓν δέ, τὰ μὲν ὀπίσω ἐπιλανθανόμενος τοῖς δὲ ἔμπροσθεν ἐπεκτεινόμενος,

ἀδελφοί. Vocative of direct address (see 1:12).

ἐγώ. Nominative subject of λογίζομαι. The first-person personal pronoun is expressed and fronted for emphasis.

ἐμαυτόν. Accusative subject of the infinitive κατειληφέναι. Fronted for emphasis. According to the rules of classical Greek, the reflexive pronoun ἐμαυτόν is syntactically superfluous because "the subject of a dependent infin[itive] is not expressed again if it is the same as the subject of the independent verb" (MHT 3:146). However, this rule is not strictly followed in Koine Greek, which frequently has the subject of the infinitive in the accusative although it is the same as the subject of the governing verb, as here (MHT 3:147–48).

οὐ. Negative particle normally used with indicative verbs. Several important witnesses (ℵ A D* P 075 33 81 104 365 614 [629] 1175 1241 ar vg^{mss} sy^{h**} bo Cl) have οὔπω ("not yet") instead of οὐ ("not"). This reading, however, appears to be a textual emendation by some copyists who "considered Paul to be too modest in his protestations" (Metzger, 548) because they interpreted his assertions ethically rather than eschatologically (Fee, 338 n. 5).

λογίζομαι. Pres mid ind 1st sg λογίζομαι. The verb means "to hold a view about someth[ing]," "think, believe, be of the opinion" (BDAG, 598.3). Paul's use of the present tense conveys his ongoing point of view (imperfective aspect).

κατειληφέναι. Perf act inf καταλαμβάνω (indirect discourse). The implied direct object of the infinitive is probably the same as with previous occurrences of the active voice of (κατα)λαμβάνω in this section (see ἔλαβον and καταλάβω in v. 12).

ἕν. Accusative direct object of an implied ποιῶ or πράσσω ("one thing [I do]"). Rhetorically, the elliptical interjectional sentence ἓν δέ ("just one thing!" [BDAG, 292.2.b]) is more effective than a reconstructed full sentence.

δέ. Marker of development.

τὰ . . . ὀπίσω. The article functions as a nominalizer, changing the adverb ὀπίσω ("behind") into the accusative direct object of ἐπιλανθανόμενος. Fronted for emphasis.

μὲν. The first element of a point/counterpoint set that correlates a clause introduced by μέν with a clause introduced by δέ (see 2:23).

ἐπιλανθανόμενος. Pres mid ptc masc nom sg ἐπιλανθάνομαι (manner). ἐπιλανθάνομαι means "to not recall information concerning some particular matter—'to forget, to not recall'" (LN 29.14). ἐπιλανθάνομαι is used here not literally but figuratively; it does not refer to Paul's amnesia but to his disregard for his past experiences (Reumann, 539; Fee, 347 n. 40). The participle modifies διώκω, providing the background information about Paul's pursuit of God's upward calling. On adverbial participles that precede the main verb, see 1:25 on πεποιθώς.

τοῖς . . . ἔμπροσθεν. The article functions as a nominalizer, changing the adverb ἔμπροσθεν ("ahead") into the dative complement of ἐπεκτεινόμενος. Fronted for emphasis.

δὲ. The second element of a point/counterpoint set that correlates a clause introduced by μέν (see above).

ἐπεκτεινόμενος. Pres mid ptc masc nom sg ἐπεκτείνομαι (manner). ἐπεκτείνομαι ("to exert oneself to the uttermost," "stretch out, strain τινί toward something" [BDAG, 361]) is a NT *hapax legomenon*. This participle also modifies διώκω, providing the background information about Paul's pursuit of God's upward calling. On adverbial participles that precede the main verb, see 1:25 on πεποιθὼς.

3:14 κατὰ σκοπὸν διώκω εἰς τὸ βραβεῖον τῆς ἄνω κλήσεως τοῦ θεοῦ ἐν Χριστῷ Ἰησοῦ.

κατὰ σκοπὸν. Spatial (direction). Fronted for emphasis. The preposition κατὰ here denotes "extension toward" (BDAG, 511.B.1.b). The noun σκοπὸν (from σκοπὸς = "goal, mark" [BDAG, 931]) is a NT *hapax legomenon*.

διώκω. Pres act ind 1st sg διώκω. On the meaning of διώκω in this context, see 3:12.

εἰς τὸ βραβεῖον. Purpose. The primary sense of βραβεῖον ("an award for exceptional performance" [BDAG, 183]) is "prize, award" for a victory in an athletic competition (BDAG, 183.a; cf. 1 Cor 9:24). The term is here used figuratively, denoting a prize for spiritual performance (BDAG, 183.b).

τῆς ... κλήσεως. Epexegetical genitive (a.k.a. genitive of apposition or genitive of definition) identifying βραβεῖον ("the prize, which is the upward call") or genitive of means modifying βραβεῖον ("the prize announced by the upward call"). The first option presumes that τῆς ἄνω κλήσεως refers to God's eschatological call, so that "the prize itself is then God's calling to life in his eternal presence" (O'Brien, 431). The second option presumes that τῆς ἄνω κλήσεως refers to God's initial call to faith. "The prize (τὸ βραβεῖον) then refers to that which is announced or promised by the call" (432). O'Brien calls this type of genitive subjective genitive, but his explanation is more suitable for a genitive of means because the act of calling (κλῆσις) is not the actual subject who offers the prize—God is—but "the means that has brought about the promised result, the prize" (Fee, 349 n. 47). The use of the term κλῆσις elsewhere in the Pauline corpus (Rom 11:29; 1 Cor 1:26; Eph 4:1, 4; 2 Thess 1:11) as a reference to the beginning rather than the completion of the life of faith tips the scales in favor of the second option.

ἄνω. An adverb ("upward[s]" [BDAG, 92.2]), which is here used as an attributive modifier of κλήσεως, standing in the first attributive position (see 1:5 on ἀπὸ τῆς πρώτης ἡμέρας).

τοῦ θεοῦ. Subjective genitive modifying κλήσεως ("God called me").

ἐν Χριστῷ Ἰησοῦ. Instrumental ("through Christ Jesus") or causal ("on account of Christ Jesus"). The PP modifies κλήσεως, explaining how or why Paul received God's upward call. Campbell argues that the second option is preferable because Paul's "pursuit of a prize . . . is grounded in God's call. It follows, then, that since the concept of being *grounded* is already in view, it may be best to regard ἐν Χριστῷ as indicating *ground*, *cause*, or *reason*" (2012, 138).

3:15 Ὅσοι οὖν τέλειοι, τοῦτο φρονῶμεν· καὶ εἴ τι ἑτέρως φρονεῖτε, καὶ τοῦτο ὁ θεὸς ὑμῖν ἀποκαλύψει·

Ὅσοι. Nominative subject of an implied copula, such as ἐσμέν or εἰσίν. Ὅσοι is a correlative pronoun "pert[aining] to a comparative quantity or number of objects or events," "how much (many), as much (many) as" (BDAG, 729.2).

οὖν. Postpositive inferential conjunction.

τέλειοι. Predicate adjective. Since Paul includes himself in the group described by this adjective, τέλειος probably means "mature" in a spiritual sense (BDAG, 995.2) or "perfect" in a moral sense (BDAG, 996.4) and not "initiated into mystic rites" (*pace* BDAG, 995.3). At the same time, Paul's disclaimer in 3:12 (Οὐχ ὅτι . . . ἤδη τετελείωμαι) and his appropriation of the designation τέλειοι here indicate that the verb τελειόω and the adjective τέλειος do not have analogous meanings (O'Brien, 435–36). This is probably an intentional wordplay that Paul uses for rhetorical purposes. "So he who is 'not yet' *teleios* ('completed') in the sense of *eschatological* hope, is 'already' *teleios* ('mature'), along with them, in terms of how they live in the present as they await the final glory" (Fee, 355).

τοῦτο. Accusative direct object of φρονῶμεν or adverbial accusative ("this way" [ESV; HCSB]). The near-demonstrative pronoun does not have a clear antecedent but probably refers to the content of vv. 12-14. Fronted for emphasis.

φρονῶμεν. Pres act subj 1st pl φρονέω (hortatory subjunctive). On the meaning of the verb, see 1:7 on φρονεῖν.

καὶ. Coordinating conjunction, linking two clauses.

εἴ. Introduces the protasis of a first-class condition. The proclitic εἰ acquired an acute accent from the enclitic τι (Carson, 49).

τι. Accusative direct object of φρονεῖτε.

ἑτέρως. Adverb ("differently, otherwise" [BDAG, 400]). A NT *hapax legomenon*. LSJ places this text in group V.3 that lists the passages in which the meaning of ἑτέρως carries negative connotations: "otherwise than should be, badly, wrongly" (cf. Silva, 187–88).

φρονεῖτε. Pres act ind 2nd pl φρονέω.

καὶ. Adverbial use (adjunctive).

τοῦτο. Accusative direct object of ἀποκαλύψει. The near-demonstrative pronoun refers back to τι ἑτέρως (Runge 2010, 381). Fronted for emphasis.

ὁ θεὸς. Nominative subject of ἀποκαλύψει.

ὑμῖν. Dative indirect object of ἀποκαλύψει.

ἀποκαλύψει. Fut act ind 3rd sg ἀποκαλύπτω. The verb means "reveal, disclose, bring to light, make fully known" (BDAG, 112). The future tense conveys Paul's expectation that God will reveal to the Philippians the matter about which they presently hold a different opinion and bring them in conformity with his own view on this subject.

3:16 πλὴν εἰς ὃ ἐφθάσαμεν, τῷ αὐτῷ στοιχεῖν.

πλὴν. Adverb used as a conjunction at the beginning of a sentence. It breaks off a discussion and emphasizes what is important: "only, in any case, on the other hand, but" (BDAG, 826.1.c).

εἰς ὃ. Used with φθάνω to indicate the state that has been attained (BDAG, 1053.3). εἰς ὃ introduces a headless relative clause (εἰς ὃ ἐφθάσαμεν) that stands in a left-dislocation (cf. Runge 2010, 287–313) and is resumed by τῷ αὐτῷ. The placement of the relative clause in the left-dislocation functions as a thematic highlighter, calling attention to the spiritual state that has already been attained, which is in the next clause regarded as a standard for the Philippians' conduct.

ἐφθάσαμεν. Aor act ind 1st pl φθάνω. The verb means "to come to or arrive at a particular state," "attain" (BDAG, 1053.3).

τῷ αὐτῷ. Dative of rule. This use of dative, which is quite rare, occurs when "[t]he dative substantive specifies the rule or code a person follows or the standard of conduct to which he or she conforms" (Wallace 1996, 157). The personal pronoun αὐτῷ resumes the headless relative clause in the left-dislocation (εἰς ὃ ἐφθάσαμεν). It is fronted as a new topical frame, marking the transition from the left-dislocation to the main clause (cf. Runge 2010, 297). The article indicates that αὐτῷ functions as an identifying adjective that means "the same" (BDAG, 153.3).

στοιχεῖν. Pres act inf στοιχέω (imperatival). στοιχεῖν is one of the only three examples in the NT (the other two are found in Rom 12:5) of an imperatival infinitive (Wallace 1996, 608; BDF §389). It does not have an expressed subject. Wallace notes that regarding its function, στοιχεῖν "more resembles a hortatory subjunctive than an imperative" (1996, 608; cf. Fee, 360 n. 35). στοιχέω means "to be in line with a pers[on] or thing considered as standard for one's conduct," "hold to, agree with, follow, conform" (BDAG, 946). The imperfective aspect of the present tense portrays such conduct as an ongoing process.

Paul's terse style has prompted some scribes to add various clarifying words and phrases. There are four major textual variants of the second half of this verse:

(1) τῷ αὐτῷ στοιχεῖν ($\mathfrak{P}^{16.46}$ ℵ* A B I^{vid} 6 33 1739 b co Hil Aug)
(2) τῷ αὐτῷ στοιχεῖν κανόνι τὸ αὐτὸ φρονεῖν (ℵ² K L P Ψ 075 630 1505 2464 $\mathfrak{M}$ sy$^{(p)}$)
(3) τὸ αὐτὸ φρονεῖν τῷ αὐτῷ κανόνι στοιχεῖν (D 81 104 365 629 1175 1241 [vg])
(4) τὸ αὐτὸ φρονεῖν τῷ αὐτῷ συνστοιχεῖν (F G)

Reading (1) is clearly superior to other readings because it has the earliest manuscript support and can best explain the rise of other variants, which seek to identify the puzzling τῷ αὐτῷ by adding the noun κανόνι, perhaps under influence of Gal 6:16 (readings [2] and [3]), and/or to explain the entire phrase τῷ αὐτῷ στοιχεῖν by adding τὸ αὐτὸ φρονεῖν after (reading [2]) or before it (readings [3] and [4]).

Philippians 3:17-21

¹⁷Become fellow-imitators of me, brothers [and sisters], and observe those who live in this way, just as you have us as an example. ¹⁸For many live, about whom I often spoke to you—but now I speak even with tears—as the enemies of the cross of Christ, ¹⁹whose end [is] destruction, whose god [is] their stomach, and whose glory [is] in their disgrace, the ones who think about earthly things. ²⁰For our commonwealth is in heaven, from which we also eagerly await a Savior, the Lord Jesus Christ, ²¹who will transform our humble body [to become] similar in form to his glorious body according to his power even to subject all things to himself.

3:17 Συμμιμηταί μου γίνεσθε, ἀδελφοί, καὶ σκοπεῖτε τοὺς οὕτως περιπατοῦντας καθὼς ἔχετε τύπον ἡμᾶς.

Συμμιμηταί. Predicate nominative. Fronted for emphasis. The noun συμμιμητής ("fellow-imitator") is a genuine *hapax legomenon* because this is the only occurrence of this term in ancient Greek literature. Paul makes a similar appeal in 1 Cor 4:16 and 11:1 (μιμηταί μου γίνεσθε).

μου. Objective genitive modifying Συμμιμηταί. The Philippians are invited to join one another in imitating Paul rather than to join Paul (in that case, μου would be a genitive of association) in imitating someone else (Wallace 1996, 130).

γίνεσθε. Pres mid impv 2nd pl γίνομαι.

ἀδελφοί. Vocative of direct address (see 1:12).

καὶ. Coordinate conjunction, linking two clauses.

σκοπεῖτε. Pres act impv 2nd pl σκοπέω. The verb means "to pay careful attention to" (BDAG, 931).

τοὺς ... περιπατοῦντας. Pres act ptc masc acc pl περιπατέω (substantival). Accusative direct object of σκοπεῖτε. περιπατέω (lit. "to walk around") is here used figuratively, "to conduct one's life," "comport oneself, behave, live" (BDAG, 803.2).

οὕτως. Adverb of manner, which is used as an attributive modifier of περιπατοῦντας, standing in the first attributive position (see 1:5 on ἀπὸ τῆς πρώτης ἡμέρας).

καθὼς. Comparative adverb. The sense of καθὼς is correlated with οὕτως: "Mark those who walk in the way that our example has set for you" (de Boer, 180).

ἔχετε. Pres act ind 2nd pl ἔχω.

τύπον. Complement to ἡμᾶς in a double accusative object-complement construction. τύπον (from τύπος) here denotes "an archetype serving as a model" (BDAG, 1020.6), "example, pattern" (BDAG, 1020.6.b).

ἡμᾶς. Direct object of ἔχετε in a double accusative object-complement construction. The switch from the singular (μου) to the plural (ἡμᾶς) may be an example of the "editorial we" (Fee, 365 n. 14), which probably includes Timothy (1:1; 2:19-23) and Epaphroditus (2:25-30).

3:18 πολλοὶ γὰρ περιπατοῦσιν οὓς πολλάκις ἔλεγον ὑμῖν, νῦν δὲ καὶ κλαίων λέγω, τοὺς ἐχθροὺς τοῦ σταυροῦ τοῦ Χριστοῦ,

πολλοί. Nominative subject of περιπατοῦσιν. This adjective is here used as a substantive (BDAG, 848.1.a.β.ℵ).

γὰρ. Postpositive conjunction that introduces a clause that explains why the Philippians should imitate Paul.

περιπατοῦσιν. Pres act ind 3rd pl περιπατέω. On the meaning of the verb, see τοὺς ... περιπατοῦντας in the previous verse.

οὕς. Accusative direct object of ἔλεγον and λέγω in a double accusative object-complement construction. The antecedent of the relative pronoun οὕς is πολλοί.

πολλάκις. Adverb ("many times, often"). Fronted for emphasis.

ἔλεγον. Impf act ind 1st sg λέγω. The imperfective aspect of the verb portrays Paul's talking about this subject as an ongoing process, whereas πολλάκις indicates that this was an iterative activity.

ὑμῖν. Dative indirect object of ἔλεγον. Paul's use of the second-person plural pronoun indicates that the πολλοί about whom he speaks here are not among the recipients of this letter.

νῦν δὲ καὶ κλαίων λέγω. This clause functions as a metacomment (cf. Runge 2010, 101–24), which interrupts the flow of the relative clause to convey Paul's strong emotions as he speaks about such people as enemies of the cross in the present.

νῦν. Adverb of time ("now").

δὲ. Marker of development from πολλάκις ἔλεγον to νῦν . . . λέγω.

καὶ. Adverbial use (ascensive).

κλαίων. Pres act ptc masc nom sg κλαίω (manner). On adverbial participles that precede the main verb, see 1:25 on πεποιθώς.

λέγω. Pres act ind 1st sg λέγω.

τοὺς ἐχθρούς. Complement to οὕς in a double accusative object-complement construction. Paul says that he often spoke to the Philippians about πολλοί as the enemies of the cross (οὓς πολλάκις ἔλεγον ὑμῖν . . . τοὺς ἐχθροὺς τοῦ σταυροῦ τοῦ Χριστοῦ). τοὺς ἐχθρούς cannot be a direct object of περιπατοῦσιν because περιπατοῦσιν is an intransitive verb (*pace* Sumney, 93). The translation, "many live as enemies of the cross," adopted in some English versions (NRSV; NIV; NCV; ESV; HCSB), is a translation according to sense that renders the accusative τοὺς ἐχθρούς as if it is a nominative οἱ ἐχθροί in apposition to πολλοί (Hellerman 2015, 217; Haubeck and von Siebenthal, 1078). The article nominalizes the adjective ἐχθρούς (from ἐχθρός = "hostile") and makes it definite (Reumann, 570).

τοῦ σταυροῦ. Objective genitive modifying ἐχθρούς ("that which is the obj[ect] of enmity" [BDAG, 419.2.b.γ]). The noun σταυροῦ functions as metonymy for the death of Christ.

τοῦ Χριστοῦ. If τοῦ σταυροῦ is understood literally, τοῦ Χριστοῦ is the possessive genitive in a broader sense ("Christ's cross"). If τοῦ σταυροῦ stands for the death of Christ, τοῦ Χριστοῦ could be viewed as the subjective genitive ("the cross of Christ = Christ's death"). If τοῦ σταυροῦ conveys the idea of crucifixion, τοῦ Χριστοῦ could be understood as the objective genitive ("the cross of Christ" = "crucifying Christ").

3:19 ὧν τὸ τέλος ἀπώλεια, ὧν ὁ θεὸς ἡ κοιλία καὶ ἡ δόξα ἐν τῇ αἰσχύνῃ αὐτῶν, οἱ τὰ ἐπίγεια φρονοῦντες.

ὧν. Possessive genitive modifying τὸ τέλος ("whose end"). The antecedent of the relative pronoun is τοὺς ἐχθρούς in v. 18.

τὸ τέλος. Nominative subject of a verbless equative clause. The implied verb is ἐστίν. The noun τέλος denotes "the goal toward which a movement is being directed," "end, goal, outcome" (BDAG, 998.3).

ἀπώλεια. Predicate nominative.

ὧν. Possessive genitive modifying both ὁ θεὸς ("whose god") and ἡ δόξα ("whose glory"). The antecedent of the relative pronoun is again τοὺς ἐχθροὺς in v. 18. The relative clause ὧν ὁ θεὸς ἡ κοιλία is connected to the previous one by asyndeton.

ὁ θεὸς. Nominative subject of a verbless equative clause. The implied verb is again ἐστίν.

ἡ κοιλία. Predicate nominative. ἡ κοιλία ("belly, stomach" [BDAG, 550.1.b]) is a distributive singular. The definite article functions as a possessive pronoun ("their stomach"), which is usually the case "when human anatomy is involved" (Wallace 1996, 215), as here. κοιλία may be metonymy for gluttony (cf. Seneca, *Ben.* 7.26; *Vit. beat.* 9.4).

καὶ. Coordinate conjunction, linking two clauses governed by ὧν.

ἡ δόξα. Nominative subject of a verbless equative clause, with the implied ἐστίν. The term δόξα here denotes "honor as enhancement or recognition of status or performance," "fame, recognition, renown, honor, prestige" (BDAG, 257.3).

ἐν τῇ αἰσχύνῃ. State or condition (BDAG, 327.2.b).

αὐτῶν. Objective genitive modifying αἰσχύνη.

οἱ ... φρονοῦντες. Pres act ptc masc nom pl φρονέω (substantival). This participle could be viewed as (1) nominative in apposition to πολλοὶ in v. 18 (Fee, 368 n. 26), (2) nominative in apposition to the logical subject of the preceding relative clauses (BDF §136.1; §137.3), or (3) an anacoluthon—an abrupt nominative without any grammatical connection to the preceding material (Lightfoot, 156).

τὰ ἐπίγεια. Accusative direct object of φρονοῦντες. The adjective ἐπίγεια ("earthly") is used as a substantive ("the earthly things"). The direct object is placed between the article and the substantival participle for emphasis.

3:20 ἡμῶν γὰρ τὸ πολίτευμα ἐν οὐρανοῖς ὑπάρχει, ἐξ οὗ καὶ σωτῆρα ἀπεκδεχόμεθα κύριον Ἰησοῦν Χριστόν,

ἡμῶν. Possessive genitive modifying πολίτευμα. The preposed pronoun is thematically salient (Levinsohn 2000, 64), calling attention to a contrast between those who think earthly things and "us" (Fee, 378 n. 14).

γὰρ. Postpositive conjunction that typically has causal and explanatory force. In this verse, however, it introduces an explanation that is based on an opposition to the preceding description of those whose end is destruction (Zerwick §472). It should be kept in mind, though, that the contrast lies in the character of Paul's argument and not in an alleged adversative meaning for γὰρ (cf. Hellerman 2015, 221). A better option is to take the explanatory clause introduced with this γὰρ not with v. 19 but with v. 17. On this reading, v. 20 offers the second reason for why the Philippians should imitate Paul and those who live like him (cf. Fee, 378).

τὸ πολίτευμα. Nominative subject of ὑπάρχει. πολίτευμα is a NT *hapax legomenon*, but in 1:27 Paul uses its cognate πολιτεύεσθε (from πολιτεύομαι). According to LN (11.71), the noun denotes "the place or location in which one has the right to be a citizen—'state, commonwealth, place of citizenship.'" Spicq, however, emphasizes the communal aspect of the term when he says that "a *politeuma* is an organization of citizens from the same place, with the same rights (*isonomoi*) in the midst of a foreign state" (TLNT 3:130).

ἐν οὐρανοῖς. Locative. Fronted for emphasis. The noun οὐρανοῖς is in the plural under Semitic influence (Hebrew שָׁמַיִם; cf. Robertson, 408; BDF §141.1). Conceptually, the term is singular, referring to heaven as the abode of God (BDAG, 738.2).

ὑπάρχει. Pres act ind 3rd sg ὑπάρχω. In this context, ὑπάρχω means "exist, be present, be at one's disposal" (BDAG, 1029.1).

ἐξ οὗ. Source. The grammatical antecedent of the relative pronoun is πολίτευμα, with which it agrees in gender and number, which supports the understanding of πολίτευμα as a concrete place. It is better, however, to regard the plural οὐρανοῖς as an *ad sensum* antecedent of οὗ because the concept of heaven is singular (BDAG, 726.2.c.β.ℵ; Lightfoot, 156). On this reading, the term πολίτευμα does not need to have the spatial sense.

καὶ. Adverbial use (adjunctive).

σωτῆρα. Accusative direct object of ἀπεκδεχόμεθα. Fronted for emphasis.

ἀπεκδεχόμεθα. Pres mid ind 1st pl ἀπεκδέχομαι. The verb means "await eagerly" (BDAG, 100). The prefix ἀπό intensifies the sense of expectation.

κύριον Ἰησοῦν Χριστόν. Accusative in apposition to σωτῆρα. The appositional information receives prominence through right-dislocation (Runge 2010, 317–35).

3:21 ὃς μετασχηματίσει τὸ σῶμα τῆς ταπεινώσεως ἡμῶν σύμμορφον τῷ σώματι τῆς δόξης αὐτοῦ κατὰ τὴν ἐνέργειαν τοῦ δύνασθαι αὐτὸν καὶ ὑποτάξαι αὐτῷ τὰ πάντα.

ὅς. Nominative subject of μετασχηματίσει. The antecedent of the relative pronoun is σωτῆρα . . . κύριον Ἰησοῦν Χριστόν (v. 20).

μετασχηματίσει. Fut act ind 3rd sg μετασχηματίζω. The compound verb (μετά + σχηματίζω) means "to change the form of someth[ing]," "transform, change" (BDAG, 641.1).

τὸ σῶμα. Accusative direct object of μετασχηματίσει. τὸ σῶμα is a distributive singular.

τῆς ταπεινώσεως. Attributive genitive describing σῶμα ("the humble body"; cf. Robertson, 496; Zerwick §41) or possessive genitive modifying σῶμα ("the body that belongs to humiliation"; cf. Fee, 382 n. 28). The noun ταπείνωσις denotes "an unpretentious state or condition," "lowliness, humility, humble station" (BDAG, 990.2).

ἡμῶν. If ταπεινώσεως is an attributive genitive, ἡμῶν is a possessive genitive modifying σῶμα ("our humble body"). If ταπεινώσεως is a possessive genitive modifying σῶμα, ἡμῶν is a possessive genitive modifying ταπεινώσεως ("the body that belongs to our humiliation").

σύμμορφον. Predicate accusative. The adjective σύμμορφον ("similar in form" [BDAG, 958]) stands in predicate relationship to τὸ σῶμα, with which it is connected by an implied infinitive of γίνομαι. Some scribes tried to clarify the link between σῶμα and σύμμορφον by adding εἰς τὸ γενέσθαι αὐτό ("so that it will become") before σύμμορφον (D¹ K L P Ψ 075 33 104 365 630 1505 2464 𝔐 sy Ir Ambr). The shorter reading is to be preferred on both internal (it represents the *lectio difficilior*) and external grounds (it is attested in ℵ A B D* F G 6 81 323 1175 1241 1739 1881 latt co Ir^lat Tert).

τῷ σώματι. Dative complement of σύμμορφον.

τῆς δόξης. Attributive genitive describing σώματι ("the glorious body") or possessive genitive modifying σώματι ("the body that belongs to glory").

αὐτοῦ. If δόξης is an attributive genitive, αὐτοῦ is a possessive genitive modifying σώματι ("his glorious body"). If δόξης is a possessive genitive modifying σώματι, αὐτοῦ is a possessive genitive modifying δόξης ("the body that belongs to his glory").

κατὰ τὴν ἐνέργειαν. Causal, denoting "the norm [that] is at the same time the reason" (BDAG, 512.B.5.a.δ). ἐνέργεια denotes "the state or quality of being active," "working, operation, action" (BDAG, 335).

τοῦ δύνασθαι. Pres mid inf δύναμαι (epexegetical to τὴν ἐνέργειαν).

αὐτόν. Accusative subject of the infinitive τοῦ δύνασθαι. Lit. "according to (the fact that) he is able" (cf. Reumann, 581) = "according to his power" (my translation).

καί. Adverbial use (ascensive or adjunctive).

ὑποτάξαι. Aor act inf ὑποτάσσω (complementary to δύνασθαι). ὑποτάσσω means "to subject, to subordinate" (BDAG, 1042.1).

αὐτῷ. Dative indirect object of ὑποτάξαι. The personal pronoun is used here in a reflexive sense ("himself"; cf. Wallace 1996, 324–25; Zerwick §210), referring to Christ. Some correctors and later copyists explicate this sense by replacing αὐτῷ with ἑαυτῷ (ℵ² D² L Ψ 6 81^vid 104 326 630 1175 1241 *pm* lat).

τὰ πάντα. Accusative direct object of ὑποτάξαι.

Philippians 4:1-3

¹So then, my beloved and longed-for brothers [and sisters], my joy and crown, thus stand firm in the Lord, dear friends. ²I entreat Euodia and I entreat Syntyche to be of the same mind in the Lord. ³Yes, I ask also you, true companion, help these women who have struggled along with me in the gospel together with Clement and my other fellow-workers, whose names [are] in the book of life.

4:1 Ὥστε, ἀδελφοί μου ἀγαπητοὶ καὶ ἐπιπόθητοι, χαρὰ καὶ στέφανός μου, οὕτως στήκετε ἐν κυρίῳ, ἀγαπητοί.

Ὥστε. An inferential conjunction ("for this reason, therefore, so" [BDAG, 1107.1]) that introduces the conclusion drawn from the preceding material and marks the beginning of a new unit (cf. 2:12).

ἀδελφοί. Vocative of direct address (see 1:12).

μου. Genitive of relationship modifying ἀδελφοί.

ἀγαπητοί καὶ ἐπιπόθητοι. The verbal adjective ἀγαπητοί ("dear, beloved, prized, valued" [BDAG, 7.2]) and the *hapax legomenon* verbal adjective ἐπιπόθητοι ("longed for, desired" [BDAG, 377]) could be seen as attributive modifiers of ἀδελφοί standing in the fourth attributive position (Wallace 1996, 310–11) or as adjectival substantives in apposition to ἀδελφοί (cf. Sumney, 98). Most English translations reflect the first option, regardless of whether they place the adjectives before the noun ("my beloved and greatly desired brothers" [LEB]) or after it ("my brothers and sisters, whom I love and long for" [NRSV; ESV]; "my brethren dearly beloved and longed for" [KJV; ASV]; "my brothers, well loved and very dear to me" [BBE]).

χαρά. Vocative in apposition to ἀδελφοί. The noun functions as a collective singular.

καί. Coordinating conjunction connecting two vocatives that are appositional to ἀδελφοί.

στέφανός. Vocative in apposition to ἀδελφοί. This noun also functions as a collective singular. στέφανός (lit. "wreath, crown") is here used figuratively, denoting "that which serves as adornment or source of pride" (BDAG, 944.2). στέφανός, which has an acute accent on the antepenult, acquired an additional accent, the acute, on the ultima from the enclitic μου (Smyth §183; Carson 1985, 48).

μου. Possessive genitive modifying both χαρά and στέφανός.

οὕτως. Adverb of manner. Fronted for emphasis. οὕτως probably refers to the preceding exhortatory section in 3:17-21.

στήκετε. Pres act impv 2nd pl στήκω. The verb στήκω ("to be firmly committed in conviction or belief" [BDAG, 944.2]) is a common term in Pauline paranesis (cf. 1 Cor 16:13; Gal 5:1; Phil 1:27; 1 Thess 3:8).

ἐν κυρίῳ. Locative, denoting the sphere in which believers are to stand firm (Fee, 388 n. 22; Campbell 2012, 162).

ἀγαπητοί. Vocative in apposition to ἀδελφοί. The second occurrence of this adjective most likely functions as a substantive.

4:2 Εὐοδίαν παρακαλῶ καὶ Συντύχην παρακαλῶ τὸ αὐτὸ φρονεῖν ἐν κυρίῳ.

Εὐοδίαν. Accusative direct object of παρακαλῶ. Fronted for emphasis. Εὐοδία is a well-attested feminine name in Greek inscriptions (BDAG, 409), but we have no way of knowing the identity of the woman addressed here.

παρακαλῶ. Pres act ind 1st sg παρακαλέω. The verb means "to urge strongly," "appeal to, urge, exhort, encourage" (BDAG, 765.2). Contrary to his habit of using παρακαλέω to make communal appeals (παρακαλῶ ὑμᾶς; see Rom 12:1; 15:30; 16:17; 1 Cor 1:10; 4:16; 16:15; 2 Cor 2:8; 10:1), Paul employs the verb here—not just once but twice—to make a personal appeal.

καί. Coordinating conjunction.

Συντύχην. Accusative direct object of παρακαλῶ. Fronted for emphasis. Συντύχη is also a well-attested name in inscriptions (BDAG, 976), but the identity of the woman addressed in this letter remains unknown.

παρακαλῶ. Pres act ind 1st sg παρακαλέω. The repetition of the verb underscores the seriousness of Paul's appeal to these two women.

τὸ αὐτό. Accusative direct object of φρονεῖν. Fronted for emphasis. The article functions as a nominalizer and αὐτό as an identical adjective. Paul used τὸ αὐτό + φρονέω earlier in 2:2. τὸ αὐτὸ φρονεῖν ("to think the same thing") can be rendered in idiomatic English as "to be of the same mind" (NRSV; NIV; ASV), "to be in agreement" (LEB), or simply "to agree" (ESV; HCSB; NET).

φρονεῖν. Pres act inf φρονέω (indirect discourse).

ἐν κυρίῳ. Causal ("because of their common bond in the Lord") or locative ("in the realm of the Lord"). Campbell argues that the locative sense is more appropriate to this context because it draws attention to the right code of conduct: "Since believers live within Christ's domain, they are expected to conform to behavior that is appropriate to it" (2012, 163).

4:3 ναὶ ἐρωτῶ καὶ σέ, γνήσιε σύζυγε, συλλαμβάνου αὐταῖς, αἵτινες ἐν τῷ εὐαγγελίῳ συνήθλησάν μοι μετὰ καὶ Κλήμεντος καὶ τῶν λοιπῶν συνεργῶν μου, ὧν τὰ ὀνόματα ἐν βίβλῳ ζωῆς.

ναὶ. Affirmative particle used in emphatic repetition, consisting "in the fact that one request preceded and a similar one follows" (BDAG, 665.c).

ἐρωτῶ. Pres act ind 1st sg ἐρωτάω. Fee (391 n. 33) suggests that the switch from παρακαλῶ (v. 2) to ἐρωτῶ indicates a switch from addressing a subordinate to addressing an equal.

καὶ. Adverbial use (adjunctive). It qualifies σέ ("also you," "you too"; cf. NRSV; LEB; ESV) rather than ἐρωτῶ ("I also ask you"; cf. HCSB; CEB).

σέ. Accusative direct object of ἐρωτῶ.

γνήσιε σύζυγε. Vocative of direct address. The adjective γνήσιε ("legitimate, true" [BDAG, 202.1]) modifies the noun σύζυγε ("comrade, companion"; lit. "yoke-fellow" [BDAG, 954]), standing in the first (anarthrous) attributive position (see 1:4 on ἐν πάσῃ δεήσει). σύζυγος is a NT *hapax legomenon*. A corresponding proper name "Syzygus," found in some translations (NJB; MSG; GW) or footnotes (NRSV), has not yet been discovered in Greek literature (BDAG, 954; Fee, 392–93 n. 40).

συλλαμβάνου. Pres mid impv 2nd sg συλλαμβάνω. The verb means "to help by taking part w[ith] someone in an activity," "support, aid, help" (BDAG, 955.4).

αὐταῖς. Dative complement of συλλαμβάνου. αὐταῖς is usually translated as "these women" to convey the feminine gender of the personal pronoun.

αἵτινες. Nominative subject of συνήθλησάν. This indefinite relative pronoun functions here as a simple relative pronoun (cf. BDAG, 730.3), whose antecedent is αὐταῖς.

ἐν τῷ εὐαγγελίῳ. Locative. Fronted as a topical frame.

συνήθλησάν. Aor act ind 3rd pl συναθλέω. On the meaning of this verb, see 1:27.

μοι. Dative complement of συνήθλησάν.

μετὰ καὶ Κλήμεντος καὶ τῶν λοιπῶν συνεργῶν. Association. The first καὶ (after μετὰ) is either pleonastic (BDF §442.13) or adverbial (adjunctive). The second καὶ (after Κλήμεντος) functions as a coordinating conjunction. The adjective λοιπῶν ("pert[aining] to being one not previously cited or included," "other, rest of" [BDAG, 602.2]) modifies the substantive συνεργῶν ("helper, fellow-worker" [BDAG, 969]), standing in the first attributive position (see 1:5 on ἀπὸ τῆς πρώτης ἡμέρας).

μου. Genitive of association modifying συνεργῶν.

ὧν. Possessive genitive modifying ὀνόματα. The antecedent of the relative pronoun is not only τῶν λοιπῶν συνεργῶν but also the named individuals in vv. 2-3 (Εὐοδίαν, Συντύχην, and Κλήμεντος).

τὰ ὀνόματα. Nominative subject of an implied ἐστίν (because neuter plural subjects typically take singular verbs).

ἐν βίβλῳ. Locative. Even though βίβλῳ is anarthrous, it is probably definite because it is followed by a defining genitive (MHT 3:179). Omission of the article is common in genitive constructions that occur in prepositional phrases, as here (MHT 3:180).

ζωῆς. Epexegetical genitive (a.k.a. genitive of apposition or genitive of definition) explaining βίβλῳ ("the book which is life") or genitive of purpose modifying βίβλῳ ("the book for life"). The anarthrous ζωῆς conforms to Apollonius' canon, which states that the head noun and genitive noun mimic each other with regard to articularity (Wallace 1996, 239). Elsewhere in the NT, the expression ἡ βίβλος τῆς ζωῆς occurs in Rev 3:5; 13:8; 17:8; 20:15; 21:27.

Philippians 4:4-7

⁴Rejoice in the Lord always! Again I will say, rejoice! ⁵Let your gentleness be known to all people. The Lord [is] near. ⁶Do not be anxious about anything, but in everything, by prayer and supplication, with thanksgiving let your requests be made known to God. ⁷And the peace of God that surpasses all understanding will guard your hearts and your thoughts in Christ Jesus.

4:4 Χαίρετε ἐν κυρίῳ πάντοτε· πάλιν ἐρῶ, χαίρετε.

Χαίρετε. Pres act impv 2nd pl χαίρω. The same encouragement (χαίρετε ἐν κυρίῳ) occurred earlier in 3:1. The adverb πάντοτε, however, indicates that Χαίρετε in this verse cannot be understood as a farewell greeting but as a repeated emphasis of joy and rejoicing as a dominant theme of Philippians (see 1:18; 2:17, 18, 28; 3:1; 4:10). This clause is connected to the previous one by asyndeton.

ἐν κυρίῳ. Causal, close association, or locative (see 3:1).

πάντοτε. Temporal adverb ("always, at all times"). πάντοτε modifies Χαίρετε.

πάλιν ἐρῶ. This clause functions as a metacomment, calling attention to Paul's repeated call to rejoice (cf. Runge 2010, 101–24).

πάλιν. Adverb "pert[aining] to repetition in the same (or similar) manner" (BDAG, 752.2). πάλιν modifies ἐρῶ and is fronted for emphasis. The clause introduced with this adverb is connected to the previous one by asyndeton.

ἐρῶ. Fut act ind 1st sg λέγω.

χαίρετε. Pres act impv 2nd pl χαίρω.

4:5 τὸ ἐπιεικὲς ὑμῶν γνωσθήτω πᾶσιν ἀνθρώποις. ὁ κύριος ἐγγύς.

τὸ ἐπιεικὲς. Nominative subject of γνωσθήτω. Fronted as a topical frame. This exhortation is connected to the previous admonition by asyndeton. The neut sg adjective ἐπιεικὲς (from ἐπιεικής = "yielding, gentle, kind, courteous, tolerant") is here used as an articular substantive that is analogous to ἡ ἐπιείκεια (BDAG, 371). Although this word group is often used to describe graciousness of someone in a position of power and authority (2 Macc 9:27; Acts 24:4; 2 Cor 10:1; 1 Pet 2:18), Wis 2:19 ("Let us test him with insult and torture, so that we may find out how gentle he is [ἵνα γνῶμεν τὴν ἐπιείκειαν αὐτοῦ] and make trial of his forbearance") shows that it can also be applied to a subordinate or an inferior.

ὑμῶν. Possessive genitive modifying ἐπιεικὲς.

γνωσθήτω. Aor pass impv 3rd sg γινώσκω. The English translation of the third-person imperative "let your gentleness be known" should not be confused with a permissive idea. The Greek verb form conveys the command that involves volition and places a requirement on the recipients of the letter (Wallace 1996, 486 n. 97). The aorist imperative does not mean that Paul demands a momentary action; rather, the aorist imperative means that the activity of making their gentleness be known is portrayed as a whole (perfective aspect). Fanning (352) notes that lexical distinctions between the ingressive sense of γινώσκω ("recognize," "come to know") and its stative sense ("be aware," "keep in mind") are particularly elusive in commands and prohibitions. Nevertheless, he suggests that Paul's use of γνωσθήτω in this verse puts emphasis "on the beginning of the occurrence or on a change from some previous conduct" (368; cf. Wallace 1996, 720).

πᾶσιν ἀνθρώποις. Dative indirect object of γνωσθήτω. The adjective πᾶσιν stands in the first (anarthrous) attributive position (see 1:4 on ἐν πάσῃ δεήσει).

ὁ κύριος. Nominative subject of an implied ἔστιν. As elsewhere in Philippians (1:2, 14; 2:11, 19, 24, 29; 3:1, 8, 20; 4:1, 2, 10, 23) and other letters of Paul (Rom 1:4; 10:9; 12:11; 16:12; 1 Cor 4:17; 6:13-14, 17; 11:23), this designation refers to Christ.

ἐγγύς. Predicate adverb. In this verbless clause, which is connected to the previous one by asyndeton, the adverb ἐγγύς (which could indicate spatial or temporal proximity) is used like an adjective functioning as a predicate of the implied equative verb (MHT 3:226; BDF §434.1).

4:6 μηδὲν μεριμνᾶτε, ἀλλ' ἐν παντὶ τῇ προσευχῇ καὶ τῇ δεήσει μετὰ εὐχαριστίας τὰ αἰτήματα ὑμῶν γνωριζέσθω πρὸς τὸν θεόν.

μηδὲν ... ἀλλ'. A point/counterpoint set that replaces anxiety with prayer. The negative substantive μηδὲν functions either as the accusative of respect or as the cognate accusative (if μηδὲν stands for μηδεμίαν μεριμνάν; cf. Moule, 34).

μεριμνᾶτε. Pres act impv 2nd pl μεριμνάω. Here μεριμνάω means "to be apprehensive," "have anxiety, be anxious, be (unduly) concerned" (BDAG, 632.1; see 2:20, where μεριμνάω has a positive connotation). Although the use of the present imperative in a prohibition does not automatically mean the cessation of an activity that is already in progress (Wallace 1996, 714–17), in this context, μηδὲν μεριμνᾶτε probably means to stop being unduly concerned (Hellerman 2015, 238).

ἐν παντί. Circumstance or condition ("in every situation") rather than temporal ("always"; *pace* Holloway, 183 n. 17). Since παντί is neuter in gender, it does not modify the feminine noun τῇ προσευχῇ but functions as a substantive ("in everything"). The PP ἐν παντί is fronted as a topical frame in the point clause, creating a marked contrast with μηδὲν in the counterpoint clause.

τῇ προσευχῇ καὶ τῇ δεήσει. Datives of means (Wallace 1996, 163, 435). Although the semantic domains of these two nouns significantly overlap, προσευχή is a broader term ("petition addressed to deity," "prayer" [BDAG, 878.1]) than δέησις ("urgent request to meet a need, exclusively addressed to God," "prayer" [BDAG, 213]).

μετὰ εὐχαριστίας. Manner. This PP does not qualify the preceding datives ("by prayer and supplication with thanksgiving") but goes with the imperative γνωριζέσθω, describing how the requests should be presented to God (cf. Silva, 199). The noun εὐχαριστία denotes "gratitude for benefits or blessings" (LN 33.349).

τὰ αἰτήματα. Nominative subject of γνωριζέσθω. αἰτήματα could be translated as "requests" or "demands" (BDAG, 30). This is the only occurrence of this term in Paul's letters.

ὑμῶν. Subjective genitive modifying αἰτήματα.

γνωριζέσθω. Pres pass impv 3rd sg γνωρίζω. Neuter plural subjects typically take singular verbs (BDF §133). On the function of a third-person imperative as a demand that involves volition, see 4:6 on γνωσθήτω. Although the use of the causative verb γνωρίζω ("to cause information to become known" [BDAG, 203.1]) may suggest that God is unaware of the needs of believers until they reveal them to God in prayer, theologically the causative effect works backward: by bringing their personal requests to God, the petitioners become aware that God knows their needs and desires (O'Brien, 493). Wallace (1996, 489) calls the imperative that is followed by καί + the future indicative a "conditional imperative" because it conveys the idea that "if X, then Y will happen." On this reading, the imperative γνωριζέσθω + καὶ (v. 7) + the future φρουρήσει (v. 7) means "*if* you let your requests be made known to God, *then* the peace of God that surpasses all understanding will guard your hearts and your thoughts in Christ Jesus."

πρὸς τὸν θεόν. Locative (motion toward). In this PP, πρὸς serves as a "marker of movement or orientation toward someone" (BDAG, 874.3).

4:7 καὶ ἡ εἰρήνη τοῦ θεοῦ ἡ ὑπερέχουσα πάντα νοῦν φρουρήσει τὰς καρδίας ὑμῶν καὶ τὰ νοήματα ὑμῶν ἐν Χριστῷ Ἰησοῦ.

καὶ. Coordinating conjunction. This unusual way of starting a sentence may be explained by taking this καὶ as part of the sequence that began in the previous verse: the imperative γνωριζέσθω (v. 6) + καί + future indicative φρουρήσει (see 4:6 on γνωριζέσθω).

ἡ εἰρήνη. Nominative subject of φρουρήσει.

τοῦ θεοῦ. Genitive of producer ("the peace produced by God"; cf. Wallace 1996, 106), subjective genitive ("the peace that God gives"; cf. Robertson, 499), or genitive of source modifying εἰρήνη ("the peace that comes from God"; cf. Sumney, 104).

ἡ ὑπερέχουσα. Pres act ptc fem nom sg ὑπερέχω (attributive). The participle modifies εἰρήνη, standing in the second attributive position (see 1:1 on τοῖς οὖσιν). ὑπερέχω here means "to surpass in quality or value" (BDAG, 1033.3). Elsewhere in Philippians, ὑπερέχω occurs in 2:3 and 3:8.

πάντα νοῦν. Accusative direct object of ὑπερέχουσα. The noun νοῦς denotes "understanding, mind as the faculty of thinking" (BDAG, 680.1.b). This is the only occurrence of this term in Philippians. The adjective πάντα modifies νοῦν, standing in the first (anarthrous) attributive position (see 1:4 on ἐν πάσῃ δεήσει).

φρουρήσει. Fut act ind 3rd sg φρουρέω. On the sequence imperative + καί + future indicative, see 4:6 on γνωριζέσθω. φρουρέω is a military term (lit. "to maintain a watch" [BDAG, 1066.1]) that here means "to provide security," "guard, protect, keep" (BDAG, 1067.3).

τὰς καρδίας ὑμῶν καὶ τὰ νοήματα ὑμῶν. Although there is a considerable semantic overlap between the meanings of καρδίας and νοήματα (see below), these two direct objects of φρουρήσει are here "emphatically separated" (O'Brien, 498), each having its own article and each having its own qualifying pronoun ὑμῶν. The replacement of νοήματα with σώματα in some Western witnesses (F G ar d MVict Pel) or the addition of τὰ σώματα after νοήματα in 𝔓16vid are scribal alterations "in order to diversify still further the domains covered by καρδίας and νοήματα" (Metzger, 549).

τὰς καρδίας. Accusative direct object of φρουρήσει. The term καρδία denotes "the causative source of a person's psychological life in its various aspects, but with special emphasis upon thoughts—'heart, inner self, mind'" (LN 26.4). LN adds in a note that "[t]hough in English the term 'heart' focuses primarily upon the emotive aspects of life, in the Greek NT the emphasis is more upon the result of thought, particularly in view of the relationship of καρδία to the Hebrew term *lēb*, which, though literally meaning 'heart,' refers primarily to the mind."

ὑμῶν. Possessive genitive modifying καρδίας.

καί. Coordinating conjunction.

τὰ νοήματα. Accusative direct object of φρουρήσει. The noun νόημα, which in the NT occurs only in the letters of Paul (here and five times in 2 Corinthians [2:11; 3:14; 4:4; 10:5; 11:3]), denotes either "that which one has in mind as product of intellectual process," "thought" (BDAG, 675.1.a) or "the faculty of processing thought," "mind, understanding" (BDAG, 675.2). The first option regards νόημα as the result of the activity of the νοῦς, whereas the second option regards νόημα and νοῦς as synonyms (cf. LN 26.14).

ὑμῶν. Possessive genitive modifying νοήματα.

ἐν Χριστῷ Ἰησοῦ. Locative (the peace of God characterizes life within the realm of Christ), instrumental (God guards the hearts and thoughts of believers through Christ), or causal (the person and work of Christ is the grounds on which the peace of God guards the hearts and thoughts of believers). For an assessment of these options, see Campbell (2012, 89–90). Campbell may be right that causal function best explains the flow of thought in 4:6-7 from anxiety, via prayer, to peace.

Philippians 4:8-9

⁸Finally, brothers [and sisters], whatever things are true, whatever things [are] honorable, whatever things [are] right, whatever things [are] pure, whatever things [are] pleasing, whatever things [are] commendable—if [there is] any virtue and if [there is] anything praiseworthy, think about these things. ⁹The things which you have both learned and received and heard and seen in me—keep doing these things, and the God of peace will be with you.

4:8 Τὸ λοιπόν, ἀδελφοί, ὅσα ἐστὶν ἀληθῆ, ὅσα σεμνά, ὅσα δίκαια, ὅσα ἁγνά, ὅσα προσφιλῆ, ὅσα εὔφημα, εἴ τις ἀρετὴ καὶ εἴ τις ἔπαινος, ταῦτα λογίζεσθε·

Τὸ λοιπόν. Adverbial accusative of time (see 3:1). Fronted as a topical frame. Although Τὸ λοιπόν could signal the end of the letter ("as far as the rest is concerned, beyond that, in addition, finally" [BDAG, 602.3.b]), it probably marks a transition to the final section of Paul's exhortation. Robertson (1146) suggests that it functions almost like οὖν, but O'Brien is more precise when he says that Τὸ λοιπόν introduces a "fresh idea, which is not logically connected with the previous sentence" (503).

ἀδελφοί. Vocative of direct address (see 1:12).

ὅσα ἐστὶν ἀληθῆ, ὅσα σεμνά, ὅσα δίκαια, ὅσα ἁγνά, ὅσα προσφιλῆ, ὅσα εὔφημα. Six relative clauses in a left-dislocation (Runge 2010, 287–313), which are jointly resumed by ταῦτα. The left-dislocation of this pendent construction draws attention to various ethical qualities that Paul wants his readers to focus on and reflect about. The statement "whatever things are true, whatever things [are] honorable, whatever things [are] right, whatever things [are] pure, whatever things [are] pleasing, whatever things [are] commendable . . . think about these things" is rhetorically more effective than a straightforward statement, "Think about true, honorable, right, pure, pleasing, and commendable things."

ὅσα . . . ὅσα . . . ὅσα . . . ὅσα . . . ὅσα . . . ὅσα. Relative pronouns "pert[aining] to a comparative quantity or number of objects or events" (BDAG, 729.2). Each ὅσα functions as the subject of the stated ἐστίν (first pronoun) or an implied ἐστίν (the other five pronouns).

ἐστίν. Pres act ind 3rd sg εἰμί. The verb is in the singular because neuter plural subjects typically take singular verbs (BDF §133).

ἀληθῆ. Predicate adjective in the first relative clause. ἀληθῆ (neut pl from ἀληθής) "pert[ains] to being in accordance with fact," "true" (BDAG, 43.2).

σεμνά. Predicate adjective in the second relative clause. σεμνά (neut pl from σεμνός) means "honorable, worthy, venerable, holy, above reproach" (BDAG, 919.b).

δίκαια. Predicate adjective in the third relative clause. δίκαια (neut pl from δίκαιος) "denotes that which is obligatory in view of certain requirements of justice," "right, fair, equitable" (BDAG, 247.2).

ἁγνά. Predicate adjective in the fourth relative clause. ἁγνά (neut pl from ἁγνός) is a cultic term that means "pure, holy" (BDAG, 13).

προσφιλῆ. Predicate adjective in the fifth relative clause. προσφιλῆ (neut pl from προσφιλής) is a NT *hapax legomenon* that "pert[ains] to causing pleasure or delight," "pleasing, agreeable, lovely, amiable" (BDAG, 886).

εὔφημα. Predicate adjective in the sixth relative clause. εὔφημα (neut pl from εὔφημος) is another NT *hapax legomenon* that means "praiseworthy, commendable" (BDAG, 414).

εἴ. Introduces the first protasis of a first-class condition. The proclitic εἰ acquired an acute accent from the enclitic τις (Carson, 49).

τις ἀρετή. Nominative subject of an implied ἐστίν. ἀρετή denotes "uncommon character worthy of praise," "excellence of character, exceptional civic virtue" (BDAG, 130.1). The indefinite pronoun τις functions as an adjectival modifier of ἀρετή ("any virtue").

καί. Coordinating conjunction, linking the corresponding elements of the two-part protasis.

εἴ. Introduces the second protasis of a first-class condition. The proclitic εἰ acquired an acute accent from the enclitic τις (Carson, 49).

τις ἔπαινος. Nominative subject of an implied ἐστίν. ἔπαινος denotes "a thing worthy of praise" (BDAG, 357.2). The indefinite pronoun τις functions as an adjectival modifier of ἔπαινος ("anything worthy of praise"). The addition of the genitive ἐπιστήμης after ἔπαινος ("worthy of praise of understanding") in some Western witnesses (D* F G ar vg[cl] Ambst) is a scribal attempt to clarify the meaning of this adjective (Metzger, 549–50).

ταῦτα. Accusative direct object of λογίζεσθε. The near-demonstrative pronoun resumes the six ὅσα clauses in the left-dislocation. ταῦτα is fronted for emphasis, marking the beginning of the apodosis of a first-class condition.

λογίζεσθε. Pres mid impv 2nd pl λογίζομαι. In this context, λογίζομαι means "to give careful thought to a matter," "think (about), consider, ponder, let one's mind dwell on" (BDAG, 598.2).

4:9 ἃ καὶ ἐμάθετε καὶ παρελάβετε καὶ ἠκούσατε καὶ εἴδετε ἐν ἐμοί, ταῦτα πράσσετε· καὶ ὁ θεὸς τῆς εἰρήνης ἔσται μεθ᾽ ὑμῶν.

ἅ. The relative pronoun introduces a headless relative clause (ἃ καὶ ἐμάθετε καὶ παρελάβετε καὶ ἠκούσατε καὶ εἴδετε ἐν ἐμοί) that stands in a left-dislocation (cf. Runge 2010, 287–313) and is resumed by ταῦτα. Within its clause, ἅ is the accusative direct object of ἐμάθετε, παρελάβετε, ἠκούσατε, and εἴδετε.

καὶ . . . καὶ . . . καὶ . . . καὶ. Each verb is preceded by the coordinating conjunction καί. This sequence of words connected with καί is an example of polysyndeton, which "produces the impression of extensiveness and abundance by means of an exhausting summary" (BDF §460.3). The initial καὶ, which at first sight appears to be superfluous, is best understood in correlation with the second καὶ, creating the "both . . . and" construction (Hellerman 2015, 249).

ἐμάθετε. Aor act ind 2nd pl μανθάνω. μανθάνω means "to gain knowledge or skill by instruction" (BDAG, 615.1). The perfective aspect of this and the next three aorist verbs indicates that Paul portrays each activity—learning, acceptance, hearing, and seeing—as a whole with no reference to any process that might have been involved.

παρελάβετε. Aor act ind 2nd pl παραλαμβάνω. If in this context the emphasis lies on receiving something transmitted by tradition (cf. 1 Cor 15:1, 3), παρελάβετε could be viewed as a technical term for the reception of Christian tradition that Paul handed over to the Philippians (O'Brien, 509–10). If, however, the emphasis "lies not so much on receiving or taking over, as on the fact that the word implies agreement or approval" (BDAG, 768.3), παρελάβετε could be rendered as "you have accepted." My translation reflects the second option.

ἠκούσατε. Aor act ind 2nd pl ἀκούω.

εἴδετε. Aor act ind 2nd pl ὁράω.

ἐν ἐμοί. Locative. The word order and the sense of ἐν ἐμοί indicate that the PP modifies εἴδετε, but its placement at the end of the relative clause may have been "for rhetorical effect, that is, to indicate in an emphatic way that everything they had learnt, received, heard, and seen had been embodied in Paul himself" (O'Brien, 511).

ταῦτα. Accusative direct object of πράσσετε. The near-demonstrative pronoun resumes the headless relative clause in a left-dislocation (ἃ καὶ ἐμάθετε καὶ παρελάβετε καὶ ἠκούσατε καὶ εἴδετε ἐν ἐμοί). It is fronted for emphasis, marking the transition from the left-dislocation to the main clause (cf. Runge 2010, 297).

πράσσετε. Pres act impv 2nd pl πράσσω. Here πράσσω means "to bring about or accomplish someth[ing] through activity" (BDAG, 860.1). The imperfective aspect of the verb form draws attention to the ongoing character of doing the things that the Philippians have learned, accepted, heard, and seen in Paul. The imperative πράσσετε, followed by καί and the future indicative ἔσται, fulfills the conditions for what Wallace (1996, 489) calls "conditional imperative" because it conveys the idea that "if X, then Y will happen." If this interpretation of the syntax is accepted, ταῦτα πράσσετε καὶ ὁ θεὸς τῆς εἰρήνης ἔσται μεθ' ὑμῶν could be understood as a conditional clause: "If you do these things, the God of peace will be with you" (cf. NAB; Sumney, 108).

καί. Coordinating conjunction linking two clauses.

ὁ θεός. Nominative subject of ἔσται.

τῆς εἰρήνης. Genitive of product ("God who produces peace," "God who gives peace"; cf. Wallace 1996, 106–7) or descriptive genitive modifying θεός ("God who is characterized by peace"). Elsewhere in his letters, Paul uses the expression ὁ θεὸς τῆς εἰρήνης in Rom 15:33; 16:20; and 1 Thess 5:23 (cf. 1 Cor 14:33; 2 Cor 13:11).

ἔσται. Fut act ind 3rd sg εἰμί.

μεθ' ὑμῶν. Association/accompaniment (BDAG, 636.2.a.γ.ℶ).

Philippians 4:10-20

[10]I rejoiced in the Lord greatly because now at last you have renewed your concern for me, for whom you were indeed concerned, but you lacked opportunity. [11]Not that I speak out of need, for I have learned, in whatever circumstances I am, to be content. [12]I know how even to live in humble circumstances, I know how also to have an abundance. In any and all circumstances, I have learned the secret both to be well fed and to be hungry, both to have an abundance and to be in need. [13]I am able to do all things through him who strengthens me. [14]Nevertheless, you have done well by taking part in my trouble. [15]And you, Philippians, also know that at the beginning of the gospel, when I departed from Macedonia, no church shared with me in the matter of giving and receiving except you alone, [16]because even in Thessalonica more than once you sent to me for [my] need. [17]Not that I desire the gift, but I desire the profit that increases to your account. [18]But I have received everything in full, and I have an abundance. I am fully supplied because I have received from Epaphroditus what you sent—a fragrant odor, an acceptable sacrifice, pleasing to God. [19]And my God will supply every need of

yours according to his riches in glory in Christ Jesus. ²⁰Now to our God and Father [be] the glory forever and ever. Amen.

4:10 Ἐχάρην δὲ ἐν κυρίῳ μεγάλως ὅτι ἤδη ποτὲ ἀνεθάλετε τὸ ὑπὲρ ἐμοῦ φρονεῖν, ἐφ' ᾧ καὶ ἐφρονεῖτε, ἠκαιρεῖσθε δέ.

Ἐχάρην. Aor pass ind 1st sg χαίρω. Ἐχάρην is sometimes viewed as an epistolary aorist (e.g., NRSV: "I rejoice"), but it is more likely that it describes Paul's joy occasioned by his reception of the Philippians' gift, which was from his perspective already a past event (O'Brien, 516; Reumann, 647; Fee, 428 n. 17).

δὲ. Marker of development, signaling the beginning of a new section.

ἐν κυρίῳ. Causal ("because of the Lord"), indicating the ultimate cause of Paul's joy (Campbell 2012, 163; Hansen, 306; O'Brien, 517).

μεγάλως. Adverb of manner ("greatly"). A NT *hapax legomenon*.

ὅτι. Introduces a causal clause that supplies the reason for Paul's joy. Although many English translations sound as if ὅτι introduces a nominal clause giving the content of Paul's joy (e.g., NRSV: ". . . that now at last you have revived your concern for me"), the ὅτι clause with χαίρω gives the reason for someone's rejoicing (BDAG, 1075.1). To convey this sense in English, it is better to render ὅτι with "because" than with "that."

ἤδη ποτὲ. An idiom consisting of the temporal adverb ἤδη ("now, already") and the particle ποτέ ("at some time or other"), which is used as a marker of culmination: "now at last" (BDAG, 434.2; 856.1). Fronted as a temporal frame.

ἀνεθάλετε. Aor act ind 2nd pl ἀναθάλλω. A NT *hapax legomenon*. ἀναθάλλω (lit. "grow up again, bloom again" [BDAG, 63.1]) is here used transitively and figuratively: "to cause to be in a state identical with a previous state," "revive" (BDAG, 63.2).

τὸ . . . φρονεῖν. Pres act inf φρονέω. The articular infinitival phrase, τὸ ὑπὲρ ἐμοῦ φρονεῖν, functions as direct object of ἀνεθάλετε (cf. Wallace 1996, 602). With ὑπέρ τινος, φρονέω means "think of someone" in the sense "be concerned about him" (BDAG, 1065.1).

ὑπὲρ ἐμοῦ. Advantage (lit. "on behalf of me"). In this PP, ὑπὲρ functions as "a marker indicating that an activity or event is in some entity's interest" (BDAG, 1030.A.1.).

ἐφ' ᾧ. Cause or purpose. Causal function is based on the idiomatic use of the PP ἐφ' ᾧ in Rom 5:12 and 2 Cor 5:4, where it stands for ἐπὶ τούτῳ ὅτι, "for this reason that, because" (BDAG, 365.6.c). Here, however, purpose seems more appropriate (cf. Zerwick §129; BDAG, 366.16), regardless of whether the antecedent of ᾧ is ἐμοῦ, i.e., Paul (cf. ESV: "you were indeed concerned for me"), or the antecedent is "'my wants, my interests,' being involved in, though not identical with, τὸ ὑπὲρ ἐμοῦ φρονεῖν" (Lightfoot, 163; cf. Moule, 132: "with regard to which"). My translation ("for whom") presumes that ἐμοῦ is the antecedent of ᾧ.

καί. Adverbial use (adjunctive). καί reinforces the repeated use of φρονέω, emphasizing that the Philippians have not only shown their concern for Paul by sending their gift but were also concerned for him during the entire time before they had the opportunity to help him in a concrete way.

ἐφρονεῖτε. Impf act ind 2nd pl φρονέω. The verb has the same meaning ("be concerned about someone") as in the previous ὅτι clause. The imperfective aspect of the verb form emphasizes the Philippians' ongoing concern for Paul.

ἠκαιρεῖσθε. Impf mid ind 2nd pl ἀκαιρέομαι. A NT *hapax legomenon*. This alpha-privative verb means "to lack an opportune time for doing someth[ing]," "have no opportunity, have no time" (BDAG, 34). The imperfective aspect of the verb points to the ongoing lack of opportunity to do something concrete for Paul.

δέ. Marker of development with adversative nuance.

4:11 οὐχ ὅτι καθ' ὑστέρησιν λέγω, ἐγὼ γὰρ ἔμαθον ἐν οἷς εἰμι αὐτάρκης εἶναι.

Οὐχ ὅτι. An ellipsis for οὐ λέγω ὅτι (BDF §480.5). Paul frequently uses this formulaic expression (2 Cor 1:24; 3:5; 7:9; Phil 3:12; 4:11, 17; 2 Thess 3:9) to qualify something in the preceding material to avoid misunderstanding. In this case, the possible misunderstanding could be that Paul is rejoicing because his needs have been satisfied or that he is asking for more assistance at present.

Οὐχ. Negative particle normally used with indicative verbs.

ὅτι. Introduces the clausal complement (indirect discourse) of an implied λέγω (see Οὐχ ὅτι above).

καθ' ὑστέρησιν. Causal, denoting "the norm [that] is at the same time the reason, so that *in accordance with* and *because of* are merged" (BDAG, 512.B.5.a.δ). The noun ὑστέρησις denotes "the condition of lacking that which is essential" (BDAG, 1044). Lit. "not that I speak as a result of want," i.e., "not that I am prompted to speak by any lack" (Zerwick and Grosvenor, 601).

λέγω. Pres act ind 1st sg λέγω.

ἐγώ. Nominative subject of ἔμαθον. It is not fronted for emphasis (MHT 3:37) but as a topical frame.

γάρ. Postpositive conjunction introducing a clause that clarifies why Paul does not speak out of need.

ἔμαθον. Aor act ind 1st sg μανθάνω. In this context, μανθάνω means "to come to a realization, with implication of taking place less through instruction than through experience or practice" (BDAG, 615.3). The perfective aspect of the aorist tense portrays Paul's experience of learning how to be content in every situation as a whole rather than as a process. "Duration is implied but the more important point is that the action is viewed as *completed*" (Fanning, 153).

ἐν οἷς. Circumstance or condition. The relative pronoun does not have a specific antecedent but most likely refers to Paul's circumstances. His use of a regular relative pronoun rather than an indefinite pronoun may indicate that he refers to his actual situation at the time of writing (ἐν οἷς εἰμι = ἐν τούτοις ἐν οἷς εἰμι; cf. Robertson, 721; Zerwick and Grosvenor, 601). His description of all kinds of experiences in the next verse (ἐν παντὶ καὶ ἐν πᾶσιν), however, suggests that Paul here probably refers to all and any circumstances in which he might find himself (Fee, 431 n. 36).

εἰμι. Pres act ind 1st sg εἰμί.

αὐτάρκης. Predicate adjective. Fronted for emphasis. αὐτάρκης ("content, self-sufficient" [BDAG, 152]) is a NT *hapax legomenon*, but a cognate noun αὐτάρκεια occurs in 2 Cor 9:8 and 1 Tim 6:6. These terms were used in the Stoic philosophical traditions to convey the concept of self-sufficiency (e.g., Seneca, *Vit. beat.* 6.2; *Ep.* 9.13; Epictetus, *Diatr.* 4.7.14). Paul, however, uses the adjective αὐτάρκης in a nontechnical sense to express his contentment derived from his complete dependence on God (see v. 13). αὐτάρκης is in the nominative because the implied subject of the infinitive εἶναι (ἐγώ) is identical to the nominative subject of the governing verb ἔμαθον (BDF §396; §405).

εἶναι. Pres act inf εἰμί. This infinitive could be seen either as a complement or as a direct object of ἔμαθον.

4:12 οἶδα καὶ ταπεινοῦσθαι, οἶδα καὶ περισσεύειν· ἐν παντὶ καὶ ἐν πᾶσιν μεμύημαι, καὶ χορτάζεσθαι καὶ πεινᾶν καὶ περισσεύειν καὶ ὑστερεῖσθαι·

οἶδα καὶ ταπεινοῦσθαι, οἶδα καὶ περισσεύειν. Two clauses in antithetical parallelism.

οἶδα. Prf act ind 1st sg οἶδα. The perfect tense has the present meaning, describing "the enduring result rather than the completed act" (Smyth §1946). In this context, οἶδα means "to know/understand how" (BDAG, 694.3), expressing knowledge acquired through experience rather than through instruction or revelation.

καὶ ... καί. It is usually assumed that these two conjunctions are correlated, creating a "both ... and" structure (cf. Sumney, 112; Hellerman 2015, 259). This interpretation would certainly be persuasive had Paul simply said, οἶδα καὶ ταπεινοῦσθαι καὶ περισσεύειν, as he does in the second half of the verse, in which the finite verb μεμύημαι is followed by four infinitives, each preceded by a καί. The repetition of οἶδα, however, is peculiar and creates a cumbersome sentence structure if the correlative interpretation of the conjunctions is accepted (e.g., LEB: "I know [how] both to make do with little and I know [how] to have an abundance"), which most English versions try to circumvent by not translating the first καί. In my view, a better approach is to interpret both occurrences of καί adverbially, the first with the ascensive sense and the second with the adjunctive sense: "even ... also" (cf. BDF §444.3; Reumann, 646, 654).

ταπεινοῦσθαι. Pres pass inf ταπεινόω. The infinitive ταπεινοῦσθαι (lit. "to be humbled") functions as the direct object of οἶδα. All infinitives in this verse are in the present tense, whose imperfective aspect highlights the durative character of each way of life that Paul experienced. Since ταπεινόω is not paired with the ὑψόω but with περισσεύω, the opposition is not between humility and exaltation but between life in economic deprivation and life in abundance. Consequently, ταπεινόω means "to live in circumstances regarded as characteristic of low status—'to live in humble circumstances, to live like those of low status'" (LN 87.63). The verb is in the passive voice, "since the discussion assumes the effect of external circumstances beyond Paul's control" (Hellerman 2015, 260).

οἶδα. Prf act ind 1st sg οἶδα (see above).

περισσεύειν. Pres act inf περισσεύω. The infinitive περισσεύειν functions as the direct object of οἶδα. περισσεύω, when used in relation to a person, as here, means to "have an abundance, abound, be rich" (BDAG, 805.1.b).

ἐν παντί. Circumstance or condition ("in every circumstance").

καί. Coordinating conjunction linking two prepositional phrases.

ἐν πᾶσιν. Circumstance or condition ("in all circumstances"). The compound phrase ἐν παντὶ καὶ ἐν πᾶσιν emphasizes the comprehensive character of Paul's experiences—ἐν παντί singly and ἐν πᾶσιν collectively (Lightfoot, 164)—which corresponds to the English idiom "in any and all circumstances."

μεμύημαι. Prf pass ind 1st sg μυέω. A NT *hapax legomenon*. As a technical term in the mystery religions, μυέω means "initiate (into the mysteries)" (BDAG, 660). Paul uses the perfect passive verb form (lit. "I have been initiated into the mystery") in a nontechnical sense to convey that he has learned the secret of being content with all kinds of circumstances. Within the sentence structure, this finite verb is parallel to the first two occurrences of οἶδα.

καὶ . . . καὶ . . . καὶ . . . καὶ. Two sets of correlated coordinating conjunctions ("both . . . and, both . . . and"), each governing a pair of contrasting infinitives: (1) *both* to be well fed *and* to be hungry; (2) *both* to have an abundance *and* to be in need.

χορτάζεσθαι. Pres pass inf of χορτάζω (complementary). χορτάζω means "to fill w[ith] food," "feed, fill" (BDAG, 1087.1).

πεινᾶν. Pres act inf πεινάω (complementary). πεινάω means "to feel the pangs of lack of food," "hunger, be hungry" (BDAG, 792.1). πεινάω and χορτάζω occur together as a pair of opposites in Matt 5:6.

περισσεύειν. Pres act inf περισσεύω (complementary). On the meaning of the verb, see περισσεύειν above.

ὑστερεῖσθαι. Pres mid inf ὑστερέω (complementary). ὑστερέω means "to experience deficiency in someth[ing] advantageous or desirable," "lack, be lacking, go without, come short of" (BDAG, 1044.5). The juxtaposition of ὑστερεῖσθαι and περισσεύειν indicates that ὑστερέω refers to economic needs.

4:13 πάντα ἰσχύω ἐν τῷ ἐνδυναμοῦντί με.

πάντα. Accusative direct object of ἰσχύω. Fronted for emphasis. The adjective πάντα functions as a substantive, referring to various circumstances described in the previous verse and summed up in ἐν παντὶ καὶ ἐν πᾶσιν. The sense of πάντα is therefore not limitless, as it is often assumed in various types of triumphalist reading, but contextually restrained (cf. O'Brien, 526; Fee, 434).

ἰσχύω. Pres act ind 1st sg ἰσχύω. ἰσχύω means "to have requisite personal resources to accomplish someth[ing]," "have power, be competent, be able" (BDAG, 484.2).

ἐν τῷ ἐνδυναμοῦντί. Instrumental or locative. Wallace notes that "ἐν + dative to express *means* can be (and often is) used of *persons*, though they are conceived of as impersonal (i.e., used as an instrument by someone else)" (1996, 373). If, then, ἐν τῷ ἐνδυναμοῦντί is understood in the instrumental sense, it conveys that Paul's ability to endure various circumstances in life comes through Christ (NRSV; NIV; HCSB; ESV; cf. Moule, 77). If the PP is understood in the locative sense, it expresses "the sphere within which Paul is able to endure. . . . Paul is able to endure hardship not because he has great power, but because he participates in the realm that he characterizes as ἐν Χριστῷ" (Sumney, 113).

τῷ ἐνδυναμοῦντί. Pres act ptc masc dat sg ἐνδυναμόω (substantival). ἐνδυναμόω means "to cause one to be able to function or do someth[ing]," "strengthen" (BDAG, 333.1). ἐνδυναμοῦντί, which has a circumflex accent on the penult, acquired an additional accent, the acute, on the ultima from the enclitic με (Smyth §183; Carson 1985, 48).

με. Accusative direct object of ἐνδυναμοῦντί.

4:14 Πλὴν καλῶς ἐποιήσατε συγκοινωνήσαντές μου τῇ θλίψει.

Πλὴν. Adverb used as a conjunction at the beginning of a sentence. It breaks off a discussion and emphasizes what is important: "only, in any case, on the other hand, but" (BDAG, 826.1.c). After the previous discussion in which Paul described his contentment in all circumstances, Πλὴν signals a concession: "*nevertheless*, though I could have dispensed with your contributions" (Lightfoot, 164).

καλῶς. Adverb ("rightly, correctly" [BDAG, 505.4]). καλῶς ποιεῖν = "be kind enough to do someth[ing]" (BDAG, 506.4.a).

ἐποιήσατε. Aor act ind 2nd pl ποιέω.

συγκοινωνήσαντές. Aor act ptc masc nom pl συγκοινωνέω (means or manner). On adverbial participles that follow the main verb, see 1:4 on ποιούμενος. In this context, συγκοινωνέω means "to be associated w[ith] someone in some activity" (BDAG, 952.1). συγκοινωνήσαντές, which has an acute accent on the antepenult, acquired an additional accent, the acute, on the ultima from the enclitic μου (Smyth §183; Carson, 48).

μου. Possessive genitive modifying τῇ θλίψει ("my trouble"). The pronoun is placed before its head noun (lit. "my the trouble"), i.e., it is preposed, which "allows the focal part of the phrase to occur at the end of the clause and thus receive extra prominence" (Levinsohn 2000, 64). Fee calls a preposed μου "vernacular possessive" (439 n. 9). The genitive case of the pronoun is odd. According to BDAG (952.1), the collocation συγκοινωνέω + τινί τινος means "to be associated/connected with someone in something," but this pattern would have been applicable had Paul said μοι τῆς θλίψεως (Fee, 439 n. 9). Instead, he placed the object of the Philippians' participation not in the genitive but in the dative (τῇ θλίψει) and used the genitive μου to qualify the matter in which they participated ("my trouble").

τῇ θλίψει. Dative complement of συγκοινωνήσαντές, designating the matter that the Philippians shared with Paul. θλῖψις denotes "trouble that inflicts distress, oppression, affliction, tribulation" (BDAG, 457.1).

Philippians 4:13-15   121

4:15 οἴδατε δὲ καὶ ὑμεῖς, Φιλιππήσιοι, ὅτι ἐν ἀρχῇ τοῦ εὐαγγελίου, ὅτε ἐξῆλθον ἀπὸ Μακεδονίας, οὐδεμία μοι ἐκκλησία ἐκοινώνησεν εἰς λόγον δόσεως καὶ λήμψεως εἰ μὴ ὑμεῖς μόνοι,

οἴδατε. Prf act ind 2nd pl οἶδα. The perfect tense has the present meaning, describing "the enduring result rather than the completed act" (Smyth §1946).

δὲ. Marker of development.

καὶ. Adverbial use (adjunctive).

ὑμεῖς. Nominative subject of οἴδατε. The expressed personal pronoun is emphatic.

Φιλιππήσιοι. Vocative of direct address.

ὅτι. Introduces the clausal complement (indirect discourse) of οἴδατε.

ἐν ἀρχῇ. Temporal. Fronted as a temporal frame. ἀρχή denotes "the commencement of someth[ing] as an action, process, or state of being," "beginning" (BDAG, 137.1). ἐν ἀρχῇ τοῦ εὐαγγελίου could be rendered as "when the gospel was first preached" (BDAG, 138.1.a); cf. Mark 1:1 for a similar construction (Ἀρχὴ τοῦ εὐαγγελίου).

τοῦ εὐαγγελίου. Objective genitive modifying the verbal noun ἀρχῇ ("beginning [of the proclaiming] of the gospel" [BDAG, 402.1.a.β]).

ὅτε. Introduces a temporal clause.

ἐξῆλθον. Aor act ind 1st sg ἐξέρχομαι. The temporal clause provides the background for Paul's description of the financial support that he received from the Philippians. Since the perfective aspect of the aorist verb form portrays Paul's departure from Macedonia as a complete action, it is impossible to know whether he received the assistance as soon as he left or at some later point.

ἀπὸ Μακεδονίας. Spatial (separation).

οὐδεμία . . . εἰ μὴ. A point/counterpoint set that corrects the negated clause ("no church shared with me in the matter of giving and receiving") by introducing an exception ("except you alone"). "The negated statement is not entirely true without the inclusion of the excepted element" (Runge 2010, 83). The collocation of the negative adjective + the exception has significant rhetorical impact because Paul does not merely say that no church offered him financial support in the early days of his ministry. He also says that the Philippians alone shared with him their material resources. By making a generalized claim that is not entirely true, Paul highlights the distinctiveness of the Philippians' gift. In this way, the excepted element is effectively emphasized. Runge argues that this rhetorical effect is achieved by placing the exceptive clause after the negated clause (85).

οὐδεμία . . . ἐκκλησία. Nominative subject of ἐκοινώνησεν. The adjective οὐδεμία modifies ἐκκλησία, standing in the first (anarthrous) attributive position (see 1:4 on ἐν πάσῃ δεήσει). In contrast to 3:6, where ἐκκλησία referred to the global Christian community, here it denotes a Christian community "living and meeting in a particular locality or larger geographical area, but not necessarily limited to one meeting place" (BDAG, 304.3.b.β).

μοι. Dative complement of ἐκοινώνησεν. Levinsohn suggests that the placement of μοι between οὐδεμία and ἐκκλησία may give extra prominence to the negative οὐδεμία (2000, 50 n. 5).

ἐκοινώνησεν. Aor act ind 3rd sg κοινωνέω. In this context, κοινωνέω ("give/contribute a share" [BDAG, 552.2]) refers to sharing financial resources (cf. Rom 12:13 and Gal 6:6).

εἰς λόγον. Replaces the dative of advantage (BDAG, 290.4.g.). λόγος here denotes "settlement (of an account)" (BDAG, 601.2.b).

δόσεως. Objective genitive modifying λόγον. When δόσις ("giving") is paired with λῆμψις, it means "debit" (BDAG, 593).

καὶ. Coordinating conjunction linking two genitives governed by the same head noun.

λήμψεως. Objective genitive modifying λόγον. A NT *hapax legomenon*. When λῆμψις ("receiving") is paired with δόσις, it means "credit" (BDAG, 259.2).

ὑμεῖς μόνοι. This combination of the nominative plural of the second-person personal pronoun ὑμεῖς and the attributive adjective μόνοι ("you alone") functions as the second, excepted, nominative subject of ἐκοινώνησεν.

4:16 ὅτι καὶ ἐν Θεσσαλονίκῃ καὶ ἅπαξ καὶ δὶς εἰς τὴν χρείαν μοι ἐπέμψατε.

ὅτι. Introduces a causal clause that explains the exceptional behavior of the Philippians mentioned at the end of the previous verse (εἰ μὴ ὑμεῖς μόνοι). Some scholars (e.g., Sumney, 116; Collange, 152; Hawthorne and Martin, 270) contend that ὅτι introduces the second clausal complement (indirect discourse) of οἴδατε. However, if that were the case, this ὅτι would be preceded by a connective καί (see, e.g., Sumney's [114] translation, which adds a nonexistent conjunction at the beginning of the clause: "*and* that even in Thessalonica you sent support for me..."). Given the absence of such a conjunction, it is better to understand the ὅτι clause as providing a justification for v. 15 (cf. O'Brien, 535).

καὶ. Adverbial use (ascensive). Since Thessalonica is in Macedonia, the ascensive καὶ functions as a qualifier of the previous statement, explaining that the Philippians supported Paul financially even before he left the province (cf. Fee, 441–42).

ἐν Θεσσαλονίκῃ. Locative. Fronted as a spatial frame.

καὶ ἅπαξ καὶ δίς. An idiom consisting of two correlative conjunctions and two adverbs (lit. "both once and twice") for "again and again, more than once" (BDAG, 97.1; Fee, 445 n. 28). The usage in 1 Thess 2:18 (καὶ ἅπαξ καὶ δίς) confirms that the idiom includes not only the καὶ that connects ἅπαξ καὶ δίς but also the καὶ before ἅπαξ.

εἰς τὴν χρείαν. Purpose or reference/respect. Since χρεία is usually anarthrous, the article probably identifies "*the* need at that time" (Fee, 446 n. 30). The omission of the preposition εἰς in some manuscripts ($\mathfrak{P}^{46}$ A D* 81 104 326 1175 1241 2464 et al.) may have been either accidental after δίς or deliberate to supply a direct object for ἐπέμψατε (Metzger, 550).

μοι. Dative indirect object of ἐπέμψατε. Some copyists replaced this unusual but better-attested dative ($\mathfrak{P}^{46}$ ℵ A B F G K Ψ 33 81 104 326 365 1175 1241 1505 1739 1881 2464 𝔐 lat) with the possessive genitive μου (D¹ L P 075 323 614 629 630 et al.) to indicate that this was Paul's need.

ἐπέμψατε. Aor act ind 2nd pl πέμπω. In this context, πέμπω means "to dispatch someth[ing] through an intermediary," "send" (BDAG, 795.2). The direct object of the verb is not expressed.

4:17 οὐχ ὅτι ἐπιζητῶ τὸ δόμα, ἀλλ᾽ ἐπιζητῶ τὸν καρπὸν τὸν πλεονάζοντα εἰς λόγον ὑμῶν.

οὐχ ὅτι. An ellipsis for οὐ λέγω ὅτι (cf. 4:11).

οὐχ ... ἀλλ᾽. A point/counterpoint set ("not this . . . but that") that negates the wrong impression that Paul seeks the gift and replaces it with the claim, expressed through the commercial metaphor, that he seeks the profit that accumulates to the Philippians' account.

ὅτι. Introduces the clausal complement (indirect discourse) of an implied λέγω (see οὐχ ὅτι above).

ἐπιζητῶ. Pres act ind 1st sg ἐπιζητέω. The compound ἐπιζητέω (ἐπί + ζητέω) means "to be seriously interested in or have a strong desire for" (BDAG, 371.2), "wish, wish for" (BDAG, 371.2.a).

τὸ δόμα. Accusative direct object of ἐπιζητῶ. δόμα denotes "gift" (BDAG, 256).

ἐπιζητῶ. Pres act ind 1st sg ἐπιζητέω (see above).

τὸν καρπὸν. Accusative direct object of ἐπιζητῶ. In this context, καρπός (lit. "fruit") is used figuratively as a reference to "advantage, gain, profit" (BDAG, 510.2).

τὸν πλεονάζοντα. Pres act ptc masc acc sg πλεονάζω (attributive). The participle modifies καρπόν, standing in the second attributive position (see 1:1 on τοῖς οὖσιν). πλεονάζω means "to become more and more, so as to be in abundance," "grow, increase" (BDAG, 824.1).

εἰς λόγον. Replaces the dative of advantage (see 4:15).

ὑμῶν. Possessive genitive modifying λόγον.

4:18 ἀπέχω δὲ πάντα καὶ περισσεύω· πεπλήρωμαι δεξάμενος παρὰ Ἐπαφροδίτου τὰ παρ' ὑμῶν, ὀσμὴν εὐωδίας, θυσίαν δεκτήν, εὐάρεστον τῷ θεῷ.

ἀπέχω. Pres act ind 1st sg ἀπέχω. As a commercial technical term, ἀπέχω means "to receive in full what is due," "to be paid in full, receive in full" (BDAG, 102.1). Paul uses this commercial term to convey that he has received the Philippians' gift (cf. GNT: "Here, then, is my receipt for everything you have given me"). ἀπέχω is usually regarded as one of the verbs whose present tense has "perfective" meaning; such verbs "denote a present state or condition and imply the occurrence of an action which produced that condition" (Fanning, 239). The "perfectivizing" sense of the present tense of ἀπέχω ("I have received") comes from the prefix ἀπο- (Moulton and Milligan, 57; Reumann, 666).

δὲ. Marker of development.

πάντα. Accusative direct object of ἀπέχω.

καὶ. Coordinating conjunction.

περισσεύω. Pres act ind 1st sg περισσεύω.

πεπλήρωμαι. Prf pass ind 1st sg πληρόω. The verb πληρόω here means "to provide for completely, to supply fully" (LN 35.33). The perfect-tense πεπλήρωμαι "repeats and intensifies the idea expressed in περισσεύω" (Hawthorne and Martin, 272), describing Paul's sense of being filled (stative aspect).

δεξάμενος. Aor mid ptc masc nom sg δέχομαι (causal). On adverbial participles that follow the main verb, see 1:4 on ποιούμενος.

παρὰ Ἐπαφροδίτου. Agency.

τὰ παρ' ὑμῶν. The article functions as a nominalizer, changing the PP παρ' ὑμῶν into the accusative direct object of δεξάμενος (lit. "the things from you").

παρ' ὑμῶν. Source.

ὀσμὴν εὐωδίας, θυσίαν δεκτήν, εὐάρεστον τῷ θεῷ. The appositional information to τὰ παρ' ὑμῶν, which receives prominence through right-dislocation (Runge 2010, 317–35).

ὀσμὴν. Accusative in apposition to τὰ παρ' ὑμῶν. ὀσμή denotes "the quality of someth[ing] that affects the mind as with an odor," "odor" (BDAG, 728.2).

Philippians 4:17-19   125

εὐωδίας. Attributive genitive modifying ὀσμήν. εὐωδία means "a pleasant or sweet-smelling odor—'aroma, fragrance'" (LN 79.46). In the LXX, the expression ὀσμὴ εὐωδίας is habitually used as a description of an acceptable sacrifice, as, for example, in Lev 1:9: κάρπωμά ἐστιν θυσία ὀσμὴ εὐωδίας τῷ κυρίῳ ("It is an offering, a sacrifice, an odor of fragrance to the Lord" [NETS]; cf. LXX Gen 8:21; Exod 29:18, 41; Lev 1:13, 17; 2:2, 9, 12; 3:5; etc.). To indicate Paul's shift from commercial to sacrificial language, many English translations render ὀσμὴν εὐωδίας as "a fragrant offering" (NRSV; REB; HCSB; ESV). Since, however, ὀσμή does not mean "offering" (see above), it is more accurate to translate the phrase as "a fragrant odor" (to express the attributive function of the genitive; lit. "an odor of fragrance"; cf. ASV; CEB; NASB).

θυσίαν δεκτήν. Accusative in apposition to τὰ παρ' ὑμῶν. The adjective δεκτήν ("pleasing, acceptable") modifies the noun θυσίαν ("sacrifice"), standing in the fourth attributive position (see 1:6 on ἔργον ἀγαθὸν).

εὐάρεστον. Another attributive adjective that modifies θυσίαν or, alternatively, an attributive adjective that modifies both nouns that are appositional to τὰ παρ' ὑμῶν—ὀσμὴν and θυσίαν. εὐάρεστος ("pleasing, acceptable") is a two-termination adjective whose usage is not related to sacrificial context. In the NT, it usually describes behavior that is pleasing to God (Rom 12:1; 14:18; 2 Cor 5:9; Eph 5:10; Col 3:20; Heb 13:21).

τῷ θεῷ. Dative of advantage. Strictly speaking, it qualifies εὐάρεστον ("pleasing to God"), but it is also applicable to the entire construction ὀσμὴν εὐωδίας, θυσίαν δεκτήν, εὐάρεστον (cf. O'Brien, 542).

4:19 ὁ δὲ θεός μου πληρώσει πᾶσαν χρείαν ὑμῶν κατὰ τὸ πλοῦτος αὐτοῦ ἐν δόξῃ ἐν Χριστῷ Ἰησοῦ.

ὁ . . . θεός. Nominative subject of πληρώσει. Fronted as a topical frame, marking a shift from "I" to "my God" (Levinsohn 1995, 63).

δὲ. Marker of development.

μου. Genitive of subordination modifying θεός.

πληρώσει. Fut act ind 3rd sg πληρόω. On the meaning of the verb, see 4:18 on πεπλήρωμαι. In some witnesses (D* F G Ψ 075 6 33 81 104 326 365 1175 1241 1505 1739 1881 latt), the future indicative πληρώσει has been replaced by the aorist optative πληρώσαι. This alteration was probably motivated by a desire to convey that what Paul says here is not a declaration about the future but merely a wish-prayer ("May my God supply . . ."). The future indicative is preferable on both external (it is attested in 𝔓⁴⁶ ℵ A B D² K L P 630 𝔐 co) and internal grounds (it represents the *lectio difficilior*). While recognizing that the manuscript evidence favors the future πληρώσει, Hawthorne and Martin (273–74) nevertheless offer several arguments in support of the optative πληρώσαι, such as that in 2 Cor 9:8 Paul "refuses to say what God *will do* in meeting... material needs" (which are primarily in view here) and that Paul frequently employs the optative at the end of his letters when he asks God to do something on behalf of his friends (Rom 15:5; 1 Thess 5:23). It should be noted, however, that these arguments presume that "[t]he future indicative (πληρώσει) states a fact promising the Philippians what God will do" (Hawthorne and Martin, 273). Such understanding of the future tense should be revised in light of recent insights in verbal aspect theory. For example, Porter argues that "[r]ather than temporal values, *the future form grammaticalizes the semantic (meaning) feature of expectation*" (1994, 44). Even if one presumes that Greek verbs in the indicative mood do encode time, the future tense "tells the *temporal relation* of the verbal action to some reference-point, usually the time of speaking: the action is presented as *subsequent* (i.e. yet to take place)" (Fanning, 122). It is therefore more accurate to say that Paul uses the verb πληρώσει in the closing section of this letter to describe something that he expects to happen in the future rather than something that will assuredly happen in the future.

πᾶσαν χρείαν. Accusative direct object of πληρώσει. The adjective πᾶσαν modifies χρείαν, standing in the first (anarthrous) attributive position (see 1:4 on ἐν πάσῃ δεήσει). Paul's use of this comprehensive adjective may indicate that he has in mind both material and spiritual needs (O'Brien, 547), but the context suggests that material needs are primarily in view (Hawthorne and Martin, 273).

ὑμῶν. Possessive genitive modifying χρείαν.

κατὰ τὸ πλοῦτος. Standard ("in proportion to his wealth"; cf. Hellerman 2015, 270).

αὐτοῦ. Possessive genitive modifying πλοῦτος. The antecedent of αὐτοῦ is θεός.

ἐν δόξῃ. Locative. ἐν δόξῃ modifies τὸ πλοῦτος αὐτοῦ rather than πληρώσει, conveying that God's riches exist in the sphere of God's glory (Fee, 453).

ἐν Χριστῷ Ἰησοῦ. If ἐν Χριστῷ Ἰησοῦ modifies πληρώσει, its sense is either locative ("in Christ Jesus") or instrumental ("through Christ"). If ἐν Χριστῷ Ἰησοῦ modifies κατὰ τὸ πλοῦτος αὐτοῦ ἐν δόξῃ, it expresses close association, conveying "that God's riches in glory are closely associated with Christ" (Campbell 2012, 91).

4:20 τῷ δὲ θεῷ καὶ πατρὶ ἡμῶν ἡ δόξα εἰς τοὺς αἰῶνας τῶν αἰώνων, ἀμήν.

τῷ ... θεῷ καὶ πατρί. Dative of possession because the verbless clause presumes some form of εἰμί. A single article governing two substantives linked by καί, neither of which is impersonal, plural, or a proper name, creates a TSKS personal construction that fits the requirements for the Granville Sharp rule, which posits that both substantives have the same referent—here God (Wallace 1996, 274). Elsewhere in Paul, θεός and πατήρ are joined together in a TSKS personal construction in Gal 1:4; 1 Thess 1:3; 3:11, 13.

δέ. Marker of development.

ἡμῶν. Genitive of relationship modifying both θεῷ and πατρί.

ἡ δόξα. Nominative subject of an implied form of εἰμί, such as the optative εἴη or the indicative ἐστίν (cf. 1 Pet 4:11). If δόξα denotes "honor as enhancement or recognition of status or performance" (BDAG, 257.3), the implied verb is in the optative. If δόξα refers to God's "glory, majesty, sublimity" (BDAG, 257.1.b), i.e., to something that God already possesses, the implied verb is in the indicative (cf. Hellerman 2015, 271).

εἰς τοὺς αἰῶνας τῶν αἰώνων. Temporal. This expression (lit. "unto the ages of the ages") reflects the Hebrew superlative construction (e.g., "song of songs") and is the equivalent of our phrase "forever and ever."

ἀμήν. Greek transliteration of the Hebrew particle אָמֵן ("surely") that functions as a "strong affirmation of what is stated," "let it be so, truly, amen" (BDAG, 53.1).

Philippians 4:21-23

[21]Greet every saint in Christ Jesus. The brothers [and sisters] who are with me greet you. [22]All the saints greet you, and especially those from the emperor's household. [23][May] the grace of the Lord Jesus Christ [be] with your spirit.

4:21 Ἀσπάσασθε πάντα ἅγιον ἐν Χριστῷ Ἰησοῦ. ἀσπάζονται ὑμᾶς οἱ σὺν ἐμοὶ ἀδελφοί.

Ἀσπάσασθε. Aor mid impv 2nd pl ἀσπάζομαι. All three occurrences of ἀσπάζομαι ("greet, welcome") in Philippians are in this (2x) and the next verse; moreover, all three clauses containing this verb are connected to the previous ones by asyndeton. The addressees are probably all believers in Philippi, as indicated in 1:1 (πᾶσιν τοῖς ἁγίοις ἐν Χριστῷ Ἰησοῦ τοῖς οὖσιν ἐν Φιλίπποις).

πάντα ἅγιον. Accusative direct object of Ἀσπάσασθε. The adjective πάντα modifies ἅγιον, standing in the first (anarthrous) attributive position (see 1:4 on ἐν πάσῃ δεήσει). When πᾶς is used with a noun without the article in the singular, as here, it emphasizes "the individual members of the class denoted by the noun," "every, any," and its meaning does not differ much from the plural "all" (BDAG, 782.1.a).

ἐν Χριστῷ Ἰησοῦ. If the PP modifies Ἀσπάσασθε, its sense could be instrumental ("by means of Jesus Christ") or relational ("in fellowship with Jesus Christ"). If the PP modifies πάντα ἅγιον, which is more likely given the word order and a similar usage in 1:1, its sense could be (1) instrumental/causal ("everyone who is a saint through Jesus Christ"), (2) locative ("every saint in the sphere of Christ's power"), or (3) relational ("every saint in union / close association with Christ").

ἀσπάζονται. Pres mid ind 3rd pl ἀσπάζομαι.

ὑμᾶς. Accusative direct object of ἀσπάζονται.

οἱ ... ἀδελφοί. Nominative subject of ἀσπάζονται.

σὺν ἐμοί. Accompaniment. The PP modifies ἀδελφοί, standing in the first attributive position (see 1:5 on ἀπὸ τῆς πρώτης ἡμέρας).

4:22 ἀσπάζονται ὑμᾶς πάντες οἱ ἅγιοι, μάλιστα δὲ οἱ ἐκ τῆς Καίσαρος οἰκίας.

ἀσπάζονται. Pres mid ind 3rd pl ἀσπάζομαι.

ὑμᾶς. Accusative direct object of ἀσπάζονται.

πάντες οἱ ἅγιοι. Nominative subject of ἀσπάζονται. The adjective πάντες has attributive function ("all the saints") although it stands in the first predicate position (see 1:1 on πᾶσιν τοῖς ἁγίοις).

μάλιστα. Superlative of the adverb μάλα. It is used as an elative, indicating "an unusual degree," "most of all, above all, especially, particularly" (BDAG, 613).

δὲ. Marker of development.

οἱ ἐκ τῆς Καίσαρος οἰκίας. The article functions as a nominalizer, changing the PP ἐκ τῆς Καίσαρος οἰκίας into the second nominative subject of ἀσπάζονται.

ἐκ τῆς ... οἰκίας. Origin/source that determines someone's belonging to or membership in a group (BDAG, 296.3.b; BDF §437; Harris, 109). This usage is especially prominent in nominalized prepositional phrases, as here (οἱ ἐκ τῆς Καίσαρος οἰκίας = "those who belong to the emperor's household"; cf. Harris, 109). The noun οἰκία could denote "a structure used as a dwelling," "house" (BDAG, 695.1), or a "social unit within a dwelling," "household, family" (BDAG, 695.2). BDAG suggests that in the current context, οἰκία "means, whether it be translated 'those in the house' or 'those in the household of the Emperor,' according to the prevailing usage, not members of the emperor's family or relationship, but servants at his court; in early imperial times they were ordinarily slaves or freedpersons" (595.3).

Καίσαρος. Possessive genitive modifying οἰκίας. Καῖσαρ, originally a proper name (Lat. *Caesar*), functions as a title, denoting "emperor" (BDAG, 498–99).

4:23 Ἡ χάρις τοῦ κυρίου Ἰησοῦ Χριστοῦ μετὰ τοῦ πνεύματος ὑμῶν.

Ἡ χάρις. Nominative subject of an implied form of εἰμί, such as the optative εἴη (if this is a wish) or the indicative ἐστίν (if this is a statement).

τοῦ κυρίου. Genitive of source modifying Ἡ χάρις.

Ἰησοῦ Χριστοῦ. Genitive in apposition to κυρίου.

μετὰ τοῦ πνεύματος. Association/accompaniment (BDAG, 636.2.a.γ.ℶ). τοῦ πνεύματος is a distributive singular that denotes "a part of human personality" (BDAG, 833.3) viewed "as the source and seat of insight, feeling, and will, gener[ally] as the representative part of human inner life" (BDAG, 833.3.b). Paul uses the same PP (μετὰ τοῦ πνεύματος ὑμῶν) in his closing benediction in Gal 6:18 and Phlm 25. Elsewhere in his undisputed letters, he uses the phrase μετὰ πάντων ὑμῶν (Rom 15:33; 1 Cor 16:24; 2 Cor 13:13) or simply μεθ᾽ ὑμῶν (1 Thess 5:28). The variant reading μετὰ πάντων, found in some witnesses (ℵ² K L Ψ 630 1505 2464 𝔐 sy), is probably a scribal substitution of the original μετὰ τοῦ πνεύματος (𝔓⁴⁶ ℵ* A B D F G P 075 6 33 81 104 365 629 1175 1241 1739 1881 latt co) with a more familiar form of the benediction that occurs in Rom 15:33; 1 Cor 16:24; 2 Cor 13:13; 2 Thess 3:18; Titus 3:15 (Metzger, 550–51).

ὑμῶν. Possessive genitive modifying πνεύματος. Many manuscripts (𝔓⁴⁶ ℵ A D K L P Ψ 33 81 104 365 630 1175 1241 1505 1739ᶜ 2464 𝔐 lat sy bo) add ἀμὴν after ὑμῶν. Despite its strong external attestation, ἀμὴν is most likely a later addition reflecting church liturgical practice. Had it been part of the original text, it would be difficult to explain why it was omitted in B F G 075 6 1739* 1881 b sa Abst et al. (Metzger, 551).

GLOSSARY

Adjectivizer—An article that transforms a nonadjective *into* an adjectival modifier. Thus, in the phrase τὸν διὰ Ἰησοῦ Χριστοῦ (Phil 1:11), the article τὸν transforms the prepositional phrase διὰ Ἰησοῦ Χριστοῦ into an attributive modifier of καρπὸν.

Adjunctive—Providing something additional and supplemental. The term is used in relation to Greek conjunctions, especially καί when it signifies "also."

Aktionsart—The kind or objective quality of the verbal action, e.g., punctiliar, durative, iterative, inceptive, etc.

Alliteration—The repetition of similar sounds in a stream of lexemes.

Anacoluthon—A logical and syntactical break in the flow of a sentence, in which a different idea and corresponding syntax begin without completing what came before.

Anaphoric—Referring back to a word or phrase that is coreferential. In the sentence "Ben went on a drive, and he liked it," the pronoun *he* refers, anaphorically, to *Ben*.

Anarthrous—Not modified by an article.

Antecedent—A word to which another word later in the discourse refers. A relative pronoun's antecedent is the preceding word about which the relative clause will provide further information.

Antepenult—The third-to-last syllable in a word, *followed* by the penult (second-to-last syllable), and ultima (last syllable).

Apodosis—The second element, providing the "then" clause after the protasis in a conditional sentence.

Articular—Modified by an article.

Ascensive—Rising or intensifying. The term is often applied to conjunctions, especially καί when it signifies "even."

Aspect—The depiction of an action, event, or state—either internally, as an an unfolding process (e.g., "I am helping"), or externally, as a unified whole (e.g., "I helped").

Asyndeton—The absence of conjunctions connecting one clause to the next, effecting a faster sense of pace or intensity of tone. This is the default mode of connecting sentences in the FG.

Attraction—Rather than taking on the case required by its function within its clause, a relative pronoun occasionally reflects or "attracts" to the case of the antecedent.

Background—Information that does not advance the narrative or storyline but, rather, elaborates, supplements, or expands upon a feature of the narrative with supporting detail.

Cataphoric—Referring forward to a word or phrase that is coreferential. In the clauses "I saw her; Jane was running," the pronoun *her* refers, cataphorically, to *Jane*.

Causative—An action or circumstance is produced or initiated by the action of the verbal element.

Clausal complement—A clause that serves as direct object. Frequently this involves the use of ὅτι after verbs of speech; e.g., in the sentence καὶ πᾶσα γλῶσσα ἐξομολογήσηται ὅτι κύριος Ἰησοῦς Χριστὸς εἰς δόξαν θεοῦ πατρός ("and every tongue should confess that Jesus Christ is Lord, to the glory of God the Father") in Phil 2:11, the ὅτι clause serves as the clausal complement of ἐξομολογήσηται.

Complement—A clause, phrase, or word required to complete a given expression. This is especially common in double accusative constructions; e.g., in the sentence "Emmet calls turtles frogs," *turtles* is the object and *frogs* is the complement. Without the complement, the expression is incomplete.

Concessive—An element introducing an idea, action, or circumstance that runs counter to the main clause. Concessive clauses are typically introduced with "although" or "even though."

Constructio ad sensum—A construction that does not correspond to the expected number or gender dictated by normal syntax, because it is responding to something inherent in the *sense* of that word rather than the word itself as a morphosyntactical entity; e.g., "The crowd is hungry and *are* getting restless." The plural *are* results from conceiving the singular crowd in terms of the multiple individuals making up the crowd.

Copula—The linking verb in an equative or copular clause, connecting a subject and predicate. In the copular clause Ὅσοι οὖν τέλειοι

("Therefore, as many as [are] mature"), the implied copula is ἐσμέν or εἰσίν.

Crasis—The formation of a single word from two words by contraction, e.g., κἀγώ for καὶ ἐγώ.

Deponency—When verbs with middle, passive, or middle/passive morphology were ascribed active meanings, they were labeled "deponent." This view has faced important challenges. Thus, the BHGNT acknowledges that middle morphology involves nuances associated with middle voice that should be taken into consideration. See Series Introduction for more.

Development—The use of δέ that signals an advance in an argument or narrative but does not convey the overt continuity or discontinuity of a conjunction or adversative.

Direct discourse—A record of the speech or thought of a character, introduced by an untranslated ὅτι and placed in quotation marks.

Double accusative construction—Some verbs can take two accusatives. In a person-thing double accusative, verbs of teaching, reminding, clothing, or asking can take an accusative direct object (the person) and an object-complement (the thing). Thus, in the sentence "I taught Eliana the song," *Eliana* is the direct object and *song* is the complement. In an object-complement double accusative, verbs of making, sending, calling, and reckoning take both an object and the object's complement in the accusative. In the clause οὐδένα γὰρ ἔχω ἰσόψυχον ("For I have no one like-minded") οὐδένα is the direct object and ἰσόψυχον is the complement.

Elide/elision—The omission of a letter in a word or of an entire word. In the former case, the closing vowel in certain prepositions or conjunctions may be omitted, as in the α in ἀλλ' ὁ θεὸς (Phil 2:27). In the latter case, an entire word is omitted and must be supplied by reference to context. In Phil 2:15, a repetition of the verb φαίνω in the clause φαίνεσθε ὡς φωστῆρες [φαίνονται] ἐν κόσμῳ ("you shine like luminaries [shine] in the world") is elided, leaving only φωστῆρες ἐν κόσμῳ.

Emphasis—Important information placed in a marked position for greater prominence.

Enclitic—A word that donates its accent to the word directly preceding it, as in πάντοτέ ἐστιν.

Epexegetical—An additional word or group of words that offer greater clarity. Infinitives can function in this way—clarifying or completing words like those relating to duty, ability, expectation, or necessity (e.g., "I hope *to eat*"). Similarly, an epexegetical use of clauses beginning with ἵνα or ὅτι function to clarify or complete an idea. When a head noun is ambiguous, an epexegetical genitive can be used to offer a particular example that clarifies the noun it modifies and may, therefore, be introduced in translation by "namely" or "which is."

Epistolary aorist—A form of the aorist indicative verb often used in epistles. It is consciously used by the author to describe his or her letter from the temporal perspective of the receiving audience. For example, in the first clause of Phil 2:28, σπουδαιοτέρως οὖν ἔπεμψα αὐτόν ("Therefore I am sending him with special urgency,") the aorist verb ἔπεμψα, while not yet completed from Paul's vantage point, is a completed action from the perspective of the Philippian audience.

Equative verb/clause—Equative clauses link subjects and predicates in constructions of the type "this is that." The verbs that do the linking (typically εἰμί, γίνομαι, or ὑπάρχω) are equative verbs. The sentence ὧν τὸ τέλος [ἐστίν] ἀπώλεια ("whose end [is] destruction") is an equative clause, and the implied ἐστὶν is the equative verb.

External evidence—A term from textual criticism, referring to the evidence of manuscripts and versions (e.g., the text-type or antiquity of particular witnesses to a reading) rather than on considerations relating to the content of the text at hand (e.g., the author's style or theology).

First-class conditional—Stipulates the truth of the protasis (by means of εἰ with an indicative verb) for the sake of argument. The apodosis takes any mood and any tense.

Focal/focus—The key piece of information in a clause, frequently highlighted by placement in a marked position.

Foreground—Events that are indispensable to or propel the storyline.

Fronting/fronted—When an element occurs earlier in the sentence than might be expected in standard word order. Typically, this refers to a preverbal location.

Genitive absolute—A dependent clause consisting of a genitive substantive and an anarthrous genitive participle that is, most of the time, independent of the verb in the main clause. The participle is usually temporal but can perform any of the adverbial functions of participles.

Genitive of . . .—*agency* specifies the agent actually doing the action; *aporetic/descriptive* describes the head noun in a very general manner and is typically used when another, more specified category cannot be determined, the "catchall" category; *relationship* specifies a social or familial relation; *comparison* usually comes after a comparative adjective and is introduced with "than" (e.g., "greater *than cats*"); *content* specifies what something contains or is full of; *direction* indicates where the head noun is moving; *subordination* specifies what is subordinated under the head noun; *place* specifies within which or where the verb it is related to occurs; *production/producer* specifies what produced the noun to which it relates; *price* specifies the value or price paid; *product* specifies what is produced by the head noun; *purpose* gives the purpose of the head noun; *separation* specifies the point of departure from which the verb or head noun separates; *source* specifies the origin of the head noun; *time* indicates the time within which something happens. Other genitive relationships include *epexegetical* (specifies or exemplifies an ambiguous or metaphorical head noun by providing a clarifying example); *partitive* (specifies the whole of which the head noun is a part), *attributive* (specifies an attribute of the head noun); *subjective* (the subject of the verbal idea contained in the head noun); *objective* (the direct object of the verbal idea contained in the head noun); *descriptive* (describes the head noun in a broad manner).

Grammaticalize—Representing semantic features by means of grammatical markers (prefixes, case endings, etc.).

Hapax legomenon—The only instance of a word recorded in a designated body of literature (in this case, the New Testament).

Headless relative clause—A relative clause without an antecedent, e.g., "Among you stands [one] *whom you do not know.*"

Hendiadys—Two words linked by καί and expressing one idea.

Imperfective (aspect)—The function of present or imperfect tenses when used by a writer or speaker to frame an action or situation as habitual, ongoing, or viewed internally. See, by contrast, *perfective aspect* and *stative aspect*.

Indeclinable—Having no inflected forms; e.g., apart from a preceding article it is impossible to know whether Ναθαναήλ is nominative, genitive, etc.

Indirect discourse—A record of the content of speech or thought introduced by ὅτι. If someone utters the sentence "I'd like to hold the baby," the indirect discourse would report the content of that utterance but not the utterance itself: "Someone said *he would like to hold the baby*."

Intermediate agent—The personal or impersonal agent by means of whom/which an action took place, though he/she/it is not the ultimate cause or initiator of the action. The intermediate agent is introduced with διά + the agent in genitive case.

Intransitive—A verb that does not take a direct object. Some verbs allow but do not require a direct object and can, therefore, function transitively or intransitively.

Lectio difficilior—A text-critical principle that states that the more difficult reading is more likely to be original.

Left-dislocation—A sentence-structuring device in which the new topic of the discourse is put at the beginning of the sentence and then picked up again with a resumptive pronoun in the main clause; e.g., "*The parents with the new baby*, they need more sleep."

Litotes—Making a statement by negating the opposite idea: "no small feat" = "quite an accomplishment." This kind of understatement typically serves as a means of emphasis.

Marked—When a word departs from standard sentence structure, frequently to highlight or emphasize the element placed in the atypical position. If subjects usually follow verbs in a given language, a subject coming before a verb would be in a "marked" position.

Metacomment—A comment about another comment. A metacomment occurs when speakers "stop saying what they are saying in order to comment on what is going to be said, speaking abstractly about it" (Runge 2010, 101). The pragmatic effect can lend solemnity or slow the pace to emphasize the importance of the subsequent utterance.

Metonymy/metonym—Substituting a word or description closely associated with something for the name/term of the thing itself. "Lend me your *ear*" is metonymy for "Lend me your [auditory] attention." In the expression "the enemies of the cross of Christ" (a wooden rendering of Phil 3:18), "the cross" (τοῦ σταυροῦ) is a metonym for the death of Christ.

Nomen actionis—The "action noun" of a clause.

Nominal clause—A group of words containing a verb and functioning as a noun.
Nominalizer—An article that converts a word, phrase, or clause (frequently adjectives and participial constructions) into substantives.
Penult—The second-to-last syllable in a word, preceded by antepenult (third-to-last syllable) and followed by ultima (last syllable).
Perfective (aspect)—The function of the aorist tense when used by a writer or speaker to depict an action or situation externally or summarily as a completed whole. See, for contrast, *imperfective aspect*.
Periphrastic construction—The combination of an anarthrous participle and a verb of being functioning together like a finite verb.
Pleonasm/pleonastic—The use of additional words beyond what is strictly necessary.
Point/counterpoint set—One statement is negated (usually by οὐ or μή) to reject a possible misconception or to establish a key point of contrast and is followed by a positive statement beginning with and emphasized by an introductory ἀλλά.
Postpositive—Not occurring first in a clause. Postpositive conjunctions include γάρ, οὖν, and δέ.
Predicate nominative/accusative/adjective—The anarthrous element in an equative clause sharing the case of the subject that it identifies, renames, or describes. In the sentence "Teddie is tough," *tough* is the predicate adjective and would occur in the nominative case.
Prominence—The state of being more significant or highlighted than other elements. In Greek this is regularly achieved by means of word order or the inclusion of words that are not strictly necessary.
Protasis—The "if" clause in a conditional sentence.
Right-dislocation—A structuring device in which grammatically dispensable information is placed outside of the main clause, thus providing post hoc elaboration of something within the main clause; e.g., "They went outside, Zoe and Lee."
Second-class conditional—The "contrary-to-fact conditional," in which the protasis assumes the falsity of a premise for the sake of argument (by means of εἰ and a secondary tense indicative, typically aorist or imperfect). The apodosis typically has ἄν and an indicative secondary tense.

Semitism—Semitic style, idiom, or sentence structure that is not normally found in composition by native speakers/writers of Greek.

Stative (aspect)—The use of verbs in the perfect and pluperfect tense by a writer or speaker to depict a state of affairs or state of being without reference to unfolding action or process. See, by contrast, *imperfective aspect*.

Synecdoche—A figure of speech in which one term is used in place of another with which it is associated, specifically involving a part-whole relationship. In the sentence, "Do you have your own wheels?" the word *wheels* stands for the entire vehicle of which it is a part.

Third-class conditional—Conveys a logical connection, a hypothetical, or a future eventuality. The protasis uses ἐάν and a subjunctive verb (any tense). The apodosis is in any tense and any mood. A "present general" condition is formed when the apodosis contains a present indicative verb.

Topical frame—A key thematic element is fronted to establish the frame of reference for the following clause. According to Runge, "The two primary uses of topical frames are: to highlight the introduction of a new participant or topic, or to draw attention to a change in topics" (2010, 210).

Ultima—The final syllable in a word, preceded by penult (second-to-last syllable) and antepenult (third-to-last syllable).

Ultimate agent—The person ultimately authorizing/initiating and, therefore, bearing final responsibility for an action without necessarily carrying out that action him- or herself. The ultimate agent is conveyed by means of the genitive with ὑπό, ἀπό, or παρά.

Unmarked—Reflects standard usage or word order and, therefore, is not highlighted by the writer or speaker for special prominence.

WORKS CITED

Alexander, Loveday. "Hellenistic Letter-Forms and the Structure of Philippians." *Journal for the Study of the New Testament* 37 (1989): 87–101.
Bakker, Egbert J. "Voice, Aspect and *Aktionsart*: Middle and Passive in Anicent Greek." Pages 23–47 in *Voice: Form and Function*. Edited by B. Fox and P. Hopper. Typological Studies in Language 27. Philadelphia: Benjamins, 1994.
Beare, F. W. *A Commentary on the Epistle to the Philippians*. HNTC. San Francisco: Harper & Row, 1959.
Beker, Johan Christiaan. *Paul the Apostle: The Triumph of God in Life and Thought*. Philadelphia: Fortress, 1980.
Bockmuehl, Markus. *The Epistle to the Philippians*. BNTC. Peabody, MA: Hendrickson, 1998.
Bruce, Frederick F. *Philippians*. GNC. San Francisco: Harper & Row, 1983.
Buth, Randall. "Participles as Pragmatic Choice: Where Semantics Meets Pragmatics." Pages 273–306 in *The Greek Verb Revisited: A Fresh Approach for Biblical Exegesis*. Edited by Steven E. Runge and Christopher J. Fresch. Bellingham, WA: Lexham Press, 2016.
Campbell, Constantine R. *Basics of Verbal Aspect in Biblical Greek*. Grand Rapids: Zondervan, 2008.
———. *Paul and Union with Christ: An Exegetical and Theological Study*. Grand Rapids: Zondervan, 2012.
Caragounis, Chrys C. *The Development of Greek and the New Testament: Morphology, Syntax, Phonology, and Textual Transmission*. WUNT 167. Tübingen: Mohr Siebeck, 2004.
Carson, D. A. *Greek Accents: A Student's Manual*. Grand Rapids: Baker Books, 1985.

Collange, Jean-François. *The Epistle of St. Paul to the Philippians*. Translated by A. W. Heathcote. London: Epworth, 1979.

Conrad, Carl W. "New Observations on Voice in the Ancient Greek Verb. November 19, 2002." Online: https://pages.wustl.edu/files/pages/imce/cwconrad/newobsancgrkvc.pdf.

Culy, Martin M. "The Clue Is in the Case: Distinguishing Adjectival and Adverbial Participles." *Perspectives in Religious Studies* 30 (2003): 441–53.

———. "Double Case Constructions in Koine Greek." *Journal of Greco-Roman Christianity and Judaism* 6 (2009): 82–106.

Culy, Martin M., and Mikeal C. Parsons. *Acts: A Handbook on the Greek Text*. Waco, TX: Baylor University Press, 2003.

Dahl, Nils Alstrup. "The Messiahship of Jesus in Paul." Pages 15–25 in *Jesus the Christ: The Historical Origins of Christological Doctrine*. Edited by Donald H. Juel. Minneapolis: Fortress, 1991.

Dalton, William J. "The Integrity of Philippians." *Biblica* 60 (1979): 97–102.

de Boer, Willis Peter. *The Imitation of Paul: An Exegetical Study*. Kampen: J. H. Kok, 1962.

Duncan, George Simpson. *St. Paul's Ephesian Ministry*. London: Hodder & Stoughton, 1929.

Dunn, J. D. G. *Christology in the Making: A New Testament Inquiry into the Originas of the Doctrine of the Incarnation*. 2nd ed. London: SCM, 1989.

———. "Once More, ΠΙΣΤΙΣ ΧΡΙΣΤΟΥ." Pages 730–44 in *SBL 1991 Seminar Papers*. Edited by Eugene H. Lovering. Atlanta: Scholars Press, 1991.

———. *The Theology of Paul the Apostle*. Grand Rapids: Eerdmans, 1998.

Ehorn, Seth M., and Mark Lee. "The Syntactical Function of ἀλλὰ καὶ in Phil. 2.4." *Journal of Greco-Roman Christianity and Judaism* 12 (2016): 9–16.

Fanning, Buist M. *Verbal Aspect in New Testament Greek*. Oxford Theological Monographs. Oxford: Clarendon, 1990.

Fee, Gordon D. *Paul's Letter to the Philippians*. NICNT. Grand Rapids: Eerdmans, 1995.

Ferguson, John. "Philippians, John and the Tradition of Ephesus." *Expository Times* 83 (1971): 85–87.

Garland, David E. "The Composition and Unity of Philippians: Some Neglected Literary Factors." *Novum Testamentum* 27 (1985): 141–73.

Gnilka, Joachim. *Der Philipperbrief.* HTKNT 10.3. Freiburg: Herder, 1968.
Guthrie, George H. "Cohesion Shifts and Stiches in Philippians." Pages 36–59 in *Discourse Analysis and Other Topics in Biblical Greek.* Edited by Stanley E. Porter and D. A Carson. JSNTSup 113. Sheffield: Sheffield Academic Press, 1995.
Hansen, G. Walter. *The Letter to the Philippians.* PNTC. Grand Rapids: Eerdmans, 2009.
Harris, Murray J. *Prepositions and Theology in the Greek New Testament: An Essential Reference Resource for Exegesis.* Grand Rapids: Zondervan, 2012.
Haubeck, Wilfrid, and Heinrich von Siebenthal. *Neuer sprachlicher Schlüssel zum griechischen Neuen Testament.* 3rd ed. Giessen: Brunnen Verlag, 2015.
Hawthorne, Gerald F. *Philippians.* WBC 43. Dallas: Word, 1983.
Hawthorne, Gerald F., and Ralph P. Martin. *Philippians.* WBC 43. Revised edition. Grand Rapids: Zondervan, 2004.
Hays, Richard B. *Echoes of Scripture in the Letters of Paul.* New Haven, CT: Yale University Press, 1989.
Hellerman, Joseph H. *Philippians.* EGGNT. Edited by Andreas J. Köstenberger and Robert Yarbrough. Nashville: B&H Academic, 2015.
———. "μορφῇ θεοῦ as a Signifier of Social Status in Philippians 2:6." *Journal of the Evangelical Theological Society* 52 (2009): 779–97.
Hengel, Martin. "Erwägungen zum Sprachgebrauch von Χριστός bei Paulus und in der vorpaulinischen Überlieferung." Pages 135–58 in *Paul and Paulinism: Essays in Honour of C. K. Barrett.* Edited by Morna D. Hooker and S. G. Wilson. London: SPCK, 1982. English trans.: "'Christos' in Paul." Pages 65–77 in *Between Jesus and Paul: Studies in the Earliest History of Christianity.* Translated by John Bowden. Philadelphia: Fortress, 1983.
Holloway, Paul A. *Philippians: A Commentary.* Hermeneia. Minneapolis: Fortress, 2017.
Jowers, Dennis W. "The Meaning of μορφη in Philippians 2:6–7." *Journal of the Evangelical Theological Society* 49 (2006): 739–66.
Kilpatrick, George Dunbar. "Βλέπετε: Philippians 3.2." Pages 146–48 in *In Memoriam Paul Kahle.* Edited by Matthew Black and Georg Fohrer. BZAW 103. Berlin: Töpelmann, 1968.
Koester, Helmut. "The Purpose of the Polemic of a Pauline Fragment (Philippians III)." *New Testament Studies* 8 (1962): 317–32.

Kurek-Chomycz, Dominika. "Fellow Athletes or Fellow Soldiers? συνα-θλέω in Philippians 1.27 and 4.4." *Journal for the Study of the New Testament* 39 (2017): 279–303.

Levinsohn, Stephen H. *Discourse Features of New Testament Greek: A Coursebook on the Information Structure of New Testament Greek.* 2nd ed. Dallas: SIL International, 2000.

———. "A Discourse Study of Constituent Order and the Article in Philippians." Pages 60–74 in *Discourse Analysis and Other Topics in Biblical Greek*. Edited by Stanley E. Porter and D. A Carson. JSNTSup 113. Sheffield: Sheffield Academic Press, 1995.

———. "Verb Forms and Grounding in Narrative." Pages 163–83 in *The Greek Verb Revisited: A Fresh Approach for Biblical Exegesis*. Edited by Steven E. Runge and Christopher J. Fresch. Bellingham, WA: Lexham Press, 2016.

Lightfoot, Joseph B. *Saint Paul's Epistle to the Philippians*. Classic Commentaries on the Greek New Testament. London: Macmillan, 1913.

Martin, Ralph P. *Carmen Christi: Philippians 2:5–11 in Recent Interpretation and in the Setting of Early Christian Worship*. Rev. ed. Grand Rapids: Eerdmans, 1983.

McGaughy, Lane C. *Toward a Descriptive Analysis of EINAI as a Linking Verb in New Testament Greek*. SBLDS 6. Missoula, MT: Society of Biblical Literature, 1972.

Metzger, Bruce M. *A Textual Commentary on the Greek New Testament*. 2nd ed. Stuttgart: German Bible Society, 1994.

Moule, C. F. D. *An Idiom Book of New Testament Greek*. 2nd ed. Cambridge: Cambridge University Press, 1959.

Moulton, James Hope, Wilbert Francis Howard, and Nigel Turner. *A Grammar of New Testament Greek*. Vol. 1: *Prolegomena*. Vol. 2: *Accidence and Word-Formation*. Vol. 3: *Syntax*. Vol. 4: *Style*. 3rd ed. Edinburgh: T&T Clark, 1957–1976.

Moulton, James Hope, and James Milligan. *The Vocabulary of the Greek Testament: Illustrated from the Papyri and Other Non-Literary Sources*. Grand Rapids: Eerdmans, 1930.

Novenson, Matthew V. *Christ among the Messiahs: Christ Language in Paul and Messiah Language in Ancient Judaism*. Oxford: Oxford University Press, 2012.

O'Brien, Peter T. *The Epistle to the Philippians*. NIGTC. Grand Rapids: Eerdmans, 1991.

Patte, Daniel. *Paul's Faith and the Power of the Gospel: A Structural Introduction to the Pauline Letters*. Philadelphia: Fortress, 1983.

Pennington, Jonathan T. "Deponency in Koine Greek: The Grammatical Question and the Lexicographical Dilemma." *Trinity Journal* 24 (2003): 55–76.

Porter, Stanley E. *Idioms of the Greek New Testament*. BLG 2. 2nd ed. Sheffield: JSOT, 1994.

———. "In Defence of Verbal Aspect." Pages 26–45 in *Biblical Greek Language and Linguistics: Open Questions in Current Research*. Edited by Stanley E. Porter and D. A. Carson. JSNTSup 80. Sheffield: Sheffield Academic Press, 1993.

———. *Verbal Aspect in the Greek of the New Testament, with Reference to Tense and Mood*. SBG 1. New York: Peter Lang, 1989.

Reed, Jeffrey T. *A Discourse Analysis of Philippians: Method and Rhetoric in the Debate over Literary Integrity*. JSNTSup 136. Sheffield: Sheffield Academic Press, 1997.

———. "The Infinitive with Two Substantival Accusatives: An Ambiguous Construction?" *Novum Testamentum* 33 (1991): 1–27.

———. "Philippians 3:1 and the Epistolary Hesitation Formulas: The Literary Integrity of Philippians, Again." *Journal of Biblical Literature* 115 (1996): 63–90.

Reumann, John. *Philippians: A New Translation with Introduction and Commentary*. AB 33B. New Haven, CT: Yale University Press, 2008.

Robertson, A. T. *A Grammar of the Greek New Testament in the Light of Historical Research*. 4th ed. Nashville: Broadman, 1934.

Runge, Steven. "Contrastive Substitution and the Greek Verb: Reassessing Porter's Argument." *Novum Testamentum* 56 (2014): 154–73.

———. "The Contribution of Verb Forms, Connectives, and Dependency to Grounding Status in Nonnarrative Discourse." Pages 221–72 in *The Greek Verb Revisited: A Fresh Approach for Biblical Exegesis*. Edited by Steven E. Runge and Christopher J. Fresch. Bellingham, WA: Lexham Press, 2016.

———. *Discourse Grammar of the Greek New Testament: A Practical Introduction for Teaching and Exegesis*. Lexham Bible Reference Series. Peabody, MA: Hendrickson, 2010.

Sanders, E. P. *Paul, the Law, and the Jewish People*. Philadelphia: Fortress, 1983.

Sellew, Philip. "Laodiceans and the Philippians Fragments Hypothesis." *Harvard Theological Review* 87 (1994): 17–28.

Shaner, Katherine A. "Seeing Rape and Robbery: ἁρπαγμός and the Philippians Christ Hymn (Phil. 2:5–11)." *Biblical Interpretation* 25 (2017): 342–63.

Silva, Moisés. *Philippians*. BECNT. Grand Rapids: Baker Academic, 2005.

Smyth, H. W. *Greek Grammar*. Revised by G. M. Messing. Cambridge, MA: Harvard University Press, 1956.

Snyman, A. H. "A Rhetorical Analysis of Philippians 1:12–26." *Acta Theologica* 25 (2005): 89–111.

Soards, Marion L. *The Apostle Paul: An Introduction to His Writings and Teaching*. New York: Paulist Press, 1987.

Sumney, Jerry L. *Philippians: A Greek Student's Intermediate Reader*. Peabody, MA: Hendrickson, 2007.

Taylor, Bernard A. "Deponency and Greek Lexicography." Pages 167–76 in *Biblical Greek Language and Lexicography: Essays in Honor of Frederick W. Danker*. Edited by Bernard A. Taylor, John A. L. Lee, Peter R. Burton, and Richard E. Whitaker. Grand Rapids: Eerdmans, 2004.

Wallace, Daniel B. *Greek Grammar beyond the Basics: An Exegetical Syntax of the New Testament*. Grand Rapids: Zondervan, 1996.

Watson, Duane F. "A Note on μορφή." *Theologische Zeitschrift* 22 (1966): 19–25.

———. "A Rhetorical Analysis of Philippians and Its Implications for the Unity Question." *Novum Testamentum* 30 (1988): 57–88.

Wedderburn, A. J. M. "Some Observations on Paul's Use of the Phrases 'in Christ' and 'with Christ.'" *Journal for the Study of the New Testament* 25 (1985): 83–97.

Witherington, Ben, III. *Paul's Letter to the Philippians: A Socio-rhetorical Commentary*. Grand Rapids: Eerdmans, 2011.

Wright, N. T. *Paul and the Faithfulness of God*. Minneapolis: Fortress, 2013.

———. *Paul in Fresh Perspective*. Minneapolis: Fortress, 2009.

———. "ἁρπαγμός and the Meaning of Philippians 2:5–11." *Journal of Theological Studies* 37 (1986): 321–52.

Zerwick, Maximilian. *Biblical Greek: Illustrated by Examples*. English ed. adapted from the 4th Latin ed. by Joseph Smith. Rome: Pontifical Biblical Institute, 1963.

Zerwick, Maximilian, and Mary Grosvenor. *A Grammatical Analysis of the Greek New Testament*. Unabridged, 3rd rev. ed. Rome: Biblical Institute Press, 1988.

AUTHOR INDEX

Alexander, Loveday, xx, 75

Bakker, Egbert J., x
BDF (Blass, Debrunner, and Funk), 3, 4, 7, 8, 9, 10, 13, 15, 20, 21, 24, 28, 29, 31, 32, 42, 43, 44, 50, 51, 52, 57, 59, 60, 65, 68, 70, 73, 75, 78, 79, 82, 86, 87, 89, 91, 92, 96, 100, 101, 106, 108, 109, 112, 113, 116, 117, 118, 128
Beare, F. W., xx, 53, 75
Beker, Johan Christiaan, 81
Bockmuehl, Markus, xix, 15, 20, 22
Bruce, Frederick F., 58
Buth, Randall, 6, 33

Campbell, Constantine R., ix, 2, 18, 19, 20, 34, 42, 48, 72, 75, 78, 85, 95, 104, 105, 111, 115, 126
Caragounis, Chrys C., xi
Carson, D. A., 21, 26, 41, 42, 43, 63, 79, 90, 95, 104, 112, 120
Collange, Jean-François, xx, 87, 122
Conrad, Carl W., x, xi
Culy, Martin M., 11, 12, 20, 40

Dahl, Nils Alstrup, 2
Dalton, William J., xx
de Boer, Willis Peter, 98
Duncan, George Simpson, xix
Dunn, J. D. G., 49, 86

Ehorn, Seth M., 46

Fanning, Buist M., 43, 107, 117, 124, 126
Fee, Gordon D., xix, xxii, 4, 5, 6, 7, 8, 10, 11, 15, 18, 19, 20, 21, 22, 24, 27, 28, 33, 34, 37, 38, 39, 41, 42, 43, 44, 46, 48, 50, 51, 52, 54, 55, 56, 58, 59, 61, 72, 76, 77, 81, 82, 84, 87, 88, 90, 91, 92, 93, 94, 95, 96, 98, 100, 101, 102, 104, 105, 115, 117, 119, 120, 123, 126
Ferguson, John, xix

Garland, David E., xx
Gnilka, Joachim, 82
Grosvenor, Mary, 7, 8, 20, 33, 51, 61, 116, 117
Guthrie, George H., xxi

Hansen, G. Walter, 2, 87, 115
Harris, Murray J., 6, 7, 9, 64, 70, 71, 72, 128
Haubeck, Wilfrid, 11, 13, 14, 87, 99
Hawthorne, Gerald F., xix, 9, 11, 37, 59, 76, 81, 88, 122, 124, 126
Hays, Richard B., xix, 26
Hellerman, Joseph H., 5, 11, 16, 18, 24, 35, 40, 41, 45, 49, 53, 61, 66, 68, 72, 76, 78, 79, 84, 88, 99, 101, 108, 113, 118, 126, 127
Hengel, Martin, 2
Holloway, Paul A., 108

Jowers, Dennis W., 49

Author Index

Kilpatrick, George Dunbar, 76
Koester, Helmut, xx
Kurek-Chomycz, Dominika, 36

Lee, Mark, 46
Levinsohn, Stephen H., xxi, xxiii, 8, 12, 21, 24, 25, 27, 30, 38, 43, 45, 49, 53, 64, 66, 67, 69, 78, 100, 120, 122, 125
Lightfoot, Joseph B., 43, 45, 47, 50, 72, 100, 101, 116, 118, 120

Martin, Ralph P., 9, 11, 37, 52, 59, 76, 81, 88, 122, 124, 126
McGaughy, Lane C., 12
Metzger, Bruce M., 3, 16, 21, 47, 48, 51, 54, 56, 57, 70, 73, 77, 91, 93, 110, 112, 123, 129
MHT (Moulton, Howard, and Turner), 4, 5, 7, 8, 14, 43, 50, 73, 78, 80, 86, 87, 92, 93, 106, 108, 116
Milligan, James, 33, 124
Moule, C. F. D., 13, 20, 21, 40, 44, 54, 59, 63, 77, 87, 108, 116, 119
Moulton, James Hope, 33, 124

Novenson, Matthew V., 2

O'Brien, Peter T., xx, xxi, 2, 4, 5, 7, 8, 14, 18, 20, 22, 34, 38, 40, 42, 46, 47, 48, 49, 50, 52, 54, 57, 58, 60, 61, 62, 63, 64, 67, 71, 72, 75, 76, 77, 78, 79, 81, 82, 83, 84, 86, 87, 88, 89, 90, 91, 92, 94, 95, 109, 110, 111, 113, 115, 119, 122, 125, 126

Parsons, Mikeal C., 12
Patte, Daniel, xx
Pennington, Jonathan T., x, xi
Porter, Stanley E., ix, xxiii, 1, 7, 8, 10, 14, 15, 17, 34, 39, 40, 44, 47, 52, 58, 60, 64, 68, 71, 74, 84, 126

Reed, Jeffrey T., xxi, 4, 10, 75
Reumann, John, xx, 2, 5, 6, 7, 8, 9, 10, 11, 14, 16, 20, 26, 27, 34, 38, 46, 48, 57, 61, 62, 67, 71, 72, 75, 76, 77, 78, 82, 84, 85, 86, 89, 91, 93, 99, 103, 115, 118, 124
Robertson, A. T., x, 6, 9, 11, 13, 14, 15, 24, 27, 30, 40, 43, 46, 48, 50, 52, 57, 58, 61, 76, 77, 80, 82, 89, 92, 101, 102, 109, 111, 117
Runge, Steven, ix, xxiii, xxiv, 6, 12, 13, 17, 21, 23, 32, 33, 39, 43, 44, 46, 58, 66, 81, 82, 83, 84, 85, 86, 87, 88, 96, 99, 101, 107, 111, 113, 114, 121, 124, 136, 138

Sanders, E. P., 81
Sellew, Philip, xx
Shaner, Katherine A., 50
Siebenthal, Heinrich von, 11, 13, 14, 87, 99
Silva, Moisés, xix, xxi, xxii, 10, 19, 21, 43, 51, 75, 82, 85, 88, 95, 109
Smyth, H. W., 26, 33, 43, 63, 104, 117, 120, 121
Snyman, A. H., 33
Soards, Marion L., xix
Sumney, Jerry L., 38, 58, 68, 80, 84, 86, 87, 88, 99, 103, 109, 114, 118, 119, 122

Taylor, Bernard A., x, xi
TDNT (Kittel), 2, 26, 35, 36, 43, 49, 75, 86, 92

Wallace, Daniel B., viii, 2, 6, 7, 8, 9, 10, 11, 12, 13, 15, 16, 18, 19, 20, 22, 26, 28, 30, 31, 32, 34, 38, 39, 40, 44, 46, 49, 50, 51, 52, 53, 54, 55, 56, 58, 59, 61, 69, 71, 74, 75, 77, 79, 80, 83, 86, 88, 91, 92, 96, 98, 100, 103, 106, 107, 108, 109, 114, 115, 119, 127
Watson, Duane F., xxi
Wedderburn, A. J. M., 2
Witherington, Ben, III, 9
Wright, N. T., 2, 50

Zerwick, Maximilian, 6, 7, 8, 9, 13, 15, 20, 23, 24, 27, 28, 29, 33, 37, 44, 45, 51, 52, 61, 62, 73, 80, 81, 86, 101, 102, 103, 115, 116, 117

GRAMMAR INDEX

Superscript is used to indicate the number of times a grammatical element appears within a verse.

accusative (adverbial), 1:27; 2:15, 18, 27; 3:1; 4:8
accusative (cognate), 4:6
accusative complement in a double accusative construction, 2:6, 20, 25, 29; 3:7, 8, 17, 18
accusative direct object, 1:4, 6, 7², 8, 9, 14, 15, 17², 22, 23, 25, 27, 30; 2:2³, 3², 4², 5², 7², 8, 9², 12, 14, 16, 19, 20, 22, 23, 25, 26, 27⁴, 28², 29², 30; 3:1, 2³, 4, 6, 7, 8², 9, 10³, 13², 15³, 17², 18, 19, 20, 21²; 4:2³, 3, 7³, 8, 9², 13², 17², 18², 19, 21², 22
accusative in apposition, 1:7; 2:25²; 3:9, 20; 4:18²
accusative of respect, 1:6; 3:8; 4:6
accusative of retained object, 1:11
accusative (predicate), 1:7, 13; 3:8, 21
accusative subject of the infinitive, 1:7, 10, 12, 13, 14; 3:8, 13, 21
adjectivizer, 1:11; 2:9; 3:6, 9², 11
adverbial accusative: *see* accusative (adverbial)
alliteration, 1:4; 3:2
anacoluthon, 2:5; 3:19
anaphoric, 1:6, 7, 18a, 21², 24², 25; 2:5, 6, 13², 23; 3:9
ἀπό (separation), 4:15
ἀπό (source), 1:2, 28

ἀπό (temporal), 1:5
aporetic genitive: *see* genitive (aporetic)
asyndeton, 2:14; 3:2, 4, 19; 4:4², 5², 21
attributed genitive: *see* genitive (attributed)
attributive genitive: *see* genitive (attributive)
αὐτός (identifying adjective), 1:30; 2:2
αὐτός (intensive), 2:24
ἄχρι (temporal), 1:5, 6

cataphoric, 1:6, 29
cognate accusative: *see* accusative (cognate)
conditional sentence (first-class), 1:22; 2:1, 17; 3:4, 15; 4:8
conditional sentence (third-class), 3:11, 12
constructio ad sensum, 2:15; 3:7, 10
crasis, 2:19, 28

dative complement, 1:3, 13; 2:6, 22; 3:10, 13, 21; 4:3², 14, 15
dative direct object, 3:3
dative (ethical), 1:21
dative indirect object, 1:29; 2:9, 19; 3:1, 15, 18, 21; 4:5, 16

dative (locative), 2:7
dative of advantage, 1:2, 7, 19, 21, 22, 27; 2:16; 3:1[2], 7; 4:18
dative of association, 1:25; 2:17, 18
dative of cause, 1:14
dative of disadvantage, 1:28
dative of manner, 1:18a[3]; 2:3
dative of means/instrument, 1:14, 27; 2:7; 3:3; 4:6[2]
dative of measure/degree of difference, 1:23; 2:12
dative of possession, 4:20
dative of recipient, 1:1
dative of respect, 1:17; 2:7, 30; 3:5
dative of rule, 3:16
dative of sphere, 3:3
descriptive genitive: *see* genitive (descriptive)
διά (causal), 1:15[2], 24; 2:30; 3:7, 8[2], 9
διά (ground), 3:9
διά (instrumental), 1:20[2]
διά (intermediate agency), 1:11
διά (means), 1:19, 26; 3:9
διά (purpose), 3:7, 8[2]
double accusative object-complement construction, 2:6, 20, 25, 29; 3:7, 8, 17, 18
double accusative person-thing construction, 1:11

εἰς (advantage), 1:5
εἰς (in place of the dative of advantage), 4:15, 17
εἰς (goal), 1:29; 3:11
εἰς (manner), 2:16[2]
εἰς (purpose), 1:10, 11, 16, 25; 2:11, 16[4]; 3:14; 4:16
εἰς (reference/respect), 1:5; 2:22; 4:16
εἰς (result), 1:12, 19
εἰς (state), 3:16
εἰς (temporal), 1:10; 2:16; 4:20
ἐκ (source/origin), 1:16, 17, 23; 3:5[3], 9[2], 11, 20; 4:22
ellipsis/elliptical, 1:18a, 18b, 22, 23; 2:2, 15, 22; 3:4, 12[2], 13; 4:11, 17
ἐν (agency), 1:30[2]
ἐν (causal), 1:1, 8, 13, 18a, 26; 2:1, 29; 3:1, 3, 14; 4:2, 4, 7, 10, 21

ἐν (circumstance/condition), 4:6, 11, 12[2]
ἐν (close association), 1:1; 3:1, 9; 4:4, 19, 21
ἐν (ground), 1:14, 26; 2:19, 24
ἐν (instrumental), 1:1, 20; 3:6, 14; 4:7, 13, 19, 21
ἐν (locative), 1:1[2], 6, 7, 9, 13, 20, 22, 24, 26, 30; 2:5[2], 13, 15[2], 19, 24, 29; 3:1, 3, 4, 6, 9, 20; 4:1, 2, 3[2], 4, 7, 9, 13, 16, 19[2], 21
ἐν (means/manner), 1:8, 9
ἐν (manner), 1:8, 9, 20[2], 27, 28; 2:29
ἐν (participation), 1:13
ἐν (reason), 2:1
ἐν (state/condition), 1:7[2]; 2:6, 7; 3:19
ἐν (temporal), 1:4; 2:10, 12[2]; 4:15
epexegetical genitive: *see* genitive (epexegetical)
ἐπί (addition), 2:27
ἐπί (causal), 1:3, 5; 3:9, 12; 4:10
ἐπί (locative), 2:17
ἐπί (purpose), 3:12; 4:10
ἐπί (temporal), 1:3
ethical dative: *see* dative (ethical)

first (anarthrous) attributive position, 1:4, 27; 2:10, 11; 4:3, 5, 7, 15, 19, 21
first (anarthrous) predicate position, 3:9
first attributive position, 1:5, 26, 30; 2:2, 30; 3:2, 9, 14, 17; 4:3, 21
first predicate position (attributive function), 1:1; 4:22
fourth attributive position, 1:6; 2:15[2]; 3:4; 4:1, 18

genitive (aporetic), 1:6, 10; 2:16
genitive (attributed), 1:22; 3:8
genitive (attributive), 2:7; 3:21[2]; 4:18
genitive complement, 1:7, 27
genitive (descriptive), 3:10; 4:9
genitive (epexegetical), 1:11, 19, 22, 27; 2:16, 17; 3:5[2], 8, 14; 4:3
genitive in apposition, 1:2[2]; 2:8, 11; 3:8; 4:23
genitive (objective), 1:1, 3, 7, 11, 12, 16, 19, 27[2], 28[3]; 2:1, 11, 16, 22, 25, 30; 3:8, 9, 10[2], 17, 18[2], 19; 4:15[3]

genitive of association, 1:7; 2:1; 4:3
genitive of comparison, 2:3
genitive of means, 2:8; 3:14
genitive of origin, 1:11; 2:17; 3:5
genitive of place, 2:8, 10
genitive of product, 2:16; 4:9
genitive of production/producer, 2:8; 4:7
genitive of purpose, 2:30; 4:3
genitive of reference, 1:25
genitive of relationship, 1:2; 2:15, 25^2; 3:1; 4:1, 20
genitive of source, 1:8, 19, 22, 25, 27; 2:1^2, 17; 3:3, 5, 10; 4:7, 23
genitive of subordination, 1:3, 8; 4:19
genitive (partitive), 1:14
genitive (possessive), 1:1, 7, 8, 13, 14, 17, 20, 28; 2:2, 6, 7, 10^2, 12^2, 25, 30; 3:8, 18, 19^2, 20, 21^5; 4:1, 3, 5, 7^2, 14, 17, 19^2, 22, 23
genitive (subjective), 1:3, 4, 5, 8, 9, 11, 19^3, 20, 25, 26, 27; 2:12^3, 17, 30^2; 3:9, 10^2, 14, 18; 4:6, 7
Granville Sharp rule, 1:7; 2:25; 4:20

headless relative clause, 3:16; 4:9
hendiadys, 1:1, 7, 20, 25; 2:1, 17
homoeoteleuton, 3:7
hortatory subjunctive: *see* subjunctive (hortatory)

ἵνα (appositional), 1:9
ἵνα (direct object), 2:2
ἵνα (epexegetical), 1:9; 2:2
ἵνα (purpose), 1:10, 26, 27; 2:10, 15, 19, 28, 30; 3:8
ἵνα (purpose-result), 1:26; 2:10, 27
ἵνα (result), 1:26; 2:10
inclusio, 2:19, 24
infinitive (appositional), 1:29^2
infinitive (cause with διὰ τό), 1:7
infinitive (complementary), 1:12, 14; 2:19, 23; 3:21; 4:11, 12^4
infinitive (direct object), 2:6, 13^2, 25; 4:10, 11, 12^2
infinitive (epexegetical), 1:23^2; 3:10, 21
infinitive (imperative), 3:16

infinitive (indirect discourse), 1:17; 3:4, 8, 13; 4:2
infinitive (purpose), 3:10
infinitive (purpose with εἰς τό), 1:10
infinitive (result), 3:10
infinitive (result with εἰς τό), 1:10
infinitive (result with ὥστε), 1:13, 14
infinitive (subject), 1:7, 21^2, 22, 24; 3:1

καθώς (causal), 1:7
καθώς (comparative), 2:12; 3:17
καί (adjunctive), 1:15, 18b, 20; 2:4, 5, 9, 18, 19, 24; 3:4, 8, 12^2, 15, 20, 21; 4:3^2, 10, 12, 15
καί (ascensive), 1:15, 20; 2:17, 27; 3:4, 8, 18, 21; 4:12, 16
καί (pleonastic), 1:15; 4:3
κατά (causal), 3:21; 4:11
κατά (reference), 1:12; 3:5, 6^2
κατά (spatial), 3:14
κατά (standard), 1:20; 2:3^2; 4:19

lectio difficilior, 2:4; 3:21; 4:19
left-dislocation, 3:7, 16; 4:8, 9
locative dative: *see* dative (locative)

μέν . . . δέ (point/counterpoint), 1:15; 2:23-24; 3:1, 13
μέσον (locative), 2:15
μετά (association/accompaniment), 4:3, 9, 23
μετά (manner), 1:4; 2:12, 29; 4:6
metacomment, 1:12; 2:2; 3:18; 4:4
metonymy, 1:7, 13, 14, 17; 3:3, 18, 19
μέχρι (degree), 2:8, 30
μέχρι (temporal), 2:8
μὴ . . . ἀλλά (point/counterpoint), 3:9
μὴ . . . ἀλλὰ καί (point/counterpoint), 2:4
μηδὲν . . . ἀλλά (point/counterpoint), 4:6
μηδὲν . . . μηδὲ . . . ἀλλά (point/counterpoint), 2:3
μὴ . . . μόνον ἀλλὰ . . . πολλῷ μᾶλλον (point/counterpoint), 2:12

neuter plural subject with singular verb, 3:7; 4:3, 6, 8

nominalizer, 1:5, 12, 27, 29; 2:2², 4², 13², 18, 19, 20, 21, 23; 3:1, 13²; 4:2, 18, 22
nominative absolute, 1:1²
nominative in apposition, 1:1; 2:15; 3:3³, 19
nominative (predicate), 1:8, 21², 22, 28; 2:11, 13; 3:3, 5³, 6, 7, 17, 19²
nominative subject, 1:2², 6, 8, 9, 15², 16, 17, 18a², 19, 20, 22, 26, 28²; 2:1⁴, 4², 5, 6, 9, 10, 11², 13, 15, 18, 19, 20, 21, 22, 27, 28; 3:3, 4³, 7, 13, 15², 18, 19³, 20, 21; 4:3², 5², 6, 7, 8⁸, 9, 11, 15³, 19, 20, 21, 22², 23

objective genitive: *see* genitive (objective)
ὅτε (temporal), 4:15
ὅτι (appositional), 1:6, 27
ὅτι (causal), 1:29; 2:16, 22, 30; 4:10, 16
ὅτι (clausal complement), 1:18a
ὅτι (clausal complement; direct discourse), 2:11
ὅτι (clausal complement; indirect discourse), 1:12, 16, 19, 25; 2:11, 16, 22, 24, 26; 3:12; 4:11, 15, 17
ὅτι (epexegetical), 1:20; 2:16, 22
οὐδεμία . . . εἰ μή (point/counterpoint), 4:15
οὐκ . . . μόνον ἀλλὰ καί (point/counterpoint), 2:27
οὐ μόνον . . . ἀλλὰ καί (point/counterpoint), 1:18b, 29
οὐχ . . . ἀλλά (point/counterpoint), 2:6-7; 4:17

παρά (agency), 4:18
παρά (source), 4:18
παραπλήσιον (locative), 2:27
participle (attributive), 1:1, 7; 2:15; 3:6²; 4:7, 17
participle (causal), 1:6, 11, 14, 16, 17, 23, 25; 2:16, 30; 3:9; 4:18
participle (concessive), 2:6; 3:4, 9
participle (conditional), 1:27³
participle (imperfect periphrastic), 2:26²
participle (indirect discourse), 2:3

participle (manner), 1:4, 11, 27, 28, 30; 2:2², 3, 4, 7², 8, 16, 30; 3:9, 10, 13², 18; 4:14
participle (means), 2:2², 7², 16; 3:10; 4:14
participle (substantival), 1:6, 10, 28; 2:13; 3:3³, 6, 8, 17, 19; 4:13
participle (temporal), 1:4; 2:7, 19, 28
partitive genitive: *see* genitive (partitive)
περί (reference), 1:27; 2:19, 20, 23
periphrasis, 2:3, 9
possessive genitive: *see* genitive (possessive)
predicate accusative: *see* accusative (predicate)
predicate adjective, 1:7, 10², 23; 2:2, 8, 15², 28; 3:1², 6³, 15; 4:8⁶, 11
predicate adverb, 2:6; 4:5
predicate nominative: *see* nominative (predicate)
πρός (motion toward), 1:26; 2:25, 30; 4:6

right-dislocation, 1:17; 3:9², 20; 4:18

second attributive position, 1:1; 2:9; 3:6, 9, 11; 4:7
subjective genitive: *see* genitive (subjective)
subjunctive (hortatory), 3:15
subjunctive with ἄν, 2:23
subjunctive with εἰ, 3:12
subjunctive with εἴ πως, 3:11
subjunctive with ἵνα, 1:9, 10, 26, 27; 2:2, 10, 11, 15, 19, 27, 28², 30; 3:8, 9
σύν (association/accompaniment), 1:1, 23; 2:22; 4:21

temporal frame, 1:30; 2:12; 4:10, 15
topical frame, 1:6, 9, 12, 13, 14, 15², 25, 26, 29; 2:9, 19, 21, 28, 29, 30; 3:4, 7, 16; 4:3, 5, 6, 8, 11, 19
TSKS construction, 1:7, 19, 20, 25; 2:17, 25; 3:3, 10; 4:20

ὑπέρ (advantage), 1:4; 2:13; 4:10
ὑπέρ (cause/reason), 2:13

ὑπέρ (degree), 2:9
ὑπέρ (reference/respect), 1:4, 7
ὑπέρ (representation), 1:29[2]
ὑπό (primary agency), 1:28; 3:12

vocative in apposition, 4:1[3]
vocative of direct address, 1:12; 2:12; 3:1, 13, 17; 4:1, 3, 8, 15

χωρίς (separation), 2:14

ὡς (comparative), 1:20; 2:15, 22
ὡς (discourse content), 1:8
ὡς (perspective), 2:7
ὡς (temporal), 2:12, 23
ὥστε (inferential), 2:12; 4:1
ὥστε (result), 1:13

www.ingramcontent.com/pod-product-compliance
Lightning Source LLC
Chambersburg PA
CBHW021357300426
44114CB00012B/1264